PERSONAL STORIES

STORIES

in PUBLIC

SPACES

PERSONAL STORIES

in PUBLIC SPACES

Essays on Playback Theatre
by its Founders

Jonathan Fox *&* Jo Salas

TUSITALA PUBLISHING

Personal Stories in Public Spaces
Essays on Playback Theatre by Its Founders

Copyright © 2021 by Jonathan Fox and Jo Salas

Published in the US by Tusitala Publishing,
137 Hasbrouck Road, New Paltz, NY 12561
www.tusitalapublishing.com

COVER AND INTERIOR DESIGN: Tilman Reitzle

BACK COVER PHOTO:
The authors at the Yokohama Noh Theater in 2018.

The authors are grateful to the following for permission
to reprint previously published material:

ELSEVIER:
Editor-in-Chief Butler, *The Arts in Psychotherapy* for Chapter 3.

ROUTLEDGE LONDON:
Editors Prentki and Abraham, *The Applied Theatre Reader
(2nd Edition)*, for Chapter 16.

Editors Chesner and Iykou, *Trauma in the Creative and
Embodied Therapies: When Words Are Not Enough*, for Chapter 17.

Editors Preston and Prentki, *The Applied Theatre Reader*,
for Chapter 21.

ROUTLEDGE NEW YORK:
Editors Solinger, Fox, and Irani, *Telling Stories to Change the World*,
for Chapter 20.

NEW VILLAGE PRESS:
Editors Cohen, Varea and Walker, *Acting Together: Performance
and the Creative Transformation of Conflict*, for Chapter 22.

ISBN: 978-1-7342250-0-6
Library of Congress Control Number: 2021930621

In memory of Daniel Feldhendler
and other Playback Theatre pioneers
no longer with us

———————————

CONTENTS

Part 3: Stories from the Field

INTRODUCTION

T HIS COLLECTION GATHERS TOGETHER SOME OF THE ESSAYS, articles, talks, and contributions to other anthologies that we have produced since the earliest days of Playback Theatre. Most have been previously published, with nine essays appearing here in print for the first time. Chapters 1, 13, 14, 15, and 18 were written expressly for this volume. We've chosen writing that reflects our evolving understanding, marks a milestone, or is significant but no longer accessible in its original publication.

The first chapter in PART 1: GROWING PLAYBACK THEATRE describes the context in which Playback first emerged and grew. Further chapters describe Playback Theatre's history and turning points. PART 2: EXPLORING IDEAS focuses on socio-political, aesthetic, and ethical aspects of the work. PART 3: STORIES FROM THE FIELD reflects on projects in the US and elsewhere.

The chapters were all written as stand-alone pieces. Many include a brief explanation of Playback Theatre itself. Some previously published pieces have been edited or expanded for inclusion here. The names of all tellers and workshop participants have been changed.

Since Playback's beginnings in 1975 we, Jo and Jonathan, have continued to practice, teach, learn, experiment, and grow in our own understanding. As writers, it has come naturally to write about our experiences and insights (although evoking this ephemeral work on the page is not simple), sometimes by invitation from editors, often simply because we want to articulate and share what we are discovering. We write independently of each other but we are each other's first and toughest editors.

We are deeply grateful to the countless people who have participated with us in the adventure of Playback Theatre, as fellow pioneers, fellow performers, students, and friends. You have contributed directly and indirectly to our learning, our thinking, and our writing. We hope that reading these essays will feel like being part of the conversations that take place so often in our living room or on a walk in the woods.

Jonathan Fox and Jo Salas
New Paltz, NY, 2020

PART 1
GROWING PLAYBACK THEATRE

1

A Changing Landscape

Jo Salas & Jonathan Fox (2020)

What was the cultural context in which Playback Theatre emerged?

THE MID-SEVENTIES, when Playback Theatre[1] was born, was an era of enormous turmoil and expansive social change on every front, with the repercussions of the Vietnam War, the ongoing struggles for civil rights and women's rights, and the rise of the counterculture which swept up large numbers of our generation. Bold new ideas took hold in the arts and technology. Many, especially young people, questioned long-held assumptions about social and family structures and often tore them down, experimenting with new patterns of connection and power.

This was the atmosphere in which we, Jonathan and Jo, found ourselves in our young adulthood, and which was the context for Playback's emergence. Each of us was directly shaped, in our different ways, by the social transformations of these years.

JONATHAN: As I emerged from university in the mid-1960s, I was not especially politically minded. Nevertheless, I strongly opposed the US fighting in Vietnam, as well as other foreign incursions by the US that seemed no more than the whims of an overpowerful bully. I turned away from the privileged path that had been set for me—that choice, of course, a privilege in itself. I accepted an opportunity as far away from New York and the corridors of power and wealth as I could—in the small, beautiful city of Wellington, New Zealand.

---

1. Over the years we and other writers have alternated between capitalizing or not capitalizing the name Playback Theatre. For this volume, we're using the capitalized version.

Living in New Zealand for a year was like going back in time. Life was simpler, slower, and more convivial. This feeling was intensified by the two years that I subsequently spent living in a tiny village in Nepal, volunteering with the US Peace Corps, to avoid being sent to Vietnam. My life there was hard, and it was lonely.[2] But again, my ideas of what was necessary for life transformed. After Nepal, as Jo and I began our married life together and soon had our first daughter, material wealth seemed so much less important to life than US culture insisted, with its relentless promulgation of commerce and capitalism.

As I sought to find my calling in those post-university and post-Nepal years, I shifted from "writer" to "theatre . . . something." In my search I was drawn to what we then called the experimental theatre. I did not embrace all that these avant-garde groups stood for, but their commitment to social liberation was stirring, as was their dedication to developing a deep ensemble and experimentation. What excited me now were crude homemade pieces developed improvisationally, where the social interactions between players were as important as the product made. I seemed to want a theatre that was personal and intimate, but how could I define it, and where would it lead me? What kind of theatre person did that?

Jo was away for several weeks when some people invited me to direct the group that became our first theatre company, It's All Grace. Once she returned and met this new group (the members all soon became good friends), we invited her to play music with us. Jo and I did not imagine that it would become a professional project—and it didn't—but we were both trying to fashion our lives as independent artists and we were ready to explore this project as a couple. Two and a half years later when I resolved to start Playback Theatre, this time with the hope that it would indeed become a vocation, it felt natural to do it together. It was a time of breaking boundaries, creating new configurations. I knew I did not want to spend my working life in an office hierarchy, as my father had. Jo and I were happy to blend life and work and pin our hopes on a collective, untried experiment.

2. See Chapter 24, "Garland of Flowers."

JO: I grew up in New Zealand. In my very early teens, I was involved first in the youth campaign for nuclear disarmament (YCND) and then in the protest movement against the Vietnam War, strenuously opposing the deployment of NZ troops for which the US was pressuring our government with clumsy threats and promises. When Jonathan and I met in New Zealand in 1966, the US political situation became more personal for me. The looming draft meant that he had to leave after a year, despite our wish to be together. Our forced two-and-half-year separation ended after our stints as volunteers in Asia (myself in the tiny nation of Sarawak, on the island of Borneo; Jonathan in the lowlands of Nepal). We arrived as newlyweds in the United States in April 1970. Two weeks later, Nixon bombed Cambodia. Campuses and communities across the country exploded in protest. National Guard troops killed four white student protesters at Kent State and eight Black students at Jackson State University. My introduction to the US was through the lens of the shock, grief, and rage caused by this violence.

It was not until 1972, when we returned to the US with our baby girl after a year and half in rural England, that we engaged fully with the new youth culture that had taken hold. The values and lifestyle of the counterculture echoed our own, evolved through our separate experiences of living in remote developing countries as well as our pared-down existence on a farm in the West Country of England—wild beauty all around, but no telephone and rarely electricity in the ancient cottage we rented, miles from any town. Communication with our distant families and friends was solely through letters, handed to us by the postman after his slow scooter ride along our potholed dirt road.

Our new American life was not isolated. But we and the friends we soon found—some in It's All Grace—lived outside "the system," with artistic interests and multiple part-time jobs instead of careers, very little participation in consumer culture, and the fierce espousal of left-wing political and social ideals. I encountered the feminist movement and began to explore what it meant to be a woman in a different mold from my mother's generation. Feminist insights reverberated deeply for me, splintering my assumptions about marriage and motherhood. I took part in a consciousness-raising group, a phenomenon of the time: five or six women sitting in a quiet room, telling stories about what was true for us, speaking what had not been spoken before, listening, not judging.

Jonathan and I shared a house with other people in a deliberate attempt at communal living. We helped to create and then taught at a new alternative high school. I made most of our clothes, often modeled on the loose traditional clothes that we'd become used to wearing in Nepal and Malaysia. It led to a small design business for a while, "Clothes for the Global Village."

With my newfound feminist courage, I insisted on some respite from constant childcare. I would lock myself in a room and read: Germaine Greer, women's poetry, Abraham Maslow, Carl Rogers, Abbie Hoffman, Doris Lessing, Eldridge Cleaver, Jane Roberts, the anthology *Sisterhood is Powerful*. At the local university's famed performing arts festival, I was exhilarated by the music of pioneers like Meredith Monk and Robert Wilson. I practiced Bach and Beethoven on my violin and gingerly tried jazz idioms, not yet ready to improvise or compose.

It was music that connected me to It's All Grace. At our outdoor performances I stood at the side, playing pre-chosen melodies on my violin. By the time a breakaway group began exploring the new vision that became Playback Theatre, I was brave enough to step onto the stage as an actor. When we moved to New York and started the original company, I acted for a while and then returned to the musician's spot, finally ready to leap into the world of improvisation.

What were the vision and influences at Playback Theatre's inception?

The stage on which the original Playback Theatre company created our first experiments consisted of boards well worn by those who came before, our mentors. On this stage, we can imagine a five-pointed guiding star.

The star's first point represented the **oral tradition**, which centers around stories. Traditionally, stories helped pass the time during the long evenings. They also contained important information. In the absence of permanent records, these stories preserved the prevailing history and moral precept of the tribe. Even though these stories, like the literature that would later emerge from them, dealt with setting, character, plot, emotion, they were always more than entertainment. In the same spirit, Playback Theatre would also be based on stories, avoiding scripts and pre-rehearsed pieces. And as in the oral tradition, the stories would portray the collective wisdom of the community. Although it was a form of improvisation—nothing planned, nothing written—Playback Theatre would have a much more serious purpose than the modern improv at a comedy club, which aimed primarily to entertain. And even more than the traditional context, which privileged the established moral order, Playback Theatre would give space for the people's voice.

The bards, griots, and singers of the oral tradition usually used an instrument to help them string together their memorized lines. So stories in the oral tradition usually had a rhythm to them, and the performance was often part of a ceremony. We would eventually work long and hard on adapting this ritual element to our work.

Another point of the star was the **creative dramatics** movement out of England, an educational approach that focused on young children in school. The pioneers of creative dramatics, such as Peter Slade and Brian Way, preferred devised (or self-developed) pieces to more commonly used written plays. Those plays inevitably starred only few, relegating everyone else to minor roles. Slade and Way valued instead safety and inclusivity, and they cherished the inherent creativity in each child. They tended to resist the pressure of large auditorium performances and prized an intimate workshop-type approach.

Experimental theatre, a major source of inspiration, was in many ways the opposite of creative dramatics. It was adult, confrontational, and rarely safe—following in the footsteps of the seminal Living Theater, founded in 1947. We eagerly adopted the credo of many groups seeking to liberate theatre from conventional theatre spaces, preferring to stage our work in community settings. We followed the advice of Jerzy Grotowski of Poland and built a "poor theatre," needing nothing but our bodies and a space to mark out as the stage. We studied the work of the many groups whose productions grew out of months of intense collaboration. We aspired to the objective of Richard Schechner, an influential US performance studies professor and director of the Performance Group, who advocated a theatre of "transformation" (stimulating lasting change in the identity of the observers—i.e. taking them somewhere from which there was no going back) rather than mere "transportation" (an entertaining experience leaving the observer unchanged). We would act out stories in the community itself, and we would have the courage to act out any story, including those that revealed personal or societal injustice.

We were influenced by **psychodrama**, the creation of J.L. and Zerka Moreno. This approach gave us a concept to understand a key objective of our improvisation—spontaneity. Spontaneity emphasized creativity, but also appropriateness, finding the right action at the right moment. It also provided a theory and method of inclusion (sociometry) that would grow in importance as our work progressed. About half of the original company came to Playback Theatre from the psychodrama network, and Zerka Moreno actively supported Playback's beginnings. (Playback's affinal relationship to psychodrama has led to some confusion about whether Playback Theatre is a therapeutic modality or not: it isn't, but can be adapted and applied in therapeutic contexts.)

The writings of the Brazilian educator, Paolo Freire, helped draw another point of the star, which we can call **social activism**. It would take years of performing in the community to refine our activist approach, but from the start we emulated a bottom-up (rather than elitist) approach to culture that emphasized embodied listening rather than presentation. We also recognized the tremendous potential of Freire's concept of critical consciousness, which argues that a sense of our own story is a prerequisite for revolutionary change. (Augusto Boal's seminal *Theatre of the Oppressed*, also inspired by Freire, was not published until 1973 and first brought out in English in 1979, by which time we had already been working for four years. It reinforced many of our ideas).

This original mix—the oral tradition, educational theatre, experimental theatre, psychodrama, and social activism—five points of light complementing and at times contrasting with each other, has significance because it was the ground we stood upon as the original idea for Playback Theatre came to life. It was perhaps an unusual combination, allowing for a simple idea to develop into a method rich in complexity. What emerged was a theatre devoted to embodying truth; to the personal accounts of ordinary people, including from those usually unheard; to an emergent creativity demanding a deep ensemble; to rhythm and ritual; to an animating approach combining workshop and performance; to an allegiance to safety without avoiding risk; and finally to a way of communicating that lies at the core of what it is to be human—our stories, which at once entertain us, enlighten us, and connect us to each other.

FOR ALL THE RICHNESS of our "guiding star," there were also disadvantages. Playback Theatre seemed not to fit anywhere. Was this because it was innovative and boundary-crossing? Arts councils rejected our applications because there was no product and no text. Our weekly 3-hour rehearsals were a part of our year-round lives, in contrast to other innovative theatre companies who often rehearsed intensively for a series of performances and then stepped back for a while. Mental health institutions dismissed our overall lack of therapeutic credentials (some of us were credentialed, others not), our public positioning of private narrative, and our welcoming of highly emotional, and therefore in their eyes, unsafe, material. Theatre of the Oppressed came the closest to the kind of theatre we embraced. But there were basic differences, including Playback's much stronger identity as an art form. Clearly, if Playback were to succeed, we would have to establish our own ground, not quite the same as anyone else's.

Since those early years, what else has emerged as a fundamental value?

We learned that it was essential for us to listen with full atten-tiveness and compassion to each teller: that without such listening, it was not possible to enact their story in a way that carried mean-ing for them and for the audience. When we were able to listen fully, on the other hand, each telling became part of a profound, enriching dialogue[3] as story responded to story in the process we now recognize as narrative reticulation.[4]

This kind of listening is rare, and difficult to achieve—rare *because* it is difficult to achieve. But it is the greatest gift that Playback has to offer. (It has been troubling, in recent years, to see that some Playback teams have apparently given up on trying to listen, instead taking the teller's story as a kind of prompt for artistic flight.)

In our ordinary lives most people neither fully listen nor are fully listened to. Our days move too fast. Everyone is preoccupied. People listen through a veil of opinion or distraction, thinking about the story they want to tell in response.

The promise of Playback is that we, the performing team, will listen to your story and, to the best of our ability, hear and embody its important meanings. It sounds simple. But it is not. The philosopher Simone Weil wrote, "Attention consists of sus-pending our thought, leaving it detached, empty, and ready to be penetrated by the object."[5] The "object" in this case is the teller's story. As actors and musicians we must listen in this empty, egoless way, not planning, not worrying, not judging. For conductors, the listening is even more demanding: while we listen with the same open ears as the actors, we are also responsible for eliciting key information and keeping an eye on the wellbeing of the teller, the actors, and the audience.

Compassion, openness, and attentiveness require maturity and self-knowledge: we have to know our own story and be able to set it aside while we listen. Our listening, ideally, is also informed

3. See Chapter 10, "What We Mean by 'Dialogue' in Playback Theatre."
4. See Chapter 13, "The Theory of Narrative Reticulation."
5. Simone Weil, *Waiting for God*. New York: Harper Torchbooks, 1973, p. 62.

by knowledge of the social context of the story we are hearing. Confidence about Playback techniques is also necessary. It's hard to listen with openness if we are trying to remember the choreography of the Playback form we're about to use.

When a performing team achieves this kind of listening, the promise of Playback can be fulfilled. Each enactment is built around a clear sense of what the story means, allowing subsequent stories to respond to it with spontaneity and authenticity.

How did Playback develop its current worldwide presence?

Playback began as a single ensemble in upstate New York. Forty-five years later, there are Playback practitioners in about seventy countries, on every inhabited continent. It has been welcomed and adapted in many cultures, despite the skepticism of some who considered public self-disclosure to be too "American" to work in countries that valued restraint and privacy. People everywhere have stories and the desire to tell them.[6]

The original company's first rehearsal space was a church hall in Beacon, NY, a Hudson River town an hour and a half north of New York City.[7] The hall was just down the road from the Moreno Institute, a magnet for psychodrama students from all over the world. Sometime during that first year, we began to hold open rehearsals and some of those international students attended them. A few fell in love with this brand-new theatre, taking home with them the rudiments and experimenting further in their own countries.

In 1980, an Australian academic saw us perform at a psychodrama conference in New York City and invited four of us to Melbourne. Word spread, and Sydney and New Zealand were added to the itinerary. In Melbourne, Sydney, Wellington, and Auckland, we led workshops and carried out public performances, joined by workshop participants who soon founded companies in those four

6. See Chapter 19, "Burundi Journal."

7. The original company's history is described at more length in our books, including Jonathan's 2015 memoir *Beyond Theatre*, which also discusses the choice to start our theatre in upstate New York, not the city.

cities. It was a turning point, expanding our horizons far beyond the Hudson Valley. Meanwhile, our training workshops at home, also starting in 1980, attracted people from other countries as well as around the US, leading in turn to invitations to train nascent companies elsewhere in North America and in Europe, Eastern Europe, Central and South America, Asia, Africa, and the Middle East.

BY THE TIME the original company was approaching the end of its active life in the late '80s, there were Playback companies in about fifteen countries. Some of us, within and beyond our company, recognized the need for a means of connecting them. A new entity came into being in 1990: the International Playback Theatre Network, to which the original company donated its legal nonprofit structure and logo. The IPTN was consciously conceived as a network rather than a professional association: we saw ourselves as artists linked by common ideals and practices rather than, say, as helping professionals bound by strict training requirements and uniform standards.[8]

Parallel with the development of the IPTN was the founding of the other main Playback institution, the Centre for Playback Theatre, a training organization founded in 1993 (originally called the Jonathan Fox School of Playback Theatre, later the School of Playback Theatre). Training had been available for years through our own workshops and those of other experienced practitioners. Many people simply learned by apprenticeship, joining a company and absorbing the basics until they were ready to perform. But along with the growth of Playback there had developed a need for more comprehensive training for those who wanted to deepen and strengthen their work, often with the purpose of building a professional presence in their communities.[9]

8. The IPTN carries out its mission of connection in several ways: sponsoring international conferences (the first in Sydney in 1992), a newsletter (formerly *Interplay*, now called *IPTN Journal*), and a membership directory. Worldwide conferences now take place every three or four years, alternating with regional gatherings. A rotating volunteer board representing 12 or 15 countries guides the IPTN's direction. Regional networks, most linked to the IPTN, operate in several parts of the world and hold their own gatherings. See www.iptn.info.

9. At this point, there are CPT-affiliated schools in seventeen countries carrying out

We had also slowly come to recognize the unique ethical demands of the Playback Theatre idea. It was certainly different from traditional theatre where "the show must go on," no matter the cost for the performers. It was equally different from therapy and the modern helping professions, which create a cocoon of privacy around personal narrative. Playback was public, and it aimed to be constructive for all involved. Without proper attention, as we learned from hard experience, tellers, audience members, and even actors could be harmed. Our increasing emphasis on training grew in part as a way to instill in new practitioners the necessary sense of responsibility.

These two organizations, the IPTN and the CPT (both now run by volunteer boards), each serve a large, active, international, and amorphous community of people, the IPTN through connection and the CPT through training. Each seeks to ensure that the fundamental values and practices of Playback Theatre are understood and upheld. Playback practitioners are artists applying their art in service to communication and a safer, fairer world. The inclusiveness that is inherent in Playback extends to its practitioners: it is a tenet of Playback that anyone can do this work. You do not have to be outstandingly talented, you do not have to be an expert. This deeply-held ideal exists in tension with a contrasting reality: offering Playback Theatre on a professional basis in the community requires considerable training and experience. Our field does not need the kinds of rules and regulations that are found in other disciplines—Playback is not the law, nor medicine, nor psychology. But we acknowledge that it can be done well or poorly, and work that is adequate in one context may not be adequate in another (as in, for example, the field of music: anyone can learn to play an instrument and find great joy in doing so alone or with others, but to engage a public audience you have to train and practice for years.) In the end, the need for training is about serving the community with effectiveness and

a coordinated curriculum, adapted for each cultural context. Students who complete the training receive a diploma. In 2013, the Centre established an accreditation system for qualified trainers, identifying benchmarks for training recognized as competent by already-established trainers. See www.playbackcentre.org.

integrity, which in turn requires a sense of standards and ethical responsibility.[10]

The enormous diversity of culture, resources, and language to be found in Playback's worldwide presence brings variation and richness. There is no single "correct" way of doing Playback Theatre, although its basic values, structures, and forms remain consistent and recognizable whether you are in San Francisco or Havana, Dublin or Johannesburg, Singapore or Cairo, Moscow or Bangalore.

Published writing has played a part. From the earliest years, we have each chronicled and explored Playback through the written word. Some of our work has been translated (*Improvising Real Life* is in ten languages at this point), making our experiences and precepts directly accessible to people in many parts of the world. Between us we have published five books about Playback Theatre as well as numerous articles and contributions to edited collections.[11] We have also encouraged writing by others, including through the essay requirement for the CPT Leadership course, which has led to a body of valuable documentation and research; and the website Playback Theatre Reflects, which publishes thoughtful, professional-quality writing about Playback.[12] Books by other Playback authors, in English and other languages, have also contributed significantly to our field.

As a theatre movement, Playback has developed a strong though not universal focus on social change. What were the steps in this evolution?

As young adults we were firmly identified with progressive values—anti-war, anti-violence, feminist, critical of the capitalist order, strongly skeptical about mainstream politics. Although not at that time very attuned to environmental issues, we chose to live quite lightly on the earth, with few material possessions. We were staunch supporters of civil rights, though with a superficial awareness of the

10. See Chapter 4, "What is 'Good' Playback Theatre?"
11. See www.TusitalaPublishing.com
12. www.PlaybackTheatreReflects.net

full complexities of racism—likewise our knowledge of the struggles of gay and lesbian people. (The term LGBTQ did not exist then.)

It was with this sociopolitical stance that we launched Playback Theatre in 1975. Like It's All Grace, it was an all-white group of people in our 20s and 30s, varied in our class and educational backgrounds. With little explicit discussion, we expected that our theatre would in some way contribute to a more just and peaceful society. After all, key to the Playback vision was the profoundly egalitarian claim that everyone has a story and deserves a place to tell it, and to be heard with compassion and respect. But our sense of Playback as a force for change was vague, not much more than an orientation for the focus on artistic realization that was in the foreground.[13] For the first few years, our attention was more on finding the rituals and aesthetic forms that would bring our vision to fruition, to render it a viable and powerful form of theatre, and to have it be recognized as such. We also strove to deepen our skills in hearing and responding to any story no matter how complex or sensitive. We experimented with many forms and structures for enacting stories, discarding most of them after a few rehearsals. A few took hold and remain basic to most Playback performing: fluid sculptures, pairs, and the five-part sequence of a Playback scene.[14]

Over time, many of us (by now including practitioners beyond the original company) came to realize that the idealistic view upon which Playback was based—that everyone's story had value—contained within it a call to social justice. Voices of the poor, of people of color, of immigrants, of women, of children—in fact, of all who do not belong to the traditional holders of power and visibility—have been actively suppressed for most of US history. Other cultures hold similar patterns. The long struggle for equity is a struggle to be heard: to tell one's story and know that it has been comprehended and remembered; for cumulative voices to burst out

13. See Chapter 2, "Culture, Community, and Playback Theatre."
14. Playback forms and the structure of a full-length scene are described in Chapter 3 of *Improvising Real Life: Personal Story in Playback Theatre, 20th Anniversary Edition* by Jo Salas. New Paltz, NY: Tusitala Publishing, 2013.

of the silence and compel change. Our Playback stage was a place where the unheard voices could be heard, the untold stories told— if our awareness, historical knowledge, and interactive skills were robust enough.

There have been inflection points throughout Playback's history, often at gatherings, that have jolted our community into aware- ness. At the international conference in Olympia, Washington, in 1995, DC Playback—a multiracial company from Washington, DC—presented a stark analysis of racism within the Playback world. Uncomfortable as it was, it launched many of us on the unending journey of learning and changing, of commitment to building an ethos that fully acknowledges the realities of privilege and injustice, and the imperative to do all we can to address them. Later gatherings—notably a regional conference in the northeast US in 2000—continued this process of education and discovery, not without stormy confrontations and tears. By no means every- one welcomed the uncompromising focus of the organizers. For us, Jo and Jonathan, it seemed salutary and necessary and we stood with the courageous people of color who insisted on mak- ing explicit the patterns of injustice that so often—out of white obliviousness or weariness and wariness on the part of those who are oppressed—go unacknowledged.

As civil rights leaders always remind us, the path to racial justice is long and maddeningly circuitous, impeded by the forces of inertia and amnesia. For example, at a more recent US gathering, an African American woman told a story in which the central point about racism—clearly present though obliquely expressed in this lyrical story—was ignored in the enactment. Another Black woman spoke up, furious at the performing team and at the mostly white audience for not intervening. Passionate discussions ensued about the importance of addressing race and racism in Playback. It became clear that almost none of the 100 or so people present knew about the intense explorations that had taken place in our community years before and had led to significant changes we thought were indelible. They weren't. It was a lesson in the need for constant attention and vigilance.

Slow as our progress might be, these ongoing disruptions to the majority-white, heterosexual, middle-class culture of Playback Theatre, and the committed follow-up on the part of those who embrace them, have prompted our stage to open itself more and more to stories that go beyond the inward-looking personal stories that had been our initial focus.[15] Many in the Playback world began in a more concerted way to use Playback to address inequities, injustices, and major fault lines both within and between our societies: international conferences and even regional gatherings can include people from 30 or 40 countries, a microcosm of our troubled and unjust world order. Political divisions and oppressions come into focus, insensitivity and injustice are rightfully challenged. At the 1997 international conference in Perth, Australia, gay and lesbian playbackers shared stories in an open workshop-performance (non-gay participants were welcome to join "us perverts," as one of the instigators said in her ironic Kiwi way). They emerged from their session to challenge the rest of the conference participants to "meet us halfway on the bridge." The European regional gathering in Amsterdam in 2014 saw friction between Russians and Ukrainians, Palestinians and Israelis, and among Dutch participants bitterly divided about a beloved Christmas tradition now seen as racist.

Even with Playback's resilient and capacious rituals, even with the listening skills that we bring, it is not easy to emerge from such moments with increased understanding as well as the inevitable bruises and frustration.

One outcome of this expanded focus on stories with societal resonance has been the use of Playback in the turmoil following natural disasters—in which inequity often plays a part.[16] After the Indian Ocean tsunami in 2004, local Playback groups offered shows for displaced people whose homes and livelihood had been lost and who were in further danger of losing their stories, silenced by shock-doctrine capitalism which swooped in to build high-rise hotels where fisherfolk used to live and work. When Hurricane Katrina hit New Orleans in 2005, there was again a need for real

15. See Chapter 6, "The Wider World."
16. See Chapter 18, "Enacting Testimony: Trauma Stories in Playback Theatre."

people's stories to be heard and shared, in contrast to the mainstream media's story. With the majority of those affected in New
Orleans being people of color, it was not a fitting project for a white
Playback group, though a number of white people were eager to
go. Guided by Pamela Freeman from Philadelphia, eleven other
practitioners of color from around the US met for a preliminary
workshop to share and strategize before traveling to New Orleans.
At the invitation of the group, Jonathan was also present, as a witness rather than either leader or participant.

JONATHAN: It was humbling to sit in that workshop as the only
white person present, taking in the sense of isolation and struggle
expressed by many group members about their progress in Playback
as well as in life. New Orleans was an even more profound experience of bearing witness: to whole devastated neighborhoods, empty
of human life; to a school audience decimated of students and staff
due to evacuations; to a church audience where a teller stood up to
tell the tragic Katrina story she had not dared to articulate before
that moment. I drove our rented van, proud of our team, happy for
once to be the supporter, not the leader.

By now, in 2020, the purposeful embrace of social justice goals
is shared by a majority of Playback practitioners. Projects have
addressed the intersectional stresses of climate action and climate
justice (the impacts of the climate crisis fall disproportionately
on communities and countries already suffering from racism and
poverty); immigration and refugees; violence against women, and
more.[17]

Although there are companies that still place more emphasis
on artistic or therapeutic work, a commitment to addressing social
inequity is integral to Playback Theatre's fundamental mission. The
fight for justice necessitates ongoing learning and self-questioning
as individuals and ensembles, a process that is inevitably fraught as
well as empowering. In majority-white countries with a colonial or
slave-owning past, or both, it has remained difficult for Playback
groups to maintain antiracism as a commitment both within their

17. See Chapter 20, "Immigrant Stories in the Hudson Valley."

ensembles and in their community participation.[18] To their credit, many Playback practitioners and groups are fully engaged in this long quest.

Our own—Jo and Jonathan's—personal involvement in social justice, including antiracism, has evolved over time. In the spirit of what is now called applied theatre, the original company performed in senior centers, group homes for people with disabilities or troubled teens, and prisons. We were willing to work in very difficult conditions. At the same time, we had only minimal awareness of race, class, and privilege. At a high school in Brooklyn, for instance, where the only white faces were teachers, the lack of congruence between the mostly Caribbean and African American children and us, with our older, white-skinned faces, was stark. We felt it but did not yet know what to do about it.

JO: In the early 1990s, I joined a study group on race and racism with six or seven other local residents, white, Black, and Latinx. Jonathan soon became a member as well. We met weekly for several years. It was an extraordinary opportunity to listen to people of very different backgrounds in response to readings and videos that we took turns suggesting—an education we have never forgotten.

As someone who did not grow up in the US, the depth and perniciousness of racism in this culture was hard to comprehend. At the 2000 Playback gathering, I was shocked as I listened to stories from participants in a caucus for white people only, understanding viscerally for the first time how white Americans have been saturated with racist myths since infancy. My experience had been different. Racism and racial injustice endure in New Zealand, with its colonial history, but there has never been slavery and its insidious, poisoned, and all-pervasive consequences. Even so, as someone who now lives in the US, I am tainted by its racism. I carry unearned privilege granted to me by my whiteness. I share the responsibility to learn, grow, and take action to build justice. For me, that means using Playback with humanity and awareness to invite and honor stories from seldom-heard voices. It means

18. See Chapter 9, "Playback Theatre, Diversity, and the Two Economies."

standing on the street to protest oppression and corruption. It means speaking up even when it is controversial to do so, both in North American and international contexts.

JONATHAN: In 1993, six years after the end of the original company, and inspired by the study group on race and racism that Jo and I belonged to, I began to teach a series of Playback Theatre courses called "Social Change." I remember having an acute sense of inadequacy in offering to explore this subject, but feeling, at the same time, that a first step—for myself and as a leader of the Playback Theatre community—had to be taken. In the next few years, I facilitated Playback workshops explicitly on this theme in the US, Germany, Japan, and Australia. Some of our colleagues felt that these kinds of workshops, with their emphasis on justice and fairness, took Playback Theatre in an unfortunately "political" direction, weakening the core value of respect for all. But Jo and I did not accept this dichotomy. To the contrary, practicing Playback with a naïve or uninformed analysis regarding social issues virtually ensured the perpetuation of a status quo where the powerful and privileged shared their stories while others stayed in the shadows. With my own privileged background, I was no doubt not the best person to lead these workshops, and yet in them we did hear and embody stories from Aboriginal Australians, Korean Japanese, Maori New Zealanders, Jewish Germans, and African Americans.

As performers and teachers, we had to gain skills in responding to the often unconscious behavior of audience members and students—the high-status white man who has no idea that he is dominating the workshop discussion; the woman whose hand flies up first at every performance; the native English-speakers who cannot remember to speak more slowly so that international students can understand them; the middle school students who parrot anti-immigrant or homophobic sentiments they've heard at home. It's a complex, delicate task to address such moments constructively and kindly in the heat of a performance or training, even harder when you are the visiting outsider in another country.

JO: In a workshop in Germany a participant—a psychotherapist and the respected supervisor of several others in the room—pushed up the corners of her eyes with her fingers as she played an Asian person. Trying to help her understand why stereotypes are hurtful, I told her about my American language teacher who mimed a Heil Hitler salute to indicate the word "German." The woman objected. "Not everyone here was a Nazi," she said. "But all Chinese people have slanted eyes." Others in the workshop understood my point, even if she did not, especially when we re-enacted the scene portraying the nature of the Chinese person, not their physical appearance. Sometimes, reaching the others who are present, whether workshop participants or an audience, is the best we can do.

With Playback now thriving in so many countries and cultures, sociopolitical issues might include class, caste, religious intolerance, gender bias, or political exclusion. In some places it is impossible for Playback companies not to attend to social justice topics: these are the stories that people come to tell.[19] In others, the political climate is so repressive that stories of injustice have to go underground.

As a long-married couple who created this work together, what can you say about gender balance in Playback Theatre?

JO: This is the most personal topic that we've ever written about. We are doing so here because our very private journey as cofounders who are also a male-female couple has implications that go beyond us, especially as gender equity and sexism in Playback Theatre have come under discussion in recent times.

When Playback began, Jonathan was thirty-two years old and I was twenty-six. We had met nine years before, at twenty-three and seventeen. On the deepest level we had quickly recognized each other as soulmates and equals. But in worldly and psychological terms, we did not feel ourselves to be equal, with discrepancies in age, family wealth, nationality, and education (he a Fulbright scholar from Harvard, myself a first-year student at the small university in New Zealand where he came to study) as well as the pervasive assumption that men's lives mattered more. The disparity

19. See Chapter 23, "Stories by Firelight."

only grew stronger when I became an immigrant to the United States, cut off from all that was familiar.

TODAY, AFTER MORE THAN fifty years of marriage and forty-five years of Playback, this asymmetry has transformed completely, at least in our personal lives. But at the time that Playback began, the imbalance in our sense of ourselves prevailed. On the path toward professional identity, Jonathan was much further along than I was. It was his vision and initiative, not mine, that led to Playback's creation. But, looking back, I contributed my own considerable creativity in the ferment of those first years when the basic concept took on flesh and grew into a viable practice. I also supported from behind the scenes, a comfortable place for me—organizing, handling publicity, writing, creating our graphics, and sewing our performing outfits. Much of the early documentation is in my voice, even my handwriting. I did not question that the work itself should be promoted as Jonathan's work, leading inevitably to the inaccurate impression that he built Playback Theatre alone. The truth is that not only did I share in its crucial early development: the other members of the original company did as well. It was a genuinely collective effort—in which Jonathan's role as leader and inspirer and the one who carried the largest burden of responsibility was nevertheless fundamental. One could not have taken place without the other.

Our private relationship was not static. Over the long years of loving and parenting and working, we learned how to face our personal wounds, self-delusions, and weaknesses and build a more mindful, egalitarian marriage. Our professional life gradually caught up, not always smoothly, but eventually enabling us to become mutually respectful and appreciative partners. The hurtful experiences that used to arise where my role was openly devalued or dismissed—by women as well as men—now happen far less frequently. But I can still be derailed by unthinking disrespect—arriving, for example, for a workshop that we've been invited to co-lead and have carefully prepared together, only to find a large sign on the door saying "Workshop with Jonathan Fox." Or having our academic host excitedly introduce Jonathan to his (male) colleagues while ignoring me as I stand awkwardly beside him. There is no graceful solution in such situations: one can either speak up and interrupt the bonhomie, or stay silent like a clod of earth.

Playback Theatre has probably attracted more women than men as practitioners. At a rough guess, women lead more than half of the companies worldwide, alone or in a leadership team. Whether woman-led or not, there are, in fact, a number of integral aspects of Playback itself that seem female in nature, at least as femaleness is traditionally understood.[20] It is a gentle, flexible form, with receptiveness at its core. But when I hear about groups led by powerful and not always sensitive men, or about a confident but inexperienced man who has claimed more stature than his knowledge justifies, or pushed aside a more qualified woman, I am reminded that Playback Theatre takes place in a world still dominated by patriarchy. Disrupting this pattern of power, as with any form of power, takes intentionality and courage.

JONATHAN: In my thirties, while profoundly influenced by the counterculture movement, I remained a product of the male-dominant cultural education of my childhood, which produced a strong compulsion to stand out and to succeed. There is no question that in my striving, I took Jo's contribution for granted, and I shined in what attention I received. I remember our company members teasing me that I was going to be famous one day. They meant, I *wanted* to be famous one day, and they were right.

But the fact is, I failed to succeed in the manner I initially had hoped for—to be recognized and respected in New York avant-garde theatre circles. Other company members did not share my aspirations. I tried too hard on my own, ending up disappointed and burned out. In retrospect, it would have been better for the company and myself if I had shared leadership with Jo and the other company members, who of course were helping and supporting me all the time.

20. See Chapter 10, "Is Playback Female?"

When I finally began to intellectually accept Jo's seminal and co-equal role, to shift in my heart, I think the price I had paid made it even harder. What was all this sacrifice for, I said to myself, if I admit it was misconceived in the first place? Jo not only performed many of the essential "behind the scenes" tasks, as she writes. She also helped us always to deal with issues of society and to honor the importance of aesthetics. Later, in many real ways, she gained more experience than I, as founder, director, and now a performer with Hudson River Playback Theatre (which does share leadership), for thirty years, while I directed the original company for only twelve.

It was a long road from our beginnings, where we both had one foot in the tradition of our parents (husband works, wife looks after the house and children). Gradually, gradually, I came to welcome our publicly standing together as equals… and to genuinely cringe when someone spoke to me with shining eyes while ignoring Jo. At a certain point, we began to refer to ourselves as cofounders and to ask our colleagues to acknowledge us as such. Most have readily accepted this change, giving recognition both to gender equity and collective creative process.

Tensions remain. One of the trials of being cofounders of what has become a worldwide movement is that inevitably there are projections. Jo and I (and to some degree our daughter Hannah Fox, an international Playback trainer who co-runs the New York School of Playback Theatre) can be both idealized and targeted in ways that have little to do with who we actually are or what we have actually done.

It is a relief to have reached old age, where I can let go of the ambitiousness inculcated in my childhood, and genuinely want others to take the limelight in my stead, including my partner and co-creator.

How has the vision of Playback Theatre changed since the early days? What might you have done differently in retrospect?

We recently came across a very early statement of the original Playback Theatre company's values:

WE BELIEVE *in the richness and wisdom of the human story; and we will devote ourselves to acting out people's stories with all of our inventiveness, sympathy, and courage.*

We believe that any story—no matter what it is—can be of importance and is capable of being rendered with meaning and beauty if we are skilled enough.

We believe in a theatre which serves.

We believe in a theatre that tries to reach everyone in the audience, and every type of audience, including the meek, the dependent, and the different.

We believe in a theatre of neighbors.

We believe in a theatre that is for the good of the actors as well as the spectators.

We believe in the spontaneity approach.

We believe in finding a balance between collective concerns and individual personhood... and between being and doing.

And we believe in artistic standards, which requires education, criticism, and the constant reach for perfection.

The understanding and practice of Playback Theatre has been deepened, refined, and complicated in the intervening years, thanks to the work of countless practitioners as well as to our own continuing learning. A similar statement written now would refer explicitly to the commitment to social justice, embedded by implication in this proclamation. But in general, these values remain the foundation of what we do.

Throughout our own years of performing and teaching we have observed, documented, and researched how Playback Theatre creates impact for its audiences and for the community. We continue to share our discoveries in our writing and teaching, offering our understanding of elements that will make the work more effective for more people—a pressing task in a world that seems to be unraveling in the face of climate catastrophe, nationalist extremism, the chokehold of white supremacy, economic breakdown, and the Covid-19 pandemic. This volume includes Jonathan's essay on the theory of narrative reticulation, a rationale that he has developed in recent years for how and why Playback works and its potential impact in counteracting isolation and despair;[21] and another essay on the Listening Hour, a variation created and used widely online during the pandemic when in much of the world face-to-face performances are impossible.[22] Jo's essays on climate-focused performances, one of which is included here, are intended to support companies wishing to play a role in climate action in their own communities.[23]

DO WE HAVE REGRETS? Might we have taken different decisions, in hindsight? Yes and yes. Individually and together we've made choices based on what we were aware of at the time, but that perspective can look different over one's shoulder. One decision with far-reaching implications was the philosophical choice to allow others to take our idea and use it, without remuneration for ourselves, in the spirit of Abbie Hoffman and the other generative pathbreakers of the '60s and '70s who shared their ideas freely. We still stand by this choice. It has led to a rich diversity in practice and has contributed to the flourishing of Playback in so many places. Looking back, however, it would have been wise to send it off with clearer guidelines and a few warnings. We could have said more emphatically in those early years that you have a responsibility to know what you're doing if you're going to do this work well and safely. We could have tried harder to ensure that would-be practitioners apprentice themselves to those who already had substantial experience. We could have emphasized formal training more than we did. We could have said by all means innovate, but not until you have actually learned the form. (In fact we have said this, but have not intervened to discourage ill-judged "improvements" based on an incomplete understanding of the work.) We could have done more to teach the pragmatic organizing skills a company needs to be a respected, effective presence in a community—and to make it clear that being a company leader is a major task and commitment that not everyone is suited for. We could have encouraged people to remain humble and honest about their own capacities

21. See Chapter 13, "The Theory of Narrative Reticulation."
22. See Chapter 8, "The Listening Hour."
23. See Chapter 15, "Playback Theatre for a Planetary Crisis."

and limitations, and to commit to carrying out the work with social awareness as well as respect and consideration for colleagues. Some of these precepts are now embedded in the Centre for Playback Theatre's Code of Ethics, as well as being folded into the teaching that we and others offer.[24]

Human nature is what it is—loving, generous, idealistic, brave, and also at times fearful, arrogant, shallow, mean-spirited. We see all of it in the Playback Theatre community. Needless to say, we are fallible ourselves. But, dispiriting as it can be to witness or learn about feuds, unfairness, and unethical behavior among practitioners, we are enormously heartened that the great majority of practitioners do good work and strive sincerely to foster kindness and respect in relation to their audiences and colleagues. Our hope is that the aspirational values of Playback Theatre—its openness to outcome, its honoring of ordinary people's stories, its commitment to voices otherwise unheard, its call to the expansiveness of the artistic imagination—will always be a sort of magnetic north which all of us can steer by.

24. See Appendix and Centre for Playback Theatre's website, www.playbackcentre.org.

2

Culture, Community, and Playback Theatre[1]

Jo Salas (1981)

PLAYBACK THEATRE is a company based in the Mid-Hudson Valley which since 1975 has been performing and teaching a form of improvisation devised by the director, Jonathan Fox. It is a form in which the real dramas of real lives, told by volunteers from the audience, become theatre pieces created on the spot by the actors. Someone once described it as "theatre of the cave," meaning that all modern permutations of theatre had their origin in the ancient impulse to communicate and dramatize one's experience, thereby integrating it both in one's psyche and in the evolution of the community.

For this kind of personal storytelling to work in the modern context of an audience who at least begin the evening as strangers, accustomed to privacy and expecting to sit back and be entertained, it is essential to create an atmosphere of safety and respect. The actors are on stage throughout the performance, open and receptive to the unknown roles they will be asked to play, and coming back to their own selves between scenes. There is an element of humility: they are there to reflect and fulfill the audience's stories. Seeing the demeanor of the actors, members of the audience feel safe enough to respond when they are invited to tell briefly something which has happened to them: a happy memory, a painful memory, a dream, a fantasy. The "Teller," guided by the director, or "Conductor," casts his or her story from the row of actors who then transform the story into a theatrical scene, using boxes and pieces of cloth

---

1. First published in slightly different form as "Culture and Community: Playback Theatre" in *The Drama Review*, MIT Press, Vol.27, 1983, along with a partial performance transcript, not included here. This original version was written in 1981.

as props, and supported by music and lighting. In this way, story following story, a collective drama is built, the subject of which is the lives of the people present.

At a performance last year in New Paltz, New York, the hometown of several members of the company, a woman called Paula got up to tell about her fear while driving in a snowstorm. She had come to several previous performances but this was her first time as a Teller. She chose an actor to play herself, and two more to become the snow. Other actors became customers in her Main Street store, where the scene began. At the climax of the scene, the actors playing the snow threatened and taunted the onstage Paula as she drove trembling homeward.

Paula, watching, laughed in recognition. After it was over, the Conductor asked her if she wanted to see a transformation, a redoing of the scene with a new ending. Paula wanted to see herself strong and triumphant over her fear and the snowstorm, and the actors created this for her.

Some weeks later I was in her store on Main Street. It was the first time I had seen her since the performance. She told me with great pleasure and pride that somehow seeing that scene had had the effect of lessening her fearfulness about driving in snow. What fear remained she was able to turn into anger and determination to master the situation. She said two other things: one was that transforming her snow panic in this way had had a similar effect on other fears in her life, and also that other audience members had been in her store at different times and had told her how they, too, were afraid of driving in bad weather and how this scene had come to mind at those frightening moments. Paula was glad to find that she wasn't the only cowardly driver in town. And the experience of telling her story in public in her own town had to some extent deepened her sense of the town as community, as her community.

WHEN SEVERAL OF US from Playback were in Australia last year, we met a man who had been part of a team whose function was to travel through parts of the outback, spending a few days in various small settlements, getting enough familiarity with each one to write a few songs, or, a play, about that little community. They would move on, leaving the song or play with the people, and it was apparent from his words and from the slides he showed us how momentous this was for the communities they visited. To have their experience in a song! Perhaps the sense of validation created in this way would encourage the villagers to write their own. Recently I was listening to a Woodstock singer singing songs about Woodstock to a Woodstock audience. Seeing the delight and engagement of the audience I felt again how vibrant and important that link is: the artist who is of the community distills the community's experience and gives it back to them. In the US on a large scale there is no shortage of movies, songs, and plays about the ongoing reality of living in this country. But it tends to be in only a few "artistic" communities such as Woodstock that the experience of being in one particular place, with its own flavor, finds its way into living art forms and back to the people.

I've come to feel that one of the main roles of Playback Theatre is to provide this service, to offer our own community the chance to recognize itself and know that it is an entity. Traditional storytellers had this function. The experience of the group, the clan, or village was heard, crafted, distilled, recorded, and told to those to whom it meant the most. The storyteller can be a shaman, a purveyor of magic and truth, acknowledged to be vital to the health of the group. Playback Theatre potentially embodies these functions and qualities, when accepted in that role by a community.

AFTER SEVEN YEARS based in the same area—the Mid-Hudson Valley, and specifically the towns of Poughkeepsie and New Paltz—there appears to be some degree of that kind of acceptance. It shows in different ways: one is the large number of familiar faces, our "constituency," who reappear regularly at performances, some of whom seek further involvement by joining classes and workshops. Another sign is the diversity of the community agencies and organizations who ask us to work with them, or perform for them. Playback Theatre is in the air of the community, to be remembered when a need arises for entertainment, for airing problems, for celebration, for a shaman.

In a conversation published in *Parabola* magazine, Peter Brook talks about the traditional function of theatre, which is to create a temporary unity out of the fragments of society by means of ritual based on a shared frame of reference.[2] Although most modern theatre has to find ways of being effective in the absence of a shared frame of reference, a "matrix of unity," the forms and rituals evolved by Playback Theatre and manifested at each performance, together with its basis in universal experience, appear to establish enough of that matrix to allow the emergence of connection and clarity. The microcosm of a Playback performance has as its cornerstones elements common to all lives: pride, chagrin, triumph, loss, expansiveness, fear, humiliation, delight, in the contexts of family and other relationships, work, and the larger world itself. Of course, the US in the 1980s has very little in common with the tribe or the village. Our public performance audiences are composed of strangers from all the variety of backgrounds and experience that a modern urban context can provide. But even in such a context, people are eager to make use of the opportunity to tell and hear life stories, although both the stories and the audience's reception of them in such a situation tend to fall far short of the levels of intimacy, electricity, and revelation that are often part of a performance with a group who already feel themselves to be a group: a conference, a congregation, a class. However, there is no audience that does not share, in addition to the currents of all lives, the desire to tell stories, and the excitement and fear associated with doing so. In the hundreds of performances we have given over the past seven years, there has never been a time when there were no Tellers.

In a Playback Theatre performance there are prescribed rituals and forms readily understood as such by new audience members, and providing continuity to those who have come before. Visually the performances are always set up in the same way: the Conductor on the stage right (left from the audience's view), seated beside the empty Teller's chair, the musician on stage left with an array of instruments spread out on the floor; between them a semi-circle

2. "Lie and Glorious Adjective: An Interview with Peter Brook." *Parabola*, Vol. 6, 3, 1981.

of actors sitting on boxes; and upstage at left a wooden structure hung with many-colored pieces of cloth, to be used as props. There are words used by the Conductor as formulae, to create certain specific effects. The procedure followed by the actors in preparing for and concluding a scene is always the same. These and the ritual elements add up to an atmosphere of respect, familiarity, and safety, in which both audience and actors are invited to be adventurous, spontaneous, and creative.

The stories told are fragments of lives, often chaotic, half-understood by the Teller, without clear beginnings, endings, and climaxes. This is the nature of everyone's ongoing experience of living in the world. It is rare for events in real lives to be easily described and contained, without staying on the level of anecdote. It is the task of the Conductor, the actors, the musician, and the lighting person to receive the raw material, filter it through their understanding and inspiration, condense some aspects of it, expand others—all without discussion—and present the Teller and the audience with a theatre piece, in which the story and the Teller are nevertheless honored. The Teller has an opportunity to comment and correct the scene, if necessary, and in stories with an unhappy outcome, the Teller may be invited to find a new ending (a "transformation"), after seeing it first of all as it happened.

This is a process which allows the Teller and the other members of the audience to see their experience crystallized and made clear and cohesive. In scenes where a transformation is appropriate it is a chance for the Teller himself or herself to be the refiner, the inspired one who crafts the raw material of life. A series of moments from the confusion of ordinary lives becomes the subject for intense artistic focus and expression, and through this the moments are celebrated, comprehended, and entrusted to the community's reservoir of knowledge of itself.

I remember our first performance in Albany, where we were unknown to our small audience, and three pictures come to mind. One is the first story told, a father's story about trouble between his two teenage sons and how he was able to help by listening and talking to one of them. And the last story of the evening, told by an elderly woman. She was at first reluctant to leave her seat in the audience to come and sit onstage. But she came. Her story was about the peaceful death of her husband, at home and surrounded by loving family, in spite of choruses of criticism and unwelcome advice from friends who thought he should have been in a hospital. Where did it come from, the desire and courage to tell these stories to a room of strangers, to entrust them to the hands of an unknown theatre company?

The third image in my mind is a small group of elderly people in the front row. They did not participate by telling stories but I saw on their faces a shining look of wonder and excitement as they realized they were invited to be the creators, to share in the act of theatre. Everywhere that we have taken Playback Theatre we have encountered this eagerness for the public and ritualized communication of personal experience. Theatre may have other functions but none more fundamental.

3

Defining Theatre for the Nonscripted Domain[1]

Jonathan Fox (1992)

THEATRE IS STRONGLY ASSOCIATED with a play in the popular mind—that is, a production which starts with a script written by a playwright. Yet there are many kinds of theatrical performance that do not make use of playwrights—a drama therapy session, for example, or a group-developed skit performed by adolescents, or the routines of a clown. The term drama has come to distinguish what might loosely be called nonscripted from scripted theatre; it is often used polemically, both by those who wish to separate themselves from the hierarchical, product-oriented literary culture and by those in the other camp who wish to keep at arm's length what seem to be unartistic and unredeemedly homespun improvisational approaches to performing. The distinctions between theatre and drama seem to depend significantly on concepts of specialization and context, and at any rate, have often not been clear. For example, Brian Way called his seminal book *Development through Drama* (Way, 1967), and Viola Spolin called hers *Improvisation for the Theatre* (Spolin, 1963), even though both focus on young actors, developmental process, and scriptless performance. The purpose of this article is to propose a definition of theatre that does not depend on play writing and which comprehends examples of oral as well as literary theatre. The discussion will demonstrate that the therapeutic uses of theatre, which are largely nonscripted, have as much claim to legitimacy as the literary theatre, in that they place a value on clients' role-playing

1. First published in The Arts in Psychotherapy, 19, 3 (1992), pages 201–207. Jonathan Fox's book *Acts of Service: Spontaneity, Commitment, Tradition in the Nonscripted Theatre* (New Paltz, NY, Tusitala, 1994) expands on these ideas.

with awareness, and indeed are part of an older tradition. In the discussion below, oral theatre, nonscripted theatre, and improvisational
theatre all refer to dramatic production that does not depend on a
written script.

Preliterary enactment

In order to understand modern scriptless theatre, we must begin
with its origins in preliterary culture. The dramatic enactments
of oral cultures—the all-night religious ceremonies, the healing
dances, the vision quests—are characteristically trance-inducing as
a means to secure a distinctly redressive outcome. It would appear
that an irrational context stimulates trance; thus Indonesian performers stimulate themselves "beyond thought" (de Zoete, 1938);
the Kung of the Kalahari sing in nonsense syllables to propel the
dancers into trance (Katz, 1982); and many cultures make use of a
hieratic language not understood by the auditors (Jenkins, 1979). In
such enactments, the performer becomes a healer, laying hands on
the ring of spectators or exorcising illness through shamanic acts.
These events are also likely to be highly communal and intimate in
nature: the performers will be known personally by the audience,
who are liable to know each other, and the line between performer
and spectator is often easily crossed.

As children of literary culture, in contrast, we have grown up
with a distinctly different model of theatre, one based on language,
tightly organized into a written composition, of which the purpose
is not redressive, but aesthetic. Furthermore, this theatre is a
primarily urban phenomenon, performed by specialists who are
not part of the same small community as the audience.

There have been many contemporary practitioners, however,
who have rejected literary theatre and sought to recreate aspects of
the preliterary model of enactment. These actors and directors are
following a path, perhaps, cleared earlier by visual artists, dancers,
and composers (Picasso, Humphreys, Stravinsky) who found inspiration in "primitivist" tribal forms.[2] They have rejected many aspects

2. According to Christopher Small (1977, p. 35), the Paris World Exhibition of 1889,
which had such an impact on the modernist painters, also featured performances, provid-

of their literary heritage and the culture of modern play production. They have welcomed ecstasy; eschewed plays; returned to the
outdoors; allowed nonactors on stage; upheld political and even
personal transformation as goals. They have allied themselves with
the fields of experimental theatre, educational theatre, community
theatre, therapeutic theatre, and comic-satiric improvisation.

Not surprisingly, in most cases, there has been a more or less
creative blend of preliterary and literary values in the fashioning
of what might be called a postliterary theatre. For example, many
experimental theatre companies which began by improvisationally
developing their own pieces ended by using playwrights; practitioners of educational and therapeutic theatre that reject scripts
nevertheless prefer to base their objectives on cognitive assumptions rather than on trance-induction and ecstasy.

Despite this mix of literary and preliterary values, the general
trend remains valid. Many practitioners have been creating alternatives to the literary/aesthetic model of theatre. The question
remains: have they left theatre, or is it appropriate to redefine
the term to embrace at least some of their nonscripted dramatic
activities? I would like to pose here a definition that suggests theatre begins before play production.

Theatre and consciousness

The psychologist Julian Jaynes (1976) draws on left-right
brain research and his own reading of prehistory to arrive at a
theory which he encapsulates in the title of his book, *The Origin
of Consciousness in the Breakdown of the Bicameral Mind*. Insofar as
his theory attempts to identify the beginning of consciousness
in human evolution, he is drawn into conclusions about prehistory which are far from proven. Nevertheless, his ideas hold
interest. His theory was sparked by modern discoveries about

---

ing performing artists with an opportunity to experience preliterary music and dance.
Artaud's interest in "primitive" places is well known (Artaud, 1958); Moreno, the founder
of psychodrama, who was also subject to Dada and Expressionist influences, advocated
a shamanic, rather than literary approach (Fox, 1987); and there are undoubtedly other
seminal figures in the nonscripted theatre who were specifically inspired by preliterary
models. The intellectual history of modern nonscripted theatre remains understudied.

the hemispheres of the brain. Basically, Jaynes suggests that in early civilization, the human brain was structured to favor right-brain functions, such as an intuitive, nonverbal, global approach to knowing. It was a time when what we would call hallucinatory "voices" were real, and individuals, lacking what we think of as mind, relied on their "bicameral" perspective for guidance. The bicameral mindset, according to Jaynes, included induction, trance, a strong communal urge termed the "collective cognitive imperative," and "archaic authorization." (p. 324)

But as left-brain functions, enabling analysis, language, objectivity, and linearity, developed, the right brain became less dominant, and in the process, "consciousness" was born. Consciousness involves nar-ratizing, "always seeing our vicarial selves as the main figures in the stories of our lives." (p. 63) A "space" for thinking becomes located inside our heads. The brain conceives of lexical metaphor, including the idea of "me." Language is a key element in the process towards left-brain dominance: "Each new stage of words literally creates new perceptions and attentions." (p. 132) Thus "subjective conscious mind is an analog of what is called the real world," enabling us to understand reality and make decisions. (p. 55)

This theory firmly connects the idea of consciousness with story. Prior to consciousness, Jaynes seems to be arguing, humans were simply in experience, responding to basic survival drives and beyond that, to the voices of divine authorization. After consciousness, the conception of an "analog I" enabled the early human to stand outside of as well as be part of the run of events because he or she could describe them. It meant the individual reconstitution of experience, and became a vital component of human life.[3]

Oliver Sacks writes about Jimmy G., a patient with Korsakov's Syndrome, which is characterized by a complete absence of nar-ratizing consciousness. To Sacks, the 20th century neurologist, it

3. Paulo Freire's definition of "critical consciousness," developed in response to 20th-cen-tury conditions in Brazil, has interesting similarities to Jaynes's concept of consciousness. Freire found that literacy followed quickly once a new mindset was taught, involving an attitude of "creation and re-creation, a self-transformation producing a stance of inter-vention in one's context." (Freire, 1973, p. 48) Of course, Augusto Boal, a major figure in contemporary non-scripted theatre, is a protégé of Freire (Boal, 1979).

seems truly as if his patient has no "soul," so fundamental is his deficiency. "To be ourselves," Sacks concludes, "we must have ourselves—possess, if need be re-possess, our life stories. We must 'recollect' ourselves, recollect the inner drama, the narrative of ourselves." (Sacks, 1987, p. 111) In short, this capacity to see our life as a story represents a major step in human evolutionary growth. It is one of our most ineradicable possessions. It is at once a preserver of what is worth remembering from the past and a pointer to what can be in the future.[4]

The importance of narratization in the development of consciousness has implications for the concept of spontaneity, which depends on skill at knowing the "story of the moment." Thus spontaneity, like storytelling, depends on consciousness. In this sense spontaneity—an individual response to an individually constructed moment—exists only in consciousness, even though many of its characteristics seem to come from the right rather than the left hemisphere of the brain. Actually, of course, spontaneity demands an integration of left and right functions and is essential to non-scripted performance.

The steps toward theatre

Diverse theories about the origins of theatre, such as play-acting, ecstatic enactment, and ritual, when fit in to Jaynes's scheme, make a certain rough sense to me.

It would seem from earliest times human beings engaged in play-acting, pretending to be angry, for example, much as other mammals do. Such play enables the learning of survival skills and makes possible a certain level of interactive contact between individuals of the species—communication, as Bateson has pointed out, which is not without sophistication because in the "as-if" of playacting the actors

4. Jaynes articulated his theories about early human development after focusing on schizophrenics who "heard voices" and epileptics who had had their cortex severed. Sacks's patients, although with different conditions, point to compatible conclusions. Sacks finds that his patients, who cannot "think" in a variety of fundamental ways, nevertheless maintain quite wonderful qualities: of contact with the concrete, of energy, of music and drawing, of loving, and of certain remarkable mental skills. These qualities he associates with the "narrative" mode of thought. Perhaps alluding to its primacy in the course of human historical development, Sacks asserts that "the narrative comes first, has spiritual priority" [over the paradigmatic]. (Sacks, 1987, p. 183)

are dealing in paradoxical meanings. However, they always remain themselves. (Bateson, 1972, p. 189)

Ecstatic enactment, action for the purpose of generating high energy required for hunting, exorcism, war, or other purposes, consists of a dance at the simplest level, involving neither role playing nor language. Surviving examples are the twirling dervishes, the Balinese sword dances, and the Kung healing dances.

Ritual enactment becomes a means of making contact with transpersonal forces. It is distinctly unspontaneous in nature, since it shuns consciousness (although the conductor of the ritual, who stands apart to the extent that he is responsible for beginning and ending the ceremony, may be in a position which invites consciousness). There is a widely held sense that in ritual enactment the actors "represent" their roles rather than "portray" them. Thus an actor is the bison. The Lakota vision dances described by Black Elk would seem to be in this category. (Neihardt, 1972)

Theatre involves three elements absent from the above. First is the portrayal of a story: It will have certain narrative characteristics, such as characters, objects, settings, events, crises. It will be a definitional experience, defined by the spectators' own story lore, and in turn contributing to the self-definition of each spectator. And it will offer counsel, wisdom, insight, ideas of value.

Second, theatre consists of actors playing a role. The Rubicon is crossed once actors "portray," i.e. accept the awareness that they are playing roles which are distinct from themselves. Such awareness is concomitant with Jaynes's "analog I." It implies the presence of the fictive element and the ability to act "oneself" and "not oneself" at the same time.

Thirdly, theatre involves performance, which can be defined as acting with awareness. Performance is rooted in intentionality and takes place before witnesses. What distinguishes theatrical from everyday performance, or a dramaturgical perspective of ordinary behavior (Goffman, 1959), is primarily the fictive element. In theatrical performance, performer and witness share an understanding about the action that "this is pretend." Without the acceptance of this paradox, the dramatic fiction breaks down, and we are left either with "nontheatre" or deceit. Thus in performing theatre, we must communicate the frame of pretend around our actions, and around that, the frame of intentionality, an awesome—and exciting—task, the ultimate form of spontaneity test, and a tease to the playful genius of our intelligence.

Fully defined, then, theatre is the performance of a story by actors in role.[5]

The most important implication of this understanding of theatre for me is that it marks the genesis of theatre at conscious-ness, not plays. It helps explain the particular position of theatre in relation to the other arts. Dance, music, and the plastic arts are forms which, while they are created and enjoyed by conscious beings, nevertheless, do not demand consciousness. Wordless, they communicate through sound, movement, shape, color, texture and other elements which precede thought. In this sense, the nonverbal arts keep their feet in the timeless past, when language was not the be-all-and-end-all of communication. Writing, on the other hand, is divorced from this primal world of shape and sound. Experiencing a poem or a novel demands skills of reading, vocabu-lary acquisition, and literary comprehension which define it as a distinctively mental activity. We do not see the colors or the move-ments, we imagine them following the understanding of abstract letters on the page.[6] Theatre is a bridge between the nonverbal and the literary arts. There is the potential for the most sophisticated linguistic expression, demanding education and thoughtfulness from the auditor, but at the same time the experience is sensory:

---

5. Of course, we must keep in mind that there never was, or could be, a neat separa-tion in the development of a literary culture between "theatre" and what went before. Undoubtedly the process of development was gradual, subtle, and full of advances and retreats in mentation. I imagine there were plenty of occurrences of actors knowingly assuming a role in the midst of the bicameral period, although then such an awareness was probably considered an aberration, just as there has been a prodigious, but inevitably somewhat unsuccessful, pursuit of ritual on the part of modern human beings.

6. Writing that is read aloud and listened to obviously falls into a different category from writing that is read by readers. Of course, the improvisational nature of the oral poet's challenge gives added dramatic impact to his recitation. We just do not have the same concern over how or whether a reader will remember the tale, although we will still be delighted and instructed by the lines. Both the reciter and the reader, however, no matter how theatrical their presentation, are not engaged in theatre for the reason that they are not in role.

the words will be spoken, by a personage standing there before you, and she may even be screaming. Theatre's involvement both with preconscious and conscious communication is the source of much of its impact and arouses resistance in individuals who desire narrower frameworks.

In considering, therefore, the "beginning" and "end" of the domain of theatre, there will thus be a significant area of theatrical expression existing between the manifestation of consciousness and literary play production. This is the zone of oral theatre. It includes Mummers plays, Topeng dramas, and contemporary nonscripted approaches from a Living Theatre piece to a psychodrama to a performance of the Mental Health Players. Each example needs to be examined in light of the definition. If there is performance, if the actors are in role, and if there is a comprehensible story, then it is theatre—even if there is no script, even if the purpose is to heal, even if the technology is crude and the community tiny.[7]

On the other end, theatre, no matter how literary, must be fed by its preliterary roots. If a theatre piece becomes too heavy with consciousness, its impact as theatre diminishes. One can assert in such a case that the ideas overwhelm the story, as is the case in certain poorly written plays. Or one can feel that a particular production is too lacking in elements of oral culture, such as spectacle, emotion, or an organic texture. Today's literary theatre involves such complexity of organization, so many distinct individuals with differentiated inputs, so elongated a period of preparation—in sum, such breakdown and bustle, that the production often loses its creative pulse. The effort in this century of Stanislavski and others to help actors stay in touch with their subconscious can be interpreted as an effort to marshal right-brain powers to avoid succumbing to a Juggernaut of theatrical left-brainedness.[8]

In his theory of the transitional object, Winnicott emphasizes the importance of the "me-not-me" paradox—of the capacity of

7. For material on Mummers Plays and (oral) Medieval entertainments, see Brody (1970) and Willeford (1969).

8. "Our subconscious gives us inspirations; yet we apparently can use this subconscious only through our consciousness, which kills it. Fortunately, there is a way out..." (Stanislavski, 1936, p. 13)

a normal infant to believe in the aliveness of its teddy bear and yet know it is not real. "Playing," he writes, "is inherently exciting and precarious. This characteristic derives not from instinctual arousal but from the precariousness that belongs to the Interplay in the child's mind of that which is subjective (near-hallucination) and that which is objectively perceived (actual, or shared reality)." Playing, Winnicott believes, leads to shared playing, which leads to cultural experience. And thence, we might add, to theatre. (Winnicott, 1971, p. 52)

Performance can be regarded as a sophisticated form of play—play with a metalevel frame calling attention to itself. My own experience suggests that mentally healthy three year-olds can do it with ease, while others, inhibited by social or developmental conditions, fail to accomplish various components of theatrical performance, including narratization, capacity for pretending, ability to play, ability to role play, awareness of engaging in these activities, willingness to engage in them in a social context (before witnesses), and management of the transitions between performance and nonperformance.[9]

The challenge of creative manipulation of such paradoxical actions is just what drew Gregory Bateson, an early cybernetician, into the field of psychology. For Bateson, schizophrenics were individuals who could not move appropriately between the domains of play and nonplay or distinguish between frames of meaning, while a fully functioning adult could easily maneuver in a world of constantly oscillating realities. In this sense human beings can be defined as *homo agens*—human as actor: well adjusted, always readjusting, able to perform or not perform appropriately. Such flexibility and creativity lies at the heart of Moreno's spontaneity theory (Fox, 1987); it is part of the "evolutionary step" (Bateson, 1972, p. 191) human beings have made towards increasingly complex and creative forms of action and awareness. As such, theatre is an appropriate vehicle for the diagnosis and treatment of individual and social problems.

9. See Chapter 12, "Is There More?"

Language in nonscripted theatre

What place does language play in theatre? It would appear that while language may not be essential to the portrayal of role and the narration of a story, it is of vital assistance. A bedfellow of consciousness, language is the natural concomitant of theatre. Yet the language of a nonscripted production will be stylistically distinct from a play. It is important to understand how.

First the compositional style will contain characteristics of oral composition. The text is likely to be created on the spot; according to Albert Lord, who did the pioneer research showing that the Homeric epics were orally composed, the "poem is not composed for but in performance." (Lord, 1965, p. 8) There is likely to be an emphasis on aggregation (as opposed to conciseness) and an acceptance of the improvisational moment (as opposed to a fixed text and set movements). To a literary ear and eye, the performance may seem underplanned and long-winded, full of repetitiveness and slow beats.

Secondly, the meaning is conveyed according to different stylistic conventions. For instance, in the contemporary nonscripted theatre an intermediary (emcee, therapist, social worker, teacher) often coordinates verbal exchanges between audience and performances, taking suggestions for action, inviting comment afterwards, and so forth. The result is an attenuated transcript, in which the drama will be interlaced by social interaction.

One consequence of this permeable line between art and non-art is a heightened sensitivity to context. The dramatic text that emerges will be informed by the social situation and is not independent of it.

As an illustration, here is a part of the transcript of a performance of Playback Theatre. Playback Theatre is an approach based on the spontaneous enactment of personal story founded by myself and the original Playback Theatre company in 1975. While it is used in artistic and social development as well as therapeutic contexts, Playback Theatre is committed at all times to a redressive purpose. (Fox, 1982, 1991; Salas, 1983, 1992) On this occasion, the Playback actors had been enacting scenes, real stories of audience members dramatized in scene form using mime and spoken improvisations. Now they were lined up two by two enacting pairs, two feelings felt at the same time, again, as suggested by audience members. The intermediary, or Conductor, asks for another conflict:

PLAYBACK MUSICIAN: This is two feelings about a parent.

CONDUCTOR: Two feelings about a parent. O.K.

MUSICIAN: Embarrassment and being touched. When my mother got up and sang on a stage in a sort of game show kind of thing.

CONDUCTOR: O.K. When your mother got up and sang on a stage in a game show, both embarrassment and being touched.

(The actors begin the enactment. Near the climax of action, Actor A's pants, inadvertently grabbed by Actor B, start to come down. Actor A says, "I feel embarrassed, but touched." Audience laughter. Applause.)[10]

In this example, the context shapes the script in a number of ways. First of all, the dramatic scene begins with a question and response exchange between intermediary and spectator. Secondly, when the unexpected begins to happen and the actor's trousers are pulled down, the actor "ad libs" in a way that restores congruence to the scene. In the literary theatre, such moments are memorable because of their rarity, while in the nonscripted theatre, the task of finding language to integrate the dramatic (fictive) and here-and-now (social) story is an ongoing, commonplace task. Thirdly, the teller is in this case one of the performers, the company musician, and her offering a moment, usually the function of the audience, makes a statement that we have one communal identity, that no one needs to be excluded from this community of memory (the phrase is from Robert Bellah et al., 1985, p. 153). Most importantly, the performer-teller's story itself makes a statement to the group as a whole, for previous to this enactment, audience members had been invited to be actors in a scene. Her "embarrassed but touched" undoubtedly also refers to

10. Recorded at the Empire State Performing Arts Center, Albany, NY, May 1981.

her reaction to their work.

This example may not seem particularly profound. Yet it points to oral theatre's dependence on context, and the multi-layered meanings of the improvisational moment. It can help us appreciate the significance of Black Elk's line, when after an enactment by the community of one of his visions, he comments that: "The experience was not a long one, but it had great meaning, because it made a picture of the relation between the people and the bison, and the power was in the meaning." (Neihardt, 1972, p. 174) At the same time, we can also appreciate Richard Schechner's despair at documenting this kind of event, when he writes about the 3,000-year-old Indian Agnicayana drama, which is still performed and has been filmed: "What I am saying is that no matter what textual documentation exists, we do not know what Agnicayana was." (Schechner, 1985, p. 59) How meaning is elucidated in improvisational drama, remains, in my view, not well understood. Turner has underscored the larger significance of tribal dramatic events with his concept of "social drama" (Turner, 1969), but his analysis does not address the semiotic in any detail. In nonscripted theatre, the "text" is created according to a process close to everyday communication, involving, it seems, a spontaneous blend of direct, indirect, and symbolic means, both linguistic and iconographic. For theatre, however, the meaning must be heightened by consciousness. The performers must create a pregnant, charged, (what Turner terms) "ergotropic" atmosphere. (Turner, 1981, p. 9)

Conclusion

Summing up, theatre can be defined as the performance of a story by actors in role. This definition includes, as well as literary theatre, an improvisation zone, in which the performers manifest consciousness—of their performative act, of their fictive roles, of their narrative art—even though they are not making use of a play. Acceptance of this zone as a valid domain of theatrical exploration might lead to fruitful developments in our understanding of modern theatre. First of all, nonscripted theatre can benefit from criticism. For the most part, it is ignored by critics, who are staunchly literary-minded. Moreover, nonscripted theatre needs attention from critics with some knowledge and appreciation of the distinct objectives of improvisational theatre production. Secondly, arts funding sources need to expand their guidelines to include non-scripted practitioners: at present without a strong ethnic make-up (in which case there may be a special category of funding), it is almost impossible (in the US) for a process-oriented ensemble to receive funding as a theatre company. Thirdly, there is need for research: to develop new methods for the documentation and analysis of oral theatre; to study the levels of context-text related communication as they become manifest in an improvisational performance; to examine the spontaneous creative process of the improvisational actor (the results might have usefulness far outside the field of theatrical studies). Finally, students of drama need educating on the distinctions between nonscripted and literary enactment; on the aesthetic vs. redressive purposes of theatre; on theatre's roots in the small community vs. its place in the modern city; and on that narratizing, self-reflexive communication of meaning that defines theatre's boundaries.

Such criticism, research, and education will help restore a new legitimacy to the idea of theatre as therapy. Therapeutic theatre need not be compared to literary theatre, either as alternative or aberration, but rather appreciated as part of a prior tradition that emerged in the healing ceremonial rituals of ancient civilizations and has been in practice ever since. While it involves story, portrayal, and performance as does literary theatre, this tradition has its distinctive characteristics of language and purpose, including a fluid oscillation between fictive and everyday reality, communality, and a deep commitment to healing both individuals and society.

References

Artaud, Antonin. (1958). *The Theatre and Its Double*. New York: Grove.

Bateson, Gregory. (1972). *Steps to an Ecology of Mind*. San Francisco: Chandler.

Bellah, Robert N.; Madsen, Richard; Sullivan, William M.; Swindler, Ann; & Tipton, Steven M. (1985). *Habits of the Heart: Individualism and Commitment in American Life*. New York: Harper & Row.

Boal, Augusto. (1979). *Theatre of the Oppressed*. New York: Urizen Books.

Brody, Alan. (1970). *English Mummers and their Plays*. London: Routledge & Kegan Paul.

de Zoete, Beryl & Spies, Walter. (1938). *Dance and Drama in Bali*. London: Faber & Faber.

Fox, Jonathan. (1982). "Playback Theater: The Community Sees Itself." In *Drama In Therapy*, Vol. II. Richard Courtney and Gertrude Schattner, Eds. New York: Drama Book Specialists, 1982.

Fox, Jonathan. (Ed.). (1987). *The Essential Moreno: Writings on Psychodrama, Group Method, and Spontaneity*. New York: Springer.

Fox, Jonathan. (1991). "Die inszenierte persönliche Geschichte im Playback-Theater" [Dramatized Personal Story in Playback Theatre]. *Psychodrama: Zeitschrift für Theorie und Praxis* (Germany). Vol. 1, Heft 1, 31–44.

Freire, Paulo. (1973). *Education for Critical Consciousness*. New York: Seabury Press.

Goffman, Erving. (1959). *The Presentation of Self in Everyday Life*. New York: Anchor.

Jaynes, Julian. (1976). *The Origin of Consciousness in the Breakdown of the Bicameral Mind*. Boston: Houghton Mifflin.

Jenkins, Ron. (June 1979). "Becoming a Clown in Bali." *The Drama Review*, Vol. 23, 49–56.

Katz, Richard. (1982). *Boiling Energy*. Cambridge: Harvard University Press.

Lord, Albert. (1965). *The Singer of Tales*. New York: Atheneum.

Neihardt, John G. (1972). *Black Elk Speaks*. New York: Pocket Books.

Rubin, William. (Ed.). (1984). *"Primitivism" in 20th Century Art*. New York: Museum of Modern Art.

Sacks, Oliver. (1987). *The Man Who Mistook His Wife for a Hat*. New York: Harper and Row.

Salas, Jo. (1983). "Culture and Community: Playback Theater." *The Drama Review*, Vol. 27, 2, 15–25.

Salas, Jo. (1992). "Music in Playback Theatre." *The Arts in Psychotherapy*, Vol. 19, 13–18.

Schechner, Richard. (1985). *Between Theater and Anthropology.* Philadelphia: University of Pennsylvania Press.

Small, Christopher. (1977). *Music, Society, Education.* New York: Schirmer Books.

Spolin, Viola. (1963). *Improvisation for the Theater.* Evanston, IL: Northwestern University Press.

Stanislavski, Constantin. (1936). *An Actor Prepares.* New York: Theater Arts Books.

Turner, Victor. (1981). *From Ritual to Theatre.* New York: Performing Arts Journal Pubs.

Way, Brian. (1967). *Development through Drama.* London: Longmans.

Winnicott, D. W. (1971). *Playing and Reality.* London: Tavistock.

4

What is "Good" Playback Theatre?[1]

Jo Salas (1999)

AS GUEST CONDUCTOR, I took part in a performance with London Playback Theatre at a weekend celebration held in support of the Beijing Women's Conference. About 80 people crowded into the performance space, an oddly shaped room upstairs at the Royal Festival Hall. The audience was very diverse: women attending the weekend festival, individuals and families who had come especially to see Playback, some elderly couples strolling by the Thames who wandered in out of curiosity. I had been warned that British audiences were not easy to engage, so I was relieved when they responded as fully as any other audience. Within minutes strong feelings had been expressed and enacted, people were laughing and crying, and the actors, musician, and I were working smoothly together in spite of our unfamiliarity with each other. As the show went on there were some inspired moments of acting, as well as occasional awkwardness or confusion. At the end of the show the applause was warm. People lingered talking to us and to each other before dispersing into the afternoon.

The other performers and I came together before we too went our separate ways. Most of them shared my feeling that it had gone well. But one young woman was in tears of frustration. "I *hated* it!" she said. She felt that the actors had missed opportunities to be as sophisticated as they could be, and, particularly, that she had failed to show the scope of her own skill.

---

1. Delivered as a keynote speech at the first academic symposium on Playback Theatre, held at the University of Kassel, Germany, in 1997. Published in *Gathering Voices: Essays on Playback Theatre*, editors Jonathan Fox and Heinrich Dauber. New Paltz, NY: Tusitala, 1999 (now out of print).

How to account for the radical difference in our perception? My judgment of success was based on my feeling that the performers, myself included, had achieved an acceptable level of performance. Our scenes and so on had been generally well shaped, and accurate in embodying the essence of the teller's experience. The audience had participated fully from the outset, in spite of the diversity of background, age, ideology, and contact with Playback. The familiar phenomenon of audience members lingering afterwards, connected to each other as they had not been before, was another sign to me that what we had done had succeeded.

But for Chloë, the unhappy actor, the audience's satisfaction meant nothing. She hadn't even noticed it. She had been focused on artistic issues to the complete exclusion of the show as a social event. To her, success was something that happened only on stage, not in the room as a whole.

PLAYBACK THEATRE is theatre, and theatre is art.

Playback is theatre not simply because that is how it has been named, but because what we do in Playback fulfills the very essence of theatre's intention: to convey human experience by enacting it in distilled form; to embody narrative and meaning in the realm of space and time.

It is also an interactive social process with the purpose of service to its audience; a purpose that most other kinds of theatre do not share.

Since Playback's earliest days, questions relating to aesthetics and to artistic standards have raised themselves constantly. Can this really be theatre if it is also service? Are we doing it well enough? Can we expect to be acknowledged by others as theatre artists? How can we recognize and measure success in Playback? How can we refine it? What do we mean by "good" Playback?

What we do is art, but not only art, and maybe not always art. Playback's effectiveness involves artistic excellence—but artistic excellence alone does not ensure success, and further, Playback Theatre can, in certain circumstances, be fulfilled by people lacking artistic sensibility, skill, or experience.

Evaluating art

All art is the manifestation of the artist's impulse to create, which itself is an urge to synthesize and to reveal. Art is the revelation of meaning—not the simple depiction of beauty or obedience to laws of form, but the artist's inspired attempt to convey her or his perception of a meaning that emerges from or underlies the randomness of common experience. For the perceiver of art, there is a sense of recognition, delight, a confirmation of truth. The philosopher Newton speaks of the artist's task as being not to create beauty where none existed, but in fact "to lift a corner of the veil and *reveal* beauty" (Newton, 1950): and by beauty, he means rightness of form and design, not necessarily harmony. Gregory Bateson (1972) discusses art in terms of pattern, meaning the presence of elements that repeat in a connected design, so that if you see one part of a pattern you also learn about the other, unseen part. The internal metaphors of a work of art contain information about wider realms—the unconscious, or the nature of reality itself—that are not directly perceivable. The artist's deliberate placement of one element in relation to another matches or illuminates the perceiver's intuition of truth: it is the fact of this relatedness, says Bateson, that is the true subject of art.

Art has the capacity to imply the presence of design, of pattern, as a feature of reality. It can affirm an ontological meaning, which is the knowledge that *being* itself is purposeful. When we raise the question of assessment of a work of art—"how good is it?"—it is this function of affirming meaning that we are asking about. As human beings, we need the affirmation that art gives us, and we want it in strong measure. We need art in order to integrate and comprehend our experience. We are disappointed, even dismayed, by inferior art. We may travel long distances and pay large amounts of money to experience "good" art. If we are artists ourselves we invest enormous effort, usually unpaid, in making our art as fine as we can possibly make it. And as artists, we are not content with anything less than an evaluative aesthetic judgment. We are pleased to know someone has enjoyed our creation; but there is a world of difference between hearing "I enjoyed it" and "This is very good." The pronouncement of value indicates the perceiver's "yes!"—

that inward recognition of meaning and truth. It indicates that the artist has succeeded, at least to some degree, in his profoundest task of lifting a corner of the veil and revealing a part of the connecting pattern that lies underneath. The creator of the world itself, according to Genesis, pronounced his work to be good when it was completed, an expression of satisfaction recognizable by any artist.

How do ordinary people, not professional critics, evaluate the art that we encounter? What is it that leads us to perceive something as good art? Do the music, literature, art, and performance that most strongly move and inspire us have anything in common?

There are elements, I believe, shared by all art that is widely recognized as being great. Whether the work is visual, written or performed, these elements include order (in the sense of purposeful design), an integrity of form with some kind of internal cohesiveness, the presence of originality, a high degree of skill in execution, evidence of conviction and inspiration on the part of the artist, and the ineffable sense that the work of art speaks of a reality beyond its own scale.[2]

If an artistic creation possesses all these qualities in abundance, it is likely to be considered by most people as great art. It will create in its audience the strongest experience of revelation of meaning. In the absence of these qualities, or of some of them, a work of art is less likely to generate a consensus of value: its impact will vary from one perceiver to another. But art that is less than great may still fulfill art's deepest purpose for some people. It is perfectly possible for an audience member to be riveted and transported by an amateur concert even if the performers lack the skill of professionals. It depends on the presence of other elements, not exclusively aesthetic: more about this later.

Evaluating interactive social events

As I said earlier, Playback Theatre is an art, and therefore subject to assessment according to the presence or absence of the elements mentioned above. However, it is more than art: a Playback event is also integrally an interactive social event, and subject to success or

2. See Chapter 11, "Searching for Beyond."

failure as such. (It is significant that there is no obvious term to refer to the realm of our work that lies beyond pure art. The absence of a familiar or fully adequate term reflects the common difficulty in comprehending and discussing what I am referring to as the "inter-active social" domain.)

We live our lives in proximity to others. The groups in which we find ourselves as children—family, neighborhood, and school—may be nurturing, or inadequate, or destructive. With maturity comes the desire to choose, to the degree possible, the nature and quality of the groups that form our social world, the people we live and work with, the groups we learn and play with.

Although most people seek out groups that are rewarding and try to avoid those that are disappointing or harmful, they are not necessarily aware of the components of successful interactive events, and therefore may not be able to consistently choose, build or maintain groups that are truly satisfying and effective. You may notice that your evening language classes run smoothly and feel enjoyable while meetings with colleagues at work leave you dissatisfied or diminished, without realizing that the difference between them is no accident. As in the domain of art, there are distinct elements that are likely to lead to fulfillment, whether in an ongoing group or in a one-time event.

Consider a family gathering, a class, or a town meeting. Although each has its own particular demands, they also share common criteria of success. These include planning and organi-zation according to the purpose of the gathering; a congenial and appropriate physical environment; an opportunity early in the proceedings for each person to be seen and heard; an atmosphere of respect; some form of participation or engagement from all present; the acknowledgment and inclusion of diverse concerns, points of view, and feelings; time management; a sense of achieve-ment in relation to the meeting's intent; and an adequate closure at the end. The more these elements are present, the more the event will be experienced as successful. In their absence, an event is felt to be a failure. Participants are likely to feel disappointed, excluded, frustrated, bored, or left wanting, depending on which aspects were inadequate. A family gathering in which some members sit silent while others laugh and chat will not be successful in bringing the family together; a town meeting that is unplanned will not make progress toward its purpose; a classroom that is too cold or crowded will not be conducive to good learning.

Moreno's method of sociometry (1937) addresses particularly the questions relating to inclusiveness and participation. He considered that in any group there is an intricately evolving pattern of relationships between members, resulting in a greater or lesser degree of inclusion and contributing therefore to the group's vitality and effectiveness. Sociometry explores this system of interconnections, with the goal of maximizing and enlivening the participation of all those present.

Groups of many different kinds—vocational, recreational, geographical—are often referred to as "communities," a word rather wistfully overused in our post-industrial era where it is common for people not to know the names of their neighbors. What does "community" mean? It is, I think, the idea of a group of people who acknowledge, value, and maintain their connectedness and their commonality. Jean Vanier, who founded a series of group homes for disabled people in France, described community as "a group of people who are yearning to bring each other forth."

The qualities that might actually lead to the creation of this kind of community are similar to those I have suggested as necessary to a successful interactive social event: the attention to inclusiveness, the care taken with environment and structure, the matching of design to purpose. Whether in an ongoing situation or within one particular event, fulfillment of these criteria can create community in Vanier's sense—a gathering of people who seek to know each other, to listen to each other, to remember and care for each other.

Playback Theatre

A Playback Theatre event is integrally both an artistic event and an interactive social event involving both complex group dynamics and sensitive one-to-one communication. If the task of art is the creation of form to express the artist's perception of meaning, then the Playback artist's task, specifically, is to create cohesive and shapely pieces of theatre based on an acute sense of the meaning of the teller's story. It is their artist's sensibility that enables Playback performers to transform moments from real lives, however simply or roughly told, into well-crafted dramas that have resonance for the audience as well as for the teller. Drawing on their aesthetic sense of story, as well as language, metaphor, and stagecraft, they create art, embodying a pattern of elements in relation to each other in such a way as to suggest the wisdom contained in a larger reality. For the audience, watching and listening is an aesthetic experience—in other words, an experience of affirmation, expansion, revelation, and delight.

This art is different from an art that only seeks to convey the artist's vision: it is an art that is committed to affirming ordinary people's experience and to fostering connections between them so that the communities we live in can grow in compassion and humanity. We strive to hone our art in order to offer it as service. Playback is a fusion, perhaps a unique one, of artistic and social phenomena. The more it can fulfill the demands of both, the more it can succeed.

Every Playback practitioner is familiar with the experience of frustration and chagrin when the process seems to fail, and with the elation that can come when it works. The assessment depends somewhat on whether you are considering a whole show or a single scene, whether it is a performance or an applied context such as a therapy or training group, whether you are a performer, a teller, or an audience member, and so on. However, I believe that the criteria I've proposed for success in art and interactive social events will consistently apply, along with some further qualities specific to Playback.

Here are two more moments from my own experience when the question of success or failure has been notable for one reason or another:

Four of us from my company, Hudson River Playback Theatre, went to perform as part of a college symposium on reproductive rights. It was several hours' drive from our home. We got there to find that the preparation for our show had been minimal. The location was the corner of a large open space with people wandering through on their way somewhere else. Very few people came for the show. We began by making personal statements relating to the theme, feeling more exposed doing this than if there had been a large audience. One of the organizers told a moving and very disturbing story about an abortion she had had many years ago. The actors enacted with passion and ingenuity. After it was over, the audience was silent. No one else wanted to tell anything. We continued as best we could, hoping to somewhat redeem the situation with the strong ending that we had planned. But shortly before the scheduled close our host jumped up and said she was sorry, she'd made a mistake about the time frame and we had to end immediately. It felt very abrupt. In spite of expressions of gratitude from some of the people who were there, we felt that our show had been a failure.

Looking back at our choices that day, I think that we failed, and I especially as the conductor, to create a safe enough space for this tiny audience who had come to explore an extremely delicate topic. Daunted by the inhospitable space and the small turnout after our long drive, we didn't sufficiently adapt our plan to the situation we found. Our own discomfort as we made our personal statements at the beginning should have warned us that the audience would probably feel similarly exposed. If we had built a better connection with them at the outset, perhaps they would have been willing to journey with us from one story to the next. But the actors' stagework, although skillful and sophisticated, could not by itself draw the audience into more participation. It was in the social domain, not the artistic, that this performance was lacking.

ANOTHER MOMENT: At the Playback Theatre conference in Finland in 1993 there were performances by a number of different groups. A few were companies who had come with all or most of their members, but most were ad hoc groups composed of representatives usually from companies with a common language, if not a common country. All the performances showed a knowledge of

Playback forms, and some were more accomplished than others, but none fully embodied the Playback spirit, in my view, until the last day, when a pick-up group of New Zealanders, Australians, and Hungarians took the stage. They had recognized in each other a kind of anarchic energy and wanted to play together, although they shared neither language nor Playback style. Their performance was a great reassurance to me: I had been wondering unhappily what was missing from all the others (all the more troubling to me since four of the groups had asked me to perform with them as a musician). Looking back on it from the perspective of a few years, I recall a joyful interactive creativity among the actors, which made up for the complete absence of actorly polish; and a no-holds-barred attitude to the audience from the conductor.[3] She faced us as though we were a many-headed organism, which we were, and teased, provoked, and cajoled us to tell our stories, not necessarily the ones we thought we wanted to tell. The large audience came alive and felt like a group for the first time in the entire conference.

Acting and other Playback criteria

The degree of success of the three performances I've mentioned (London, Finland, and New York) can be accounted for in a general way by the presence or absence of the qualities that I listed earlier as criteria for value in art—artistic form, skill, and inspiration, etc; and in social events—skillful attention to inclusiveness, environment, and structure, etc. There are also elements that are specific to Playback Theatre, some that are clearly in the realm of art, others that are simultaneously questions of art and non-art.

In a public performance, the audience wants, expects, and deserves an aesthetic experience. How do we, the Playback artists, ensure that they get it?

Like any other artists, Playback performers strive to find form in which to embody meaning. The primary artistic task in Playback is the transformation of personal stories into theatre pieces, works of

3. The conductor was Mary Good, the founder of Melbourne Playback Theatre, an influential pioneer who died in 2020.

art with integrity of form and design. In our work, the meaning we seek to convey is the meaning embedded in the teller's experience.

The tools with which Playback performers (including musician and conductor) make such transformations are those of the stage, beginning with aesthetic concerns like the visual set-up. Most importantly, there is the quality of the actors' performance. Good actors use movement freely and creatively. They know how to move and position themselves on stage in order to embody the story and to create an aesthetic, evocative stage picture at every moment. They use language with accuracy, economy, and gracefulness. During scenes, they make imaginative and judicious use of the boxes and cloth props. There is a co-creative give-and-take between actors and musician. They have mastered the different demands of specific forms—fluid sculptures, pairs, etc. The ritual framing of the show and each segment within it is fulfilled with presence and dignity.

The quality of acting itself goes beyond the specific use of movement, voice, etc. Playback Theatre requires a particular kind of acting which we can call *authentic* acting, as opposed to the more stylized acting familiar from television, film, and most other kinds of theatre, however naturalistic. In Playback acting, the actor does not use a code to depict emotion but draws her portrayal directly from her sense of the teller and his story.

At its best, this kind of acting can be as powerful and inspired as that of great traditional actors, whose genius is precisely their quality of authenticity built on prodigious skill and training. However, formal theatre training may not be a good preparation for Playback acting. Traditional actors are used to basing their performance on a script, not an empathic sense of an actual, present human being, and their technique may distance them from teller, audience, and fellow performers. They may also find it challenging to summon the generosity that Playback actors need: part of Chloë's difficulty in the London performance was her concern to make an impression as an actress rather than a sense of service to the audience.

Experienced Playback actors use a high degree of artistic awareness and skill in their acting: authentic acting does not mean that it is unmediated by an aesthetic consciousness. But because authenticity is the key, it is sometimes possible for completely inexperienced actors to produce very good acting drawing on nothing but empathy and spontaneity. On the other hand, people with a little experience—enough to have lost their beginner's innocence, but not enough to have acquired artistic skill—sometimes fall into serious mistakes in their acting. The problems are often in their attempts to depict story or emotion nonliterally—brandishing a piece of red cloth to show anger, for example, or following the teller's actor around the stage in a clumsy attempt to "be" his inner self. Brand-new actors in their innocence do not think of being anything but literal, while sophisticated actors know how to move fluently and clearly between literal and symbolic action on stage.

The music in Playback is another area where artistry is key. Again, spontaneity and empathy on the musician's part can go a long way toward making up for a lack of musical talent or training. But the aesthetic quality of a performance will be greatly enhanced by music that is expertly and sensitively played.

In addition to these artistic considerations, there are elements indivisibly in the realms both of art and of social interaction, and equally essential to Playback's success. There is the faithfulness of the enactment to the teller's story, which depends on attentive and empathetic listening on the part of conductor, actors, and musician.[4] There is the co-creativity between actors, between actor and musician, between the conductor and the rest of the team. This includes the elusive quality of improvisation itself, which operates on a constant reciprocity of offers, in turn deriving from the performers' sense of the story and where it needs to go in order to be fulfilled. There is the shape of the event itself: the structure of the performance, how to begin, how to end, with decisions based both on an artistic sense of design and on the particular needs of the context and the audience. And encompassing all, the ritual and ceremony that underlie the entire performance, expressed in the quality of the performers' presence, the music, and the palpable sense of occasion—the "heightened dramatic event" (Fox, 1994).

4. See section on listening in Chapter 1, "A Changing Landscape."

The role of the conductor

The conductor embodies the fusion of art and social action: every aspect of the role carries both an aesthetic and an interactive consideration. It is the conductor who must greet and warm up the audience at the outset of the show; nothing is more crucial to the event's success. If the conductor in this initial moment is able to acknowledge and include all the disparate elements of the audience, to show a sensitivity to subgroups of age, culture, ethnicity, or background, to create a sense of ease in those who are new to Playback and eagerness in people who have come before, to establish an easy pattern of question and response, to direct the focus to the show's theme if there is one, then the performance is likely to unfold in a way that is satisfying to all. As the show proceeds, the conductor must remain attuned to the developing dynamics of the audience, the themes that emerge, the stories that may be untold but present. In his or her interactions with each individual teller, the conductor must create an immediate and genuine rapport, then elicit the story with grace and economy, maintaining contact with the rest of the audience while listening for the essence of the teller's experience, crystallizing it into the form of a story, and ensuring that the actors have enough but not an excess of information. As the performance draws to an end, the conductor will probably be the one to guide a closure, to draw attention to the collective story that has emerged, perhaps to thank the hosts, or to announce upcoming further events.

Are these tasks social or artistic? They are tasks that we are more familiar with in social events; but in Playback they must also be fulfilled with an aesthetic attention to form, design, and style. A Playback actor's adequacy is measured by his basic performance skills in combination with his attunement to the teller, the story, and his fellow performers; a Playback conductor by her assurance and skill in handling group and interpersonal connections, and by the elegance and integrity of her own demeanor.

Some conductors have, in addition to these qualities, a charm or force of personality that might be called charisma. When combined with the essential skills of the conductor, charisma can be a positive factor that draws audiences into warmth and connection. However, charisma without skill and integrity can exert power in a way that is dangerous and incompatible with "good" Playback, drawing trust to a conductor who does not deserve it.

In my examples of success and failure above, fulfillment of both *artistic* and *social* considerations accounted, in my opinion, for the success of the London and Finland performances. In London, Chloë's criticism only emphasized the fallacy of assessing a show by looking solely at what is happening on stage—in effect, by ignoring all but purely artistic criteria. In the reproductive rights performance, our artistic proficiency was not enough to make up for our shortcomings in the interactive realm.

Context and standards

In a Playback performance there is an implicit contract regarding standards between the Playback team and the audience. The audience has come to see professional theatre, they have paid at the door, and they legitimately expect to see competent work. They will be disappointed and critical if the performance falls below a basic level of artistic skill. Although no audience assessment will be unanimous, there will be a general consensus about the line between adequacy and inadequacy in the use of stage, voice, movement, and the artistic shaping of scenes.

The contract is different in non-performance contexts, where stories are enacted not by a company but by members of a training or therapeutic group where there is no separately defined audience. In a therapy group, the emphasis is entirely on the process, and there may be little if any attention paid to artistic skills. The same is true using Playback with groups of managers, teachers, or social workers to help them focus on current issues in their workplace. In such settings, the participants are not expected to be skillful performers, and artistic skill on their part is not necessary to the success of the work.

However, this inherent flexibility of standards in Playback does not extend to the conductor. In any context, with any group, with any purpose, the social and interactive aspects of Playback must be

expertly handled if the work is to fulfill itself. Whether in performances, workshops, or other applications, a sociometric awareness
of the group is essential—acknowledging individuals and subgroups,
choosing tellers, being alert to structures of influence and allegiance.
Playback's purpose is always to bring people together, to affirm the
individual and the group. Without mastery of the conductor's role,
this fundamental goal cannot be achieved.

Problematic Playback Theatre

Inevitably, as Playback has been adopted by enthusiasts around
the world, a few have developed practices based on a fundamental mis-
understanding of Playback Theatre's purpose. Such work can never
meet the criteria for "good" Playback, because it is built on distortion.

One such misapplication is the performance of Playback in a
comedic, entertainment manner, with little skill in sociometry or
subtle communication on the part of the conductor, and insufficient
respect for the story on the part of the actors. These companies may
enjoy success in the sense that their audiences are enthusiastic and
they may be in demand for contracted performances. However,
their work is not good Playback: the deeper meaning of the stories is
ignored or lost, the dynamics and themes of the event remain undeveloped, and the audience is entertained without being affirmed in
their humanity.

Another pitfall for Playback performers, particularly conductors, is the mishandling of Playback's therapeutic dimension. All
Playback Theatre is broadly therapeutic in the sense that the
process is potentially and ideally healing for all present, including the performers. Telling one's story publicly, seeing it reflected
back, realizing that it is accepted and valued by others is a healing
experience for the teller. For the audience, as well, there is an integration and affirmation that strengthens the connections between
them. If the basic criteria for successful Playback are met, this
healing potential will be fulfilled. But some performers do not
trust the story to carry its meaning on its own terms: instead,
with the goal of being more therapeutic, they force a "psychological" interpretation, usually with the effect of limiting instead of

deepening the meaning. Actors may do this through an interpretive enactment of the scene, conductors through interpretive
questions and comments during the interview. (Interpretation in
the psychological sense means imposing one's therapeutic insight
on the story; it is distinct from artistic interpretation, the filtering
of the story through one's artistic sensibility, a process which is
integral in Playback.)

I once watched a conductor with a teller who told a brief but
resonant story about how she survived her childhood by singing
to herself whenever her family seemed too crazy. The conductor
probed and delved until she elicited further information about the
teller's birth and her present relationship to her family. In the enactment the teller's original story, rich with image and metaphor like a
small, enigmatic painting, was buried in a rambling framework of
psychological detail.

A third danger area is the failure to understand Playback's
vigor as theatre and its roots in oral tradition (Fox, 1994), offering it
instead as a quasi-religious New Age experience replete with can-
dles and prayers, weak in cultural reference and artistic integrity.

"Good enough" Playback Theatre

In an essay called "The Face of the Story," Mimi Katzenbach
(1994) describes Playback's remarkable capacity to embody meaning simply in the enactment itself. If the story is heard and enacted
with empathy and an intuitive grasp of its essences, then all its
multiplicity of allusion to myth, history, and psychological truth
will be present and it is unnecessary, even a detraction, to make it
more explicit. Playback scenes are not superficial versions of stories
told to therapists. The story's meaning is in the face that it shows
us; what we see there is enough.

Fortunately, the majority of Playback performers are committed to its fundamental purposes. They understand the dual
requirement for artistic and interpersonal sophistication; they
are artists enough to respect the aesthetic qualities of story itself
without distortion in the direction of psychological interpretation.
And they achieve what we might call "good enough" Playback,

on the analogy of Bettelheim's idea of "good enough" parenting: Playback that generally fulfills both the artistic and interactive criteria to an adequate degree despite inevitable shortcomings.

In striving to fulfill the work as best they can, every company faces choices about how collectively oriented they want to be. What is more important to the group, the highest possible standards of performance or a democratic access to conducting, acting, and music? Do you leave the conducting in the hands of the most skilled, or do you commit to training everyone to conduct? Do you rotate roles during a performance as an expression of equality, in spite of a possible drop in standards? The guideline of "good enough" Playback is the final determinant of how a group balances the sometimes conflicting demands of democracy and excellence.

The idea that "good enough" Playback Theatre depends on fulfilling the criteria for success both in art and in interactive social events has implications for training. Whether in companies or in workshops, new performers can be encouraged to develop an artist's sensibility—an aesthetic awareness of form and design, and a commitment to art's purpose of revealing meaning through inspired metaphor and image. They can also, from the beginning, learn about the need for sensitivity and skill in communication and in guiding the functioning of a group.

Many people come to Playback with a background in one but not both of these areas—artists who are unsophisticated in human relationships, or helpers and healers who are undeveloped as artists. Training that emphasizes the importance of both sides can help people acquire the balance that is essential.

Trance, subjectivity and judgment

The response to art and the perception of value is necessarily subjective. In Playback, subjectivity of response has a special meaning, because of the marked difference in perspective between audience member, teller, and performers.

For Playback or any theatre to work, there must be an engagement on the part of the audience so that they allow themselves to believe in the illusion of another place and time, whether it is the Forest of Arden or the teller's childhood home. This is a kind of trance, willingly entered into by audience members. Part of the conductor's job is to entrance, to induct audience and teller into an altered state for the duration of the enactment (while remaining firmly out of trance herself). Even the actors are mildly in trance. While they remain fully aware of themselves and each other, thinking about the story and what needs to happen, they are also caught up in the reality conjured by their acting. The music is a powerful trance inducer, altering the state of the teller, audience, and actors from the first notes of the setting-up music.

The stronger the trance, the stronger the perception of success and of artistic value. The trance is almost always strongest for the teller, and weakest for the performer. All Playback performers have had the experience of a teller praising them warmly after a scene that they felt they had done poorly. Audience members may also let themselves believe in a story in spite of occasional mistakes or awkwardness in the enactment. (But if the performance is not "good enough" Playback, the trance will not work and audience and teller will remain unmoved.)

The peculiar strength of the teller's trance means that in non-performance situations, such as workshops, training groups, or therapy contexts, stories may be enacted with great success by people who lack skill or artistic sensibility—success in the sense that the teller and other group members feel that the story has been fulfilled satisfactorily in spite of the inexpert acting. Leading children's therapy groups, I have seen tellers completely transfixed by enactments that were clumsy and superficial, just barely adhering to the story, even though the young actors were doing as well as they could. The teller would readily project her story onto the action and feel satisfied that it had been reflected fully.

Subjectivity of response also means that the perception of artistic merit will vary according to context and expectation, as we discussed earlier. I remember a two-hour workshop for recreation workers in which a man told a story about being taken as a child to see Hooverville, the shantytown of homeless people who lived in New York's Central Park during the Depression. The man's father hoped to teach his son to appreciate the privilege and security that he had. But what Victor, the teller, remembered was the moment when a boy his own age stared back at him, a burning challenge in his eyes. In a flash Victor understood this boy's human dignity, and that it was wrong to stare as though he were an animal in a zoo. In the enactment the man who played the homeless boy fulfilled the climactic moment with unforgettable intensity and truth. He was fully invested in the role and its meaning. An experienced actor could not have done better.

He was probably to some degree in trance, believing so deeply in the reality of the boy in Hooverville that his belief informed his portrayal. Another element in the impact of his acting was the context itself, a workshop in which no one had previous experience with Playback or any other kind of performing. My co-leader and I therefore had no expectation of skillful acting and were possibly more impressed than we might have been by someone in our own company doing the same thing.

This subjectivity and flexibility of standards is not unique to Playback, but in fact a component in any realm of art. Context and expectation play a part in any audience's experience of any performance. There is always an interplay between what is actually offered by the artists, on the one hand, and what the audience brings to it, on the other. The same is true of non-performance art forms such as literature or painting. Value is ultimately a co-creation of artist and perceiver, which accounts for the genuine artistic meaning found at every point along the spectrum of actual accomplishment.

Playback's fulfillment

In my small town there lives a world-famous pianist who performs here once or twice a year. His most recent concert fell on the same night as one of our Playback shows. I was very sorry to miss it: this man's music is a treasure, a consummation of the art of the keyboard. As my imagination went from his concert, an all-Bach solo recital, to our Playback Theatre show, the difference between these two kinds of performances was very clear.

Much as I love the magic of Playback's mercurial creativity, I also sometimes want the grandeur and perfection of art that is painstakingly developed and rehearsed.

Playback is not great art. It cannot meet art's most rigorous criteria, because it is of the moment. Although performers may develop their skills for years, becoming elegant and compelling both in their acting and in the aesthetic transformation of life into theatre, their on-the-spot enactments cannot, by their nature, be built of the highly crafted language and choreography of formal theatre. However, like other art which may not attain greatness, it nevertheless has the power, depending on context and audience perception, to fulfill art's deepest purpose: the revelation of pattern and ontological meaning.

Those moments when Playback reaches a peak of brilliance, those moments that we all recognize and remember, are invariably times when there has been a perfect fusion between the artistic and the interactive aspects of playback. They may happen in any setting, with inexperienced actors as well as with trained performers. In a non-performance setting, it can seem like a kind of miracle when the group members reach into themselves and discover an artist's sensibility for the first time. In my experience, this quantum leap is always called forth by a strength of emotion toward the teller and his story. It has nothing to do with a conscious striving; it is a response to humanity combined with the potency of the artist's reaching for form. The remarkable thing is that the newly achieved level of artistry invariably creates a similar leap in the group's understanding of each other. It is a process of synergy in which the art and the group interaction mutually enhance each other.

In performance, the conductor's attunement to the audience and to the teller combines with the actors' empathy, accuracy, inspiration, and teamwork to create theatre that can be matchless in its beauty and truth. An entire performance is unlikely to remain on such a soaring level; Playback is also "Rough Theatre," in Peter Brook's phrase (1968), with the inherent unevenness of any art whose creative process is unmasked and visible to all.

Conclusion

Playback Theatre belongs rightfully in the realm of art; it seeks to fulfill art's fundamental purpose of revealing meaning through the aesthetic distillation of experience and perception. It is also integrally an interactive and altruistic social event. To be judged as "good," Playback must fulfill the criteria for success in both these realms, as well as in those unique to Playback itself.

The degree of skill required from the actors varies according to context. In performance situations, the performers must have sufficient artistry and experience to achieve "good enough" Playback if they are to satisfy audience and teller. In non-performance contexts, Playback can fulfill its purpose without a high degree of skill from the actors: stories may be told and enacted with satisfaction for the teller and the group as a whole in spite of a lack of experience and acting ability.

In any context, however, the conductor's artistry and interpersonal skill is necessary to Playback's fulfillment. The conductor's role is an embodiment of Playback's fusion of art and social action, both within and outside of performance.

And in any context, performance or otherwise, there is the possibility of those moments that show us the ideal fulfillment of Playback's promise: the ephemeral, magical fusion of artistry and humanity.

References

Bateson, Gregory. (1972). "Style, Grace, and Information in Primitive Art." In *Steps to an Ecology of Mind*. New York: Ballantine.

Bettelheim, Bruno. (1987). *A Good Enough Parent*. New York: Vintage.

Brook, Peter. (1968). *The Empty Space*. New York: Avon.

Fox, Jonathan. (1994). *Acts of Service: Spontaneity, Commitment, Tradition in the Nonscripted Theatre*. New Paltz, NY: Tusitala.

Katzenbach, Mimi. (1994). "The Face of the Story." Unpublished essay.

Moreno, J.L. (1937). "Sociometry in Relation to Other Social Sciences." Sociometry 1.

Newton, Eric. (1950). *The Meaning of Beauty*. New York: McGraw Hill.

Salas, Jo. (1990). "Aesthetic Experience in Music Therapy." *Music Therapy*, Vol. 9, 1.

5

A RITUAL FOR OUR TIME[1]

Jonathan Fox (1999)

EVERY PLAYBACK THEATRE ACTOR is familiar with the disconcerting experience that often comes just when a performance is over. An audience member will come up, shake your hand warmly as if in congratulation, and say: "But tell me. What is the purpose of it anyway?"

We groan inwardly, because to answer such a philosophical question when we are still vibrating from the last teller's story is pretty tough. Unfortunately, even in calm moments, far away from the stage lights and applause, it's not much easier.

For in fact the Playback process is not simple to describe or understand. One reason is its flexibility: it can be adapted to many different specific needs in education and mental health as well as function as artistic theatre. This means that as a method it spans the conventional categories of theatre, psychology, and education.

Nevertheless, the question is valid: What *is* the purpose of Playback Theatre?

In this essay, I will attempt to frame an answer. I will discuss the theme first from the point of view of the community—that is, the groups which experience Playback Theatre, either in ticketed performances or a special setting (such as school, workplace, or community center). Then I will turn to the Playback performers themselves and some of the challenges they face in fulfilling the promise of their form.

1. First published in *Gathering Voices: Essays on Playback Theatre.* Eds Dauber & Fox. New Paltz, NY: Tusitala, 1999. This essay was an addendum to Jo Salas's "What Is 'Good' Playback Theatre?", adding a circle of "ritual" to the intersecting circles of art and social interaction.

Red threads

I'd like to begin with some stories.

The teller, a woman in her twenties, tells about being on a trek in Asia and getting lost. She and her friend were far from a village. Darkness was falling, and no one came to help. The setting was strange and scary. There was nothing to do but camp out in a kind of shepherd's hut. The teller felt miserable at their bad luck. But nothing bad happened. In fact, they woke up to find themselves in an incredibly beautiful spot, surrounded by rhododendrons, with snow-capped mountains in the distance. Terror had turned into joy; threat into blessing.

The story that followed right after took place in New York City:

A middle-aged woman tells about meeting the daughter of an acquaintance of her mother's, a woman from overseas—a country in Asia, to be exact. The teller (who used to live in New York, but had moved away) had expected to have to show the visitor around. She feared it would be a troublesome and perhaps boring afternoon. As it turned out, the young woman was not only kind and interesting, but also very knowledgeable about the city. In fact, as the day progressed the teller realized that the young woman was showing her around. Instead of being the leader, she was being led; instead of the giver, she was being given to. It was a pleasant surprise.

Let me point out some features of this storytelling process. These two stories form a kind of point and counterpoint for each other. While they both share a theme of unexpected happiness, in the first there is no guide, or bringer of joy, while in the second there is such a figure in the presence of the young woman. The counterpoint creates a kind of dialogue. It is as if in the first story the teller is saying, "Sometimes we are lost and alone, and it turns out all right." And the second teller answers, "That may be true, yes. And it is also true that sometimes, even when we are *not* lost and alone, we can have a surprise and find ourselves guided by a stranger, finding new pleasure in old territory."

It is important to remind ourselves here that in this example the process of the tellers coming forward was spontaneous; the conductor did not invite one kind of story or another. Yet even though each teller told her own personal tale, the stories connected on a social level. This "red thread" can be understood as containing a kind of folk wisdom.[2]

Another feature of this process is that inevitably, there is not one thread, but many. For instance, the first teller has an epiphany in a remote spot in Asia; while in the second story, Asia, in the form of the young immigrant, comes to the West ("You don't have to go to the other side of the world"). In the first story, joy follows fear, disappointment, and despair, while in the second, there is nothing so dramatic ("Even a boring obligation can turn into something unexpectedly wonderful.") In the first story, the teller is a young adult, while in the second story, the teller is old enough to be the mother of the first ("Adventure is for youth, to be sure, but even when you are my age, such joy can still be found"). In Playback these "messages" are communicated through the medium of enacted story, through movement, color, music, and metaphoric action.

A third feature derives from the context. We have learned that the story elements, in addition to speaking to the community in a general way, usually relate very specifically to the circumstances of the group. In this case, the audience comprised students at the start of a long training workshop. It is natural at such a time for students to be fearful of getting overwhelmed and "lost." Others often worry that the course might be dull and unchallenging. In this case, the course was a PT training, and both tellers, each in her way, seemed to be reminding their peers to trust in the spontaneity process.

The way the red threads carry through a Playback event is so rich that as conductor I like to let the process be as undirected as possible, worried that if I make too many suggestions, I will in fact restrict this often unconscious form of dialogue (there are special cases where I act otherwise—see section below on Shamanic Conducting).

2. See Hoesch, Folma, "The Red Thread" in *Gathering Voices: Essays on Playback Theatre* (Tusitala, 1999).

Now let me go to a second event, which took place during a Playback Theatre workshop in the USA on Social Change. There were twelve participants, ten white people and two African Americans. During the first two days the stories were about white children experiencing the reality of living in a racially divided land.

In one, the teller at age five witnesses prejudice for the first time as she sees her aunt speak insultingly to a beloved servant. In another, the teller tells about being a teenager as the family moves to the suburbs to get away from Black neighbors.

Following these stories, with the encouragement of the leader, one of the African Americans tells.

It is a story about his grandfather, in whose house he had grown up—in particular, his grandfather's personal dignity and high standards for his family. There is a strong incident of racism in the story, in the form of grave injustice suffered by the grandfather at work. But there is a stronger theme of overcoming racism. In fact, the teller never knows what his grandfather suffers until much later, when he learns about it as an adult, because the grandfather had kept it from the children.

In the unfolding of the stories in this workshop, the same contrapuntal elements are present. What stands out here is that with the story of the Black teller, we hear from the "other voice." One of the strongest features of Playback Theatre is that it allows diverse voices to be heard in a context of empathy.

A final point: the stories told by the white participants were not heroic tales, nor were they victim stories. Instead they were accounts involving shameful deeds of their own families, painful to share and to watch. Such honesty enables a confrontation with truth that is all too rare in a human society where countries and their institutions often demand heroic official histories. Playback Theatre honors the people's voice, be it joyful or ashamed, triumphant or oppressed. One of its purposes is to let this voice be heard, before witnesses, in all its richness and variety.

Restoring oral traditions

What we have seen so far in these examples is the presence of a special kind of discussion taking place through the tellers' stories.[3] It is not an ordinary discussion, because it occurs through scenes enacted on a stage. We find more action and fewer words than in ordinary discussion. Moreover, the emphasis is not cognitive. Ideas may be inherent in the stories; we may be able to read a message or moral in them. Often insight will follow the enactment. But ultimately, the Playback stories are *stories*, with setting, character, plot, and image. And as in stories, the value, or meaning, often reveals itself only indirectly. For example, in the stories described above, there are points being made not only about racism and prejudice in America, but about adults' behavior to children and the place of human dignity.

These aspects bring us back in touch with the oral tradition, which is rooted in sensory perception and welcomes emotion. The modern professional world has tended to champion other values. Playback has often been looked upon suspiciously by institutions, because it appears "soft," and does not focus directly on problems or return concrete solutions. Actually, today, more than two decades after Playback first started, there is a more receptive climate to Playback's holistic kind of communication because scholars have been reframing the argument. Sensory interaction with the environment, iconic thinking, need for narrative, and the marriage of feeling and thought are fundamental, it is now believed, to the human mind.[4] Thus Playback now can be appreciated for the fullness of its approach to communication, which will often provide the *conditions* necessary to find a truly enduring answer.

Since Playback Theatre engages many aspects of our intelligence, it penetrates our consciousness in a particularly profound manner. Amazingly, we remember the stories we see in Playback Theatre. I even remember the first story I ever conducted, almost

---

3. See Chapter 10, "What We Mean by 'Dialogue' in Playback Theatre."

4. See Abram, David, *The Spell of the Sensuous*. New York: Pantheon, 1996; Sacks, Oliver, *The Man Who Mistook His Wife for a Hat*. New York: Harper & Row, 1987; Bruner, Jerome, *Actual Minds, Possible Worlds*. Cambridge: Harvard University Press, 1986; Gardner, Howard. *Frames of Mind*. New York: Basic Books, 1983.

thirty years ago. The teller is a person I see only once in ten years, but the truth contained in her story, which was about getting lost and finding her way, has also remained with me and acts as a kind of ever-present guide as I go about my life.

The concept of discourse implies exchange between equals, and there is an implied belief in Playback Theatre that if we can speak and listen to each other in this deep way, good will come of it. In a Playback performance, we are *all* experts, in that we all have stories with potential answers embodied within them—this holds for the youngest child, the humblest adult, the most wizened elder. The task of the Playback leader or team is to create the atmosphere in which the folk feel free to come forth and tell.

Those of us who have been telling, acting out, and witnessing Playback stories over a long time know the value of this communal telling. It is one of the reasons, I believe, why there tends to be so little turnover in Playback Theatre performing companies: the process is life-enhancing on such a deep level that we want to stay involved.

To sum up what we have concluded so far, Playback Theatre offers a kind of community conversation through stories, and this conversation, even though it contains not one, but many themes, and is often indirect in making its points, gives scope for the expression of a popular truth.

Awake to the world

Not always, but often enough that we recognize it as normal, the audience feels *good* after Playback Theatre. Of course, this is true of most theatre as entertainment. But in this case, the feeling is deeper, since the subject of the play is the audience themselves, their life-world. The process of identifying one's own story and witnessing another's often leads to a feeling of communal renewal.[5]

This renewal takes place on a number of levels. The first is individual. I can best illustrate it by noting the changes in a teller's body tension during the enactment of his story. At the start, he will be more or less tense. He may still be searching for the precise thing to tell. He may not quite trust the conductor sitting next to him,

5. See Chapter 13, "The Theory of Narrative Reticulation."

asking questions. He may feel shy of the others watching. Once the enactment begins, the body tenses in another way. There is excitement and intense engagement now, as he watches the actors take on the challenge of portraying his life. Then, when the actors hit a chord of truth, capturing the essence of what he was trying, so imperfectly and incompletely, to convey, there is a sudden relaxation, often accompanied by a sigh. Then there is a final body shift, once the enactment is completed, and the teller can take in the empathic response of the audience. The teller returns to his chair in a very different state than when he left it. He is likely to be smiling (sometimes through lingering tears). It is not easy to describe this new state-of-being: He is "in touch." He feels "lighter."

The second level is social. The Playback experience reduces the sense of alienation often felt by the inhabitants of the modern community. Of course, Playback now exists in a variety of places, from large cities to small towns, and in many different cultures. But despite this variety, it can be generally said that more often than not in a public setting the audience comes as strangers to one another. Thus there is always a tension in the audience as well as among prospective tellers, since there is no way of knowing what the play will be about or how it will be handled. Members of the audience are naturally wary. This wariness will be present even among a group that is already established, such as a school class or a group of fellow workers. The social integration that is such an important part of the Playback experience works to dispel the fear of being among strangers, planting in its stead a sense of connectedness. Audience members often are amazed that they are able to participate in a personal and meaningful experience with people who only hours ago felt so distant. Their aloofness is transmuted into a correspondingly strong openness to discourse, and even afterwards, as they exchange comments, often a joyful feeling.[6]

Finally, the very sensuousness of live theatre, with its sights and sounds, images and rhythms, helps bring us out of our shell and

6. John Stevenson has written about the habit of Playback audiences to remain chatting in the hall after a performance, as if they were attending a celebration. See Stevenson, John, "The Fourth Wall and the Third Space," (unpublished essay for School of Playback Theatre), 1995.

open us up to the physical world around us. For those of us living in cities and caught up in cerebral matters, the Playback experience constitutes a wake up for our senses.

Taking into consideration these mood effects on the individual, social, and environmental level, we can say that overall, Playback Theatre focuses the individual and group energy in such a way that the audience undergoes a trance experience, often feeling both energized and relaxed afterwards, along with a sense of physical and psychological renewal. We come away from the performance awake and open to the world. This effect is not unlike what people have experienced since time immemorial after special communal ceremonies. After Playback Theatre we can hear once more the leaves making music in the trees, see again the sunlight dancing on the water; enjoy pleasurable and supportive contact with others; find new hope.[7]

On the threshold of the new

One can easily imagine other kinds of discourse-enhancing activities, such as a public debate, classroom discussion, or even a therapy session. And one can easily bring to mind other kinds of relaxing, enlivening experiences, such as a yoga class, ballroom dancing, or a walk in the forest. What is not so common, perhaps, is an experience that accomplishes both. What makes this possible in Playback is its nature as a heightened dramatic event.

By comparison, we might think of a wedding or a funeral in our times. Or communal dances in other times that had the purpose of preparing hunters for the hunt, or healers to lay hands on the sick. These kinds of rituals are utterly serious and intended to produce transformation.[8]

It is commonplace to say that our modern age has seen a decline in ritual, such that many people today hardly know its power. Thus Playback Theatre is often asked to perform a more limited task, such

---

7. For more on this subject see *Acts of Service: Spontaneity, Commitment, Tradition in the Nonscripted Theatre* by Jonathan Fox, Chapter 3, "Preliterary Drama." New Paltz, NY: Tusitala, 1994.

8. See Turner, Victor, *Dramas, Fields, and Metaphors*. Ithaca, NY: Cornell University Press, 1974.

as to teach shy adolescents expressiveness, or company managers team-building techniques. And it can accomplish these objectives, but in my view only in the framework of the more profound goal associated with a ritual.

The Playback Theatre event frequently begins with flatness. The audience, unfamiliar with the form and its ritual process, waits suspiciously. But slowly, as the ritual unfolds and people get caught up in it, feelings rise, with the inevitable consequence that a fully undertaken Playback event will be strongly emotional. The music will play a haunting refrain. The actors will render a scene with particular power. The conductor will use just the right word at the right time. And suddenly a teller will spring out of her chair, to tell a story that comes from a buried corner of her soul. And this story will spring another teller into a deep nexus of feeling and memory. This letting loose of emotional energy is a natural part of the ritual.

Sometimes the informality of the Playback Theatre stage, in which actors are present as themselves, often relating to the audience between stories in a human way, is deceptive. Moreover, Playback can take place anywhere, in rooms belonging to everyday life, with virtually no equipment. But there is nothing informal about the ritual.

NOT LONG AGO IN ISRAEL, I conducted a demonstration of Playback in a university classroom for community workers. The conditions were not stable—people came and went; there was little sense of decorum in the crowded classroom space. Nevertheless, I proceeded. Space was cleared for a stage; at its rear was put a row of chairs for audience actors. To the right of the stage I placed two chairs, for myself as conductor and the teller, who would come from the group. In short, the ritual space was set. In my manner, I tried to give a sense of the temporal aspect of ritual as well: at a certain point, my words became more formal, their pace slow and rhythmic.

The first teller told an everyday tale of waking up in the morning. Volunteers from the audience acted it out. Then a second teller came forward and told a life-threatening secret of twenty years. The secret was that he had been a political radical in another country and had committed violent, illegal acts against an unlawful, repressive regime. The public revelation of this secret at this particular time in Israel's troubled history, when violent terrorism had just been the cause of innocent death, was in itself potentially explosive. The teller, in choosing to tell the story, traversed a boundary of normal acceptance and even safety, in the evident hope that the ritual frame would provide a context for understanding. As conductor I did not hesitate to follow through with the enactment of the scene, even though it involved killing. Held by the ritual, actors from the audience enacted this difficult tale as fully as they had the first. This willingness alone was a sign of deep interpersonal acceptance of the teller. Inevitably, there was a flood of response after the enactment; the ritual holding was even more important after the story than before. We enacted many fluid sculptures to express the different reactions of the witnesses. The result was a charged atmosphere. The outcome might well have been chaotic, but the order held—individuals with very diverse perspectives were able, in the Playback ritual, to listen to one another. Social discourse took place on a profound level, and the teller, for the first time since he had fled to Israel, could stand openly before his neighbors.

Anthropologist Victor Turner uses the word "liminal" to describe how participants in a ritual go to the threshold of normality—and then beyond. His studies in Africa led him to his concept of "social drama," in which community problems are dealt with through ecstatic ceremony. Thus for Turner, rituals, with their departure from everyday order, can create a field for creativity, in which the collective can leap beyond, as it were, what had been possible before. This is what happened in the Israel example. The teller crossed a threshold of disclosure, and carried his listeners with him in the process, such that the audience could regard the pressing social issue of terrorist violence from a fresh perspective, that of the terrorist himself.

This inherent power of the PT ritual is why, despite its flexibility, Playback Theatre does not always fit into the narrow confines of commissioning organizations, who want to be sure the show is "light," or focuses on team-building, or who want to avoid certain topics. It is also why Playback Theatre groups can fail—from their own insufficient grasp of heightened dramatic events. It takes a long time to grow into the role of leading Playback rituals.

Rituals of transformation, with their climate of bursting possibility, are not risk-free. If the representative of a potential client group grasps the idea of dramatic ritual inherent in Playback, she will naturally want an assurance that those leading the ritual have the necessary knowledge to conduct it properly. This is only appropriate.

Often, however, an institutional representative's hesitation comes from a fear of feelings, from the very idea of a heightened event taking place. Then the problem lies with the representative, her institution, even the society at large, but not, I believe, with the Playback actors. Indeed Playback Theatre will succeed in teaching specific outcomes, such as young people to express themselves more freely or managers to work better together when the dramatic ritual is allowed to flower fully. In such a case, there may be other far-reaching benefits for the group as well.

Widespread lack of understanding about rituals and their usefulness means that the most crucial part of a Playback event often takes place long beforehand, in the planning discussions. Host organizations need to be clear that Playback creates a ritual that will stir feelings and respond to problems only indirectly; that everyone present will have an equal voice; and that there is a great potential for creative breakthroughs in these rituals.

More and more institutions are calling on Playback Theatre to conduct rituals, especially at moments of transition. Examples of such occasions are orientation sessions (beginnings) and retirements (terminations). Playback Theatre groups are also called upon at times of crisis, when the need for a strong method as well as a strong container is clear. And Playback teams are often called on to perform for a particular group at regular intervals. Thus students in their first week of nursing school could share through PT their feelings about the start of their training, including stories about what inspired them towards nursing. A university faculty department that was being discontinued invited Playback to their final party. A married couple in crisis are each invited to share their stories in Playback, offering them a new way to see the other's perspective. The monthly Playback performances, open to all, that are performed by so many companies throughout the world provide a regular place for individuals in their communities to share moments of their lives in an ongoing way. These and many other examples attest to Playback's effectiveness in providing groups with a positive way to learn from the past and look to the future.

The Playback performer's triad

Let us now turn to the Playback practitioners themselves. Jo Salas, in "What Is 'Good' Playback Theatre?"[9] emphasizes that all Playback Theatre is art. To briefly summarize her careful argument, she claims it should convey a sense of coherent design, integrity of form, originality, and skill in execution. In this spirit, many Playback companies practice hard in order to live up to the artistic demands of Playback Theatre, working on their staging, dynamics, use of metaphor, improvisation skills, as well as spending many hours improving their mastery of the basic PT dramatic forms.

But art alone is not enough. Playback Theatre is also an interactive social event, Jo argues, in which much time is spent focusing away from the stage (greeting the audience, introducing the performance, eliciting feelings, invoking stories, interviewing the teller, and so forth). Managing an interactive social event requires a wholly different set of skills. These include good planning and organization, providing the right physical environment, giving those present a chance to be heard, and creating an atmosphere of respect.

Good Playback must fulfill the criteria of success in both these realms. Jo concludes that good Playback resides in a zone where these elements become indistinguishable from one another. To me this is an important formulation.

Typically Playback Theatre groups lean towards one side or another. Either they come primarily from an artistic background and are interested in theatrical performing, or they come primarily from a mental health or educational background and are interested more in what we might call the workshop. The former camp has more

9.   See Chapter 4, "What is 'Good' Playback Theatre?"

expressive skills, the latter more group process skills. Sometimes, they even look critically at each other. The "artists" are impatient with process concerns; the "therapists" are disdainful of theatrical elements. Such side-taking misses the point. All Playback practitioners need to develop capacities in *both* domains, no matter what their special interest or emphasis.

If what I have been describing above is true, however, there is a third aspect that is no less important than art and social interaction in creating good Playback—ritual. Creating ritual demands different skills yet again: the invocation of a transpersonal dimension, an adherence to rules of conduct; building ecstatic emotional energy; the sparse, rhythmical, highly specialized use of language; and a goal of transformation. To lead the ritual properly, actors focus on their presence on stage. They carefully practice the manner of their listening to the story, setting up a scene, giving the acknowledgment afterwards. The conductor learns to keep the ritual moving forward, no matter what kind of teller or story; be a guardian of truth (finding the "deep story"), and knowing just when the rules of Playback conduct should be adhered to and when they should be relaxed.

Thus a good Playback actor and leader must be skilled in a triad of roles—as an artist, a host, and a shaman.

This is no light task. It is why serious Playback practitioners spend years in apprenticeship and learning.

There are numerous areas where the requirements of these domains seem to place opposite demands on the actors. The art of PT allows aesthetic distance, while the ritual demands involvement. The socially interactive aspect allows for a relaxed, informal contact, while the ritual demands transpersonal intensity. It is an objective of the artist to entertain and delight the audience; the host to establish trust and put people at their ease; and the shaman to engender an atmosphere of enchantment and even confusion as a stepping stone to entering what has been called the "other thought."

So how do you plan your opening? Something funny and/or dramatic (artistic)? A clear explanation of what will happen, followed by introductions all around (socially interactive)? Or a slow rhythmical talk, with musical accompaniment, that may not even seem to make much sense (shamanistic)? Clearly, the Playback practitioner needs not only to have skills in each domain, but also to be able to blend paradoxical elements effectively. Often, in fact, an opening, while it may lean to one side or another, will accomplish objectives in each of the domains.

If we think of ritual as being a part of this triad upon which the Playback experience is based, then there follow certain considerations for the practitioner. I would like to mention some of them here.

First, even though the Playback process is spontaneous, the ritual has its rules: the teller must come to the chair; the teller must stay in the chair during the enactment; the teller must tell a personal story. The actors stand when picked for a role; the actors do not talk during the interview. The conductor does not interrupt the enactment; the conductor checks in with the teller after the enactment; the conductor dismisses the teller from the chair. These are *some* of them.

Without the clear framework provided by the rules, spontaneity can quickly turn into chaos, creativity to confusion. With it, the members of the audience feel safe enough to let themselves go into trance, allowing unforeseen breakthroughs.

The need for ritual in Playback goes beyond differences between kinds of PT groups, be they professional performing or intimate living room groups. It goes beyond differences in audience size: as much attention must be paid to these formalities with a group of four (teller, conductor, actor, and witness) as with a group of four hundred.

Because of their intensity, rituals place a heavy personal demand on their shamans, and it is essential to take time beforehand to assume the role and afterwards to release it. "Artistic" PT groups sometimes err in modeling themselves on the professional theatre, arriving in time to do a minimum amount of theatrical warming-up and departing as soon as the show is over; while the process-oriented groups sometimes err in trying to give feedback right away and "discuss" the event. Rituals, however, require a specific kind of warm-up and cool down. After being a conductor in Playback, for example, it sometimes takes me more than twenty-four hours to return to what I would consider a normal state. And this is after I have been in a state of disturbance for up to two days beforehand.

The idea of Playback as service has its locus in this ritual function. Although the artist and the shaman share certain qualities—both are often "called" to their work, for example—there is a fundamental difference. The artist's paramount concern is the creation of his or her art, demanding an ultimate loyalty to personal vision, while the shaman's focus resides in others. In a Playback performance, when these roles are in apparent conflict—for instance when the artistic integrity of a show is threatened by a disabled teller whose manner may be slow and halting—there is no doubt in my mind that the shaman role takes precedence. I am not there to look brilliant, or ultimately to create art for art's sake. Nor are my actors. We are there to conduct a process. It has inspired this person to come forward and tell. It is our responsibility to accept the teller and the story fully and to rise to the challenge of creating an atmosphere of deep attention in the audience. Such situations are common in Playback, especially when the ritual is strong, for it is then that the isolated feel safe enough to come forward.

Playback's grounding in ritual is perhaps a reason why it can flourish in many different cultures, with different artistic and social traditions. The warm-ups may differ throughout the Playback world, and the actors may have very different styles, but the ritual is constant. It provides the safety, and paradoxically, the power.

Life-and-death stories

Playback actors of moderate experience sometimes complain about a particular Playback event being dull. "The stories weren't deep," they say. "They were only anecdotes." In time, they will hopefully learn to "hear" the archetypal image inherent in any—even the most mundane-seeming—story. More often than not, however, the sequence of Playback stories does contain enough evident seriousness, as well as humor, so that by the end even fledgling actors feel satisfied that indeed, something beneficial *has* emerged from the void.

Occasionally, however, what we might call a life-and-death story is told, someone's core experience. Then the ritual is most important. At such times the feeling of risk is palpable; there is fear that the teller may "flip out" or that a feeling of chaos may overwhelm everyone.

As an example, I would like to quote from Deborah Pearson, an Australian Playback practitioner who has traveled widely. She tells about being guest conductor for a Playback performance at a school in Finland when the children had only five minutes before learned about the death of a fellow student in a car accident. If Playback is thought of as entertainment, or even as education, one might well argue that this was not the moment for it. Better cancel, and leave the school community to deal as best it can with its shock and grief. If, on the other hand, Playback is thought of as healing ritual, then perhaps it is just the moment for it, with one important caveat. It is essential that the company, and especially the conductor, be able to hold the emotions of the crowd and provide a safe place for public mourning.

(Many Playback actors know inside themselves that they are not yet ready to contain such strong events, and even if they have the artistic and social interactive skills, they will back away—as they should. And if any of the actors should worry why in their regular performances they are not getting deeper stories from their audiences, it is simply because the audiences sense that the actors are not ready yet to hold them.)

In this particular case, Deborah and her group of Finnish actors, responding to the need for a community healing ritual, did not retreat in the face of community crisis. They went ahead with the performance, ready to enact whatever difficult feelings anyone needed to tell. The young audience responded to the offer of the Playback actors. They told about their feelings, and saw them acted out. There were two full stories told and performed. The ritual was accomplished. After the performance, Deborah writes:

> I noticed the heads were not hanging down so much as they left the room, and there was more energy. More of them had cried some tears during the performance. More of them were sitting

closer to each other. I felt we had come at exactly the right time to look after them so they had more strength to continue with their grieving in the next few days and months to come.[10]

There is another important aspect to this ritual holding function in Playback. In the excitement of the spontaneous moment, audience members will fail to follow the "rules." One will stand up and criticize the story. Another will want to jump onto the stage. A third will come to the teller's chair and try to manipulate the Playback team. At such times the conductor must respond with speed and assurance, knowing when to be permissive and when to be a fierce keeper of the rules. To carry out this task requires not only knowledge and experience, but also personal strength and even wisdom.[11]

Shamanic conducting

One last point: it is important to observe that in order for discourse to take place and liveliness to be enhanced, the keepers of the ritual not only need to hold the audience, but sometimes guide it as well. A strong, cohesive group, comprised of autonomous individuals, needs little guidance. They will create just the discourse they need, and find their own sources of liveliness during the course of the event. But in reality, few groups are so enlightened. Problematic individuals are often present, such as the man (it is usually a man) who has *many* comments, *many* feelings, *many* stories to tell. Sometimes the group as a whole is suffering from a belief or attitude that hinders the unfolding of the ritual experience. For example, they may be afraid of feelings, or they may feel that stories are only valid if they have a happy ending. Finally, it is often prevailing views of the society as a whole that can block the process. An example here might be the reluctance of those who consider themselves in any way isolated from the majority—such as an immigrant, a person of color, a very old person—to step up and tell.

In such situations, the Playback performers need to have both courage and cleverness in steering around impediments. For example,

10. From an article by Deborah Pearson in a publication by the Playback company Terinateatteri Mielikuva, Helsinki, Finland, 1998.
11. See Chapter 12, "The Theory of Narrative Reticulation."

in spite of Playback's core dictum that "anyone can tell," the conductor needs to *manage* (control) the man who wishes to tell too much, so that there will be space for others. The company needs to use all their artistry and humanity, as high practitioners of improvisational theatre and interactive social events, to charm and disarm any group into being open to feelings. They also need to withstand the need for resolution after a sad or painful story, knowing that inherent in their ritual process is the sure promise of transformation. Most importantly, they need always to keep a sharp nose out for prejudice and injustice, which often reveals itself as much from those who are silent as from the lips of those who speak. The ritual demands as much.

The idea of Playback performers as "supportive" can be clarified by looking at an example of social prejudice. In order to counteract an atmosphere of politeness, or even acceptance of a prejudiced statement or story from the audience, the team will need to exert a fierce allegiance to the idea of social equality. This will involve supporting those isolated or vulnerable *by being tough* with those who voice a prejudicial view. This does not mean casting aspersions; rather it means insisting on what is necessary to keep the ritual constructive.[12]

At a summertime performance on an American university campus, the conductor made immediate contact with a group of African American teenagers who had arrived together by asking them who they were. Normally it might be thought of as too forward to single out a specific audience group, but in this case contact was preferable to silence and reinforcement of societal patterns of isolation and alienation ("Those Black teenagers might cause trouble, let's just ignore them, what are they doing here, anyway.") When one said they were part of a summer job program, the conductor, in preparation for a fluid sculpture, asked him how it was going. At this point, their counselor/supervisor broke in, saying it was going "wonderfully." Accepting this response, the conductor passed it on to the actors, and they acted out the counselor's "wonderful." But it was important not to leave it at that, for the adult had answered for the (teenage) child. So the conductor repeated the question,

12. See Chapter 6, "The Wider World."

saying, "Let's hear from one of the program participants." The risk here on the artistic level was that the actors would get a second "wonderful," and the improvisation might begin to feel boring. On the social level the risk was that *none* of the youngsters would want to speak publicly about how they felt.

What actually happened was that one child did speak up. He said something interesting and full of feeling, which the actors then made into one of the high points of the show. The conductor's assertiveness paid off, and a prejudice concerning the rights of adults over children was not indulged.

ANOTHER EXAMPLE of the shaman as guide took place during the Social Change workshop cited at the beginning of this essay. To recap the situation: there had been two stories told by white tellers about the role of Black people in their childhood lives, in which the tellers spoke from the perspective of embarrassed witnesses to prejudice. It was a strong theme. Undoubtedly more whites would come forward with stories that would help them assuage their sense of guilt. At this point, however, I intervened, deliberately asking for a story from one of the two Black participants. Such intervention runs counter to the basic Playback practice, emphasized earlier, of accepting stories from anyone at any time. This was also a request not without risk, for there was a distinct chance that the two singled out might refuse to tell. But the alternative was riskier—repeating an endemic prejudicial pattern of behavior that gave a voice to white but not Black citizens. Thus guidance was essential. In the event, an African American told his story. The discourse continued in a constructive direction, towards the hearing of different voices, and vitality had a chance.

Conclusion

For the second performance of our fledgling Playback company, more than two decades ago, we made arrangements to visit the children's ward of a general hospital. The staff allowed us to come because they often welcomed volunteers of all sorts, and in their eyes we offered simply entertainment for the children.

They had no idea of the ritual power of our form (or they might have had second thoughts). We wore clown-like overalls; we sang a children's song; we were funny and disarming. And yet... since our goal was something more than entertainment, we insisted on performing at visiting hour because we wanted parents to be present. We stuck to our form of inviting individual tellers, even if the bed had to be rolled forward for the child teller to be seen and heard. And we acted out stories—of the children, of the parents, and even the nursing staff. Two memories stand out for me of that day. First, the children told aspects of their experience one sensed they could not tell in ordinary conversation, such as the scary feeling of waiting in a holding room prior to an operation. Second, the experience transformed the atmosphere of the ward: prior to our performance, the children were lethargic and the parents worried behind their comforting smiles. But afterwards, there was eager conversation, and a much lighter mood prevailed that I would even call joyful. It was only our second Playback performance, we hardly knew what we were doing, yet one could feel the power of the Playback ritual working.

I came to Playback Theatre from the pursuit of experimental theatre in the period following the Vietnam War. I thought of myself as a theatre artist. In the course of Playback's development, I studied psychodrama to learn the group process skills necessary to conduct interactive social events, recognizing how art and social interaction had to be skillfully blended in order to make Playback work. Without fully realizing it, I strove during this time to teach my company, my students, and myself the demands of ritual. For it is the ritual component of Playback Theatre that takes it to our core being, helping us feel newly alive; and it is this ritual component that allows the kind of discourse necessary to transform a dysfunctional or outworn social order.

It happens through our stories. It happens through dance, image, and music. And it happens because of citizen actors who are willing to learn a challenging art on behalf of their communities.

References

Abram, David. (1996). *The Spell of the Sensuous.* New York: Pantheon.

Fox, Jonathan. (1994). *Acts of Service: Spontaneity, Commitment, Tradition in the Nonscripted Theatre.* New Paltz, NY: Tusitala.

Hoesch, Folma. (1999). "The Red Thread: Storytelling as a Healing Process." In *Gathering Voices: Essays on Playback Theatre.* Eds H. Dauber and J. Fox. New Paltz, NY: Tusitala.

Salas, Jo. (1993). *Improvising Real Life: Personal Story in Playback Theatre.* Dubuque, IA: Kendall/Hunt. 3rd edition 1999, New Paltz, NY: Tusitala.

Salas, Jo. (1999). "What is 'Good' Playback Theatre?" In *Gathering Voices: Essays on Playback Theatre.* Eds H. Dauber and J. Fox. New Paltz, NY: Tusitala.

Stevenson, John. (1995). "The Fourth Wall and the Third Space." Unpublished essay for School of Playback Theatre.

Turner, Victor. (1974). *Dramas, Fields, and Metaphors.* Ithaca, NY: Cornell University Press.

6

THE WIDER WORLD: PLAYBACK THEATRE'S SCOPE AND RESPONSIBILITY[1]

Jo Salas (2003)

SEVERAL YEARS AGO I began to feel restless with the exclusively personal focus of most Playback Theatre stories, especially in public performances. I felt sure that our personal stories were connected to much larger stories, including the huge tides of history. And I knew that I myself was often deeply affected by events that were not part of my own life. I wanted very much for our Playback stage to widen—to become a place where we could collectively acknowledge these connections between the personal and the political.

In public shows I began to invite stories that acknowledged these links. But no matter what invitation or suggestion I made, the stories remained purely individualistic—often wonderful, of course, memorable, revelatory, and so on—but focused purely on what happened within the scope of our audience members' individual experience.

It was clear that it was going to take more than a gentle invitation. We—my company, Hudson River Playback Theatre, and I—decided to create a Playback Theatre version of the Living Newspaper. (The tradition of the Living Newspaper goes back at least as far as revolutionary Russia, when news was brought to illiterate populations by actors who enacted the pressing stories of the day.

---

1. First published as "The Wider World" in *Interplay*, the newsletter of the International Playback Theatre Network, April 2003, one month after the US invasion of Iraq. This expanded version includes further comments about Playback performers' social responsibility and our options in responding to stories expressing prejudice.

Later, J.L. Moreno experimented with a psychodramatic version.[2])

We quickly ran up against a number of problems. Some were technical—it seemed that to act out news stories effectively we needed to plan and rehearse them, at least minimally. Some were philosophical—should we, the company, choose the stories, or let the audience suggest them? What if someone chose a story that we were not willing to enact? The most challenging problems were to do with our own process. Our own political differences came to the surface—and, more fundamentally, our different views about the importance of bringing the political/social world into our work. Sometimes a news story was vetoed by company members who didn't know about it and didn't want to know about it. "Our audiences come to enjoy themselves, not to be dragged down by depressing stuff like this," one person said.

In spite of all these hurdles, we performed a Living Newspaper in a number of shows. And we found that when the wider world was presented so strongly, it enlarged the parameters of the stories. Tellers still told about love and loss and family and work and nature. But they also remembered times when their lives confronted them with social injustice, when they were challenged to be courageous or altruistic, often as witnesses: when they were directly aware of the vast, messy business of people struggling in a post-colonial, capitalist, racist society.

We pulled back from the Living Newspaper, failing to find a format that really worked in the middle of a Playback show. But we had launched ourselves on a path of engagement and discovery—a path of slow but steady growth in the direction of taking responsibility, paying attention, acknowledging our own connections to history and social reality, facing our own identity in the world which is a part of every story we tell and hear, whether we know it or not.

The exploring we have now done together—through our own stories, through much discussion, through searching and sometimes

2. See "Morenos Stegreiftheater in New York" in the *Jahrbuch für Psychodrama, Psychosoziale Praxis & Gesellschaftspolitik 1993*. Ferdinand Buer (Ed.). Opladen, Germany: Leske + Budrich, 1993.

conflict—has brought us collectively to a place where, although we are not political clones, we share an awareness of right and wrong in the world. And we know that stories of the wider world belong on our Playback stage as much as stories of the inner life.

The discoveries we have made together enable us to enlarge the picture easily and organically. Broadening the frame of reference at the outset of a show leads to a broader and deeper pool for the stories that will follow. We often mention what's happening in the world in our personal introductions at the opening of a show. Our warm-up questions always include a question such as "What's something in the news recently that's had an impact on you?" People respond. The conductor may make reference to a social or political reality relevant to the event, like the public performance we did in an area much celebrated in our upstate region for its Huguenot history. I happened to know some of the untold stories of this famous street: the stories of the slaves who lived and died in each one of the picturesque old houses. My brief mention of this overlooked history made it possible for a teller (he told me later) to come forward with a very strong story about tragic discrimination in his own Asian culture.

Prejudiced tellers

With or without such an invitation, stories sometimes bring in the wider world in ways that are uncomfortable for the performers and the audience. Playback is built for dialogue: what better way to listen to each other?[3] But what happens, playbackers often ask, if someone tells a story that embodies an offensive point of view? What if you have a racist teller, for example? It's essential for the Playback team—not just the conductor—to be alert to any kind of intolerance or disrespect and to find a way to address it without sacrificing the teller. Not easy: such moments seem to pit the necessity to uphold our values squarely against the commitment to honor the teller. But we must do it, for our own integrity, for those in the audience who are offended by the teller's ignorance or prejudice, and so that the teller has a chance to learn from seeing his story.

3. See Chapter 8, "What We Mean by 'Dialogue' in Playback Theatre."

The performing team has several options. Firstly, the conductor can—and should—find a way to distance herself from what is problematic in the story, making it clear that she does not share the biased assumption that the teller is expressing. ("A big Black guy came over and I was terrified." "Why were you terrified?" says the conductor, refusing to be complicit in the stereotype that all Black men are dangerous.) Secondly, the actors can make sure that their enactment brings out the humanity of the victims of the teller's prejudice. Another opportunity comes after the enactment, while the actors are still in position on the stage. In that brief, but important moment of checking in with the teller, the conductor can allow space for an expression of insight or realization. She might even invite the teller to look at the actor playing the target of their bias: "I wonder how that person might have felt inside."

After the teller returns to the audience, and depending on the impact of the story and the vulnerability of the teller, you might use short forms to reflect other audience members' feelings about seeing the story. Or you can be alert to—or invite—a subsequent story that may address the issues of the earlier one. The dialogue continues.

Lastly, the ending of a show can provide a fertile opportunity to revisit a hurtful story. Hudson River Playback Theatre ends its shows with a collage of moments inspired by the stories and short forms, focusing not on memorable moments but on the stories' untold aspects. We try to shine a light on the story from a different angle, using our empathy and imagination. After a story that embodied injustice, whether recognized by the teller or not, the object can become the subject. The Arab store owner, irrationally feared by the teller after 9/11, expresses his own fear. The homeless woman who refused the wealthy teller's gift of a worn-out sweater tells her side of the story.

We have learned in this way that we can embrace any story, giving it its due attention and respect, knowing that we are still upholding the ideals of awareness and justice.[4]

---

4. In the most extreme, and extremely rare, situation, a performer or team has the right to decline to enact a story. Ultimately, we are human beings with values and integrity.

FROM THE AUDIENCE, I watched my company do a public show four days after the beginning of the US invasion of Iraq, to which all of us were passionately opposed. In the previous rehearsal, the performers had told their own stories in preparation: we knew that the war was likely to emerge as the main theme of the show. They also prepared themselves to be open to pro-war stories. In the show, some of their opening statements conveyed anguish about what was happening. But the conductor's welcome made it clear that stories from any point of view were welcome. We are here to listen to each other, she said. In that particular audience there was only one audience comment not clearly opposed to the invasion: a man talked about his trust that the government knew more than the rest of us. The actors reflected his feelings, different from their own, knowing the capacity of Playback to hold varying points of view and deepen understanding for everyone.

Playback Theatre has an important role to play in our communities during this time of war where truth, as they say, is the first casualty. In this situation, as well as in the perennial struggles for justice on any front, it is our responsibility to fulfill this role by examining our own participation in the social/political world, and educating ourselves about our society. When we, the Playback team, are prepared and unified in this goal, our audiences will embrace this much-needed opportunity to tell stories about the wider world and how they are part of it.

PART 2
EXPLORING IDEAS

7

Playback Theatre, Diversity, and the Two Economies[1]

Jo Salas (2005)

SOMETIMES IN MY COMPANY'S school performances we vary
the usual Playback format by getting the kids to help us create a
composite story, knowing that every detail they contribute will come
from their own experience. I want to tell you a composite story,
drawn from the experiences of many different Playback Theatre
groups including mine. There are other stories on this theme which
could be told, of course. But this one is common and may sound
familiar to some of you.

Jerome is a 28-year-old African American man. He has a
job as a stock manager in a big warehouse—he's worked there
for five years and has been promoted every year. He is proud of
this, and proud of having a steady job that pays enough to cover
at least basic living expenses—a lot more security than Jerome
grew up with. His father left his family when Jerome was five,
and his mother found it so hard to manage that she had to let her
parents take care of her three children for several years. When
Jerome finished high school, college wasn't even a possibility. His
whole family needed him to start earning as quickly as possible.
Now, ten years later, his sisters are working too, but his mother
has never quite got herself on her feet. Jerome sends part of his
paycheck to her every two weeks.

Jerome is usually too tired after work to do much besides watch
television. But one Friday night his friend Anne insists that he come
with her to some kind of theatre show. "I don't know, Jerome, but I

---

1. Keynote address at the 2005 International Playback Theatre Symposium, Arizona
State University, Tempe, Arizona.

think you'll like it," she says. "It's really different—not like regular theatre at all. They act out stories that people in the audience tell." Jerome is intrigued, and he likes Anne. So he goes.

From the very beginning of the performance he's riveted. He's never seen or imagined anything like this. The actors seem like real people. They face the audience, and ask them questions, and listen to what people say. And then they act out the stories that they hear and it's like magic—suddenly there's a play, and music, and the audience is laughing or sometimes crying, and it's all being made up right on the spot. Jerome finds himself wondering what it might be like to go up onto the stage and tell a story. He even starts imagining what it would be like to be one of those actors, acting out a story. They seem like nice people though they're all very different from him. All of them are white.

As the show is coming to an end, the leader says: "We're looking for new actors, and we're especially interested in people of color. Let us know if you'd like to come and visit a rehearsal."

Jerome doesn't say anything to Anne or to the performers, who are chatting with audience members over tea and brownies, but he slips one of their brochures into his pocket.

Two weeks later he calls the director. "I don't have any experience as an actor," he tells her. "That's not necessarily a problem," she says. "We can train you, if you feel and we feel that Playback Theatre is something you can do."

Jerome goes to a rehearsal. They don't call it an audition, but obviously they're checking him out. The rehearsal is fun, though somewhat strange. Everyone is amazingly friendly. They praise Jerome warmly when he plays a main character in someone's story. He feels, too, that he did it well. He remembers what it was like seeing the show, and again has the conviction, deep inside, that he can do this, he *wants* to do this. He wonders how he could explain it to his co-workers, and decides he wouldn't even try.

Jerome starts going to weekly rehearsals. He is thrilled to be learning this work, to become an actor, an artist. He's never been around such a warm-hearted, playful group of people. They talk a lot about their feelings. He knows they're sincere, but it's not totally comfortable for him. Being the only Black person makes it harder. But he loves listening to the stories, and the challenge of making theatre out of a fragment of a life. He loves the give-and-take of this kind of acting.

He starts performing, very nervous at first, though the others shower him with praise and encouragement. By now Jerome knows and likes all the company members as individuals, not just as an amorphous body of kindly white people. He's become good friends with John, one of the actors, a social worker. John's the one he calls when he can't get to rehearsal because of overtime or yet another crisis with his mother.

Jerome is anxious about something that's coming up: the company is going to do some shows in schools. He knows that Katherine, the director, is very eager for him to take part. "It will really help the kids of color to have an African American actor," she says. They talk about race a lot in the company. They want to "increase their diversity," as they put it. Jerome appreciates what they're trying to do—it's a lot better than the casual racism that's part of daily life for him and every other Black person he knows—but it still feels awkward.

Jerome hates to disappoint Katherine and the company, but there's no way he can take time off from his job to do daytime shows. Most of the other performers can arrange to be available— they either work part-time or they have full-time jobs where they can occasionally take a day for something else. But the warehouse doesn't operate like that. You either show up or you're fired.

Katherine is understanding though regretful. She raises something else: she wants Jerome to take a five-day Playback Theatre training in the summer. "All of us have gone to this training program, Jerome, and it's great. It really deepens our skills." She tells him that if it's hard to pay for it, the program offers scholarships. All he'd have to do is fill out an application. Jerome doesn't know what to tell her. He would love to do the training. He loves the idea of learning more, and meeting other people who do Playback Theatre. But July is the busiest time at the warehouse. No one takes their vacation in July. Besides, he only gets ten vacation days a year and he usually takes this time to see his family in Virginia.

It's hard to tell this to Katherine. She's so nice, and she's been so helpful. "I'll try," he says, but it's just a way of delaying the moment of telling her it's impossible.

SUMMER IS APPROACHING. At rehearsal the company talks about the school shows, which are going well, though very demanding. Jerome listens, sad that he isn't part of it. Sometimes they talk about the workshops that several of them are planning to attend. They all think that Jerome is going too, because he still hasn't been able to tell them that he's not.

"See you in July!" they say, when they have their final rehearsal for the season. Jerome feels guilty. He's also begun to feel resentful. It seems so easy for them all. None of them have parents who need their help. None of them have jobs that keep you on your feet for eight or ten hours a day and pay barely enough to get by.

During the summer he thinks of the company less and less. He's vaguely aware when the time for the workshop comes and goes. He's too busy to wonder for more than a moment what it would have been like to be there.

In the fall he doesn't make it to the first rehearsal, or the second or third. His phone rings with concerned messages from company members. "Jerome? Are you OK? We miss you." After a while the calls stop.

That's Jerome's story. A promising young actor of color, a welcoming company, and he leaves after less than a year. What's going on here, and what can we do to make this a less common Playback story? To explore these questions, we need to look at aspects of our history, our current directions, and our assumptions about ourselves as a field.

I want to talk first about what the writer Lewis Hyde called the "gift economy," and how this idea relates to Playback Theatre.[2] His idea, which he explores very fully and wonderfully in his book

2. See also Chapter 12, "Is There More?"

The Gift,[3] is that alongside the market economy, in which goods and services are bought and sold—the whole basis of western economic life—there is and always has been an economy in which things are valued in non-monetary ways and exchanged only or significantly as gifts. He makes his point in part by talking about odd pockets of western culture where the gift economy is unchanged—for example, the conviction shared by most people and reflected in the law that kidneys and livers and other organs can only be donated, not sold. But, more relevantly for our purposes, he talks about how the gift economy also still exists in the areas of art and healing.

Here's part of what Hyde says about art in the introduction: "It is the assumption of this book that a work of art is a gift, not a commodity. Or, to state the modern case with more precision, that works of art exist simultaneously in two 'economies,' a market and a gift economy. Only one of these is essential, however: a work of art can survive without the market, but where there is no gift there is no art." He goes on to say: "That art that matters to us—which moves the heart, or revives the soul, or delights the senses, or offers courage for living, however we choose to describe the experience—that work is received by us as a gift is received. Even if we have paid a fee at the door of the museum or concert hall, when we are touched by a work of art something comes to us which has nothing to do with price."[4]

I imagine that you recognize this from your own experience as artists, your own drive to make art both within Playback Theatre and beyond and to offer it regardless of monetary compensation. And you recognize it as well as from your own experience of looking at paintings, watching performances, listening to music, reading literature. When art moves us, we feel given to.

Hyde also talks about healing in relation to the gift economy— and about healthcare, which in most ways is extremely commodified these days, in the US more than anywhere else in the world. In more traditional societies, healing, like art, was given and not sold. The healer was called to his or her work, and gave it as a service.

3. Lewis Hyde, *The Gift: Imagination and the Erotic Life of Property*. New York: Vintage Books, 1979.
4. Ibid, p. xii.

This work was valued and supported by the community. But it was not quantified and traded like tangible goods. It was not separated from the altruistic impulse of the healer.

That understanding is lost, to some degree, in our modern times. But in some ways it persists. The healthcare professions are still full of people who have chosen their work because of a deep calling to help others. They expect and need to earn money too, but if money was their main priority they would have chosen other careers.

There is no clear dividing line between gift and market economy work. Many professions combine both—they lie somewhere on a spectrum between work that is given unconditionally, with no expectation or possibility of financial recompense, at one end, and work in which the idea of service is irrelevant, at the other. As Hyde says: "Few jobs are pure gift labors, of course—although a nurse is committed to healing, she is also an actor in the marketplace—but any portion of gift labor in a job will tend to pull it out of the market and make it a less lucrative profession."[5]

I first encountered Hyde's ideas in 1983 in an article called "The Gift Must Always Move."[6] It made a huge impression on me. I wasn't sure why. It wasn't until I read his book many years later that I realized the profound relevance to the work we are doing in Playback Theatre. Suddenly, much of what had felt like frustrating, stubborn contradictions made sense in a new way.

As we all know, doing Playback Theatre brings all kinds of gift-economy rewards that have nothing to do with money: artistic satisfaction, belonging, a sense of usefulness, recognition, the gratitude and admiration of audiences, a sense of relationship, spiritual meaning, and more. As Hyde says, "It is the cardinal difference between gift and commodity exchange that a gift establishes a feeling-bond between two people, while the sale of a commodity leaves no necessary connection."[7] Sometimes all this is enough. Sometimes it is not.

5. Ibid, p. 107.

6. Lewis Hyde, "The Gift Must Always Move" in *CoEvolution Quarterly*, No.35, Fall 1982.

7. Hyde, 1979, p. 56.

When we began Playback Theatre, back in 1975, it was with the artist's impetus to create theatre, along with the activist's impetus to create change. It was, obviously, not about making money. Jonathan and I—a young couple with a small child—and our fellow members of the original company came together as idealists and explorers, operating completely within the gift economy. We started performing, occasionally at first, and then more often. Our early performances, still mostly during evenings or weekends, were manageable even for those who had fulltime jobs. But the burgeoning behind-the-scenes work, carried out mostly by Jonathan and to some degree by me, soon brought the two of us to what I'll call the "volunteer viability" point: the point where the gift economy comes right up against the market economy.

The "volunteer viability" point isn't a fixed place. It varies from one person to another and from one culture to another. It's the point where your unpaid activity simply has to become remunerative or you will starve. Or you give it up. If you are someone who has support from a well-paid spouse, or you have some inherited wealth, you may never get to this point—you can spend all your life working without financial compensation. If you're middle class, you can probably take the risk of a very low or uncertain income, at least for a while, knowing that if things get too tight you can step back and get a regular job, and if some kind of emergency happens to you, your family and friends can help you out. Your volunteer viability point will depend on how long you can put up with lack of security and material comfort, as well as other factors. For someone who lives from paycheck to paycheck, or who is working two jobs just to meet basic needs, who has no safety net from extended family, the volunteer viability point comes up very quickly.

Jonathan and I were in the middle-class category—we had no money other than what we earned, and we did not own property, but we had the kind of education and family backgrounds that would, if necessary, protect us from destitution. Jonathan, particularly, had a deep drive and commitment to keep developing Playback in spite of the hardship. As a young family, we lived for many years below the poverty line in order to stay with our art.

Some other company members were sufficiently passionate about Playback to make similar sacrifices, so we had a team that could say yes to whatever work came up. We all got paid just enough to survive, but never enough to relax.

When I started a new company in 1990, after the first one ended, it was with the clear intention that we would not go this route. I just wanted to do Playback Theatre. I did not want all this worry about money. But there is an inherent and inevitable drive to grow, like the force within a plant that impels it to become tall and strong and fruitful. If you suppress this force you might stagnate and die. We embraced it, and at this point, my 15-year-old company is very active and very engaged. We have accepted the challenge to be as available to our community as we can. Along with all the excitement and satisfactions, it means considerable financial responsibility, considerable stress, and dilemmas that are so far unsolved.

It has been helpful to have the conceptual framework of the two economies, which we did not have back in the original company days. My company needs to earn money, but we accept that our basis is in the impulse of art, healing, and social change. Ultimately, we all do Playback because we love it and believe in its power for good, and because we find it deeply rewarding to create theatre together. Much of our work is contracted and paid, but weekly rehearsals and monthly public shows are not, and it is important to us to maintain this level of gift economy functioning. We feel that there would be a danger in putting all of our work on a paid basis, even if we could. "If I am right to say that where there is no gift there is no art," writes Lewis Hyde, "then it may be possible to destroy a work of art by converting it into a pure commodity."[8]

WE'RE GOING TO TURN now toward another very important focus for many Playback Theatre groups, and that is the growth of social awareness and responsibility. This dimension was part of the original vision, but the focus during Playback Theatre's first 15 or 20 years was primarily on the significance of the story for the teller and the immediate audience, rather than attending to the relationship

8. Hyde, 1979, p. xiii.

of the stories to the broadest and deepest social/political realities. More recently, playbackers all over the world have expanded
their sphere of attention to the larger social context, seeing that all
stories, all groups, exist in relation to it. And that our wonderful
theatre, though always based in the primacy of the subjective story,
can be offered as a means of dialogue and connection in ways that
go far beyond the simply personal.

An important part of that focus, at least here in the US, has
been the interwoven issues of race, racism, and class—or rank and
privilege, as these issues are also referred to. Many of us by now
have realized—and it's a learning process often characterized by
reluctance and pain as well as exhilaration—that the Playback
community itself has been unintentionally exclusive of people who
are not white or middle class. No one ever wanted it to be this way,
but in a society as contaminated by racism and the enduring legacy
of slavery as ours is, social entities that originate in the white middle
class are almost certain to remain there unless there is a concerted
and conscious commitment to change.[9]

A consequence of this courageous and growing awareness
is that many Playback Theatre companies are working hard to
increase their diversity—to recruit people of different racial,
cultural, and class backgrounds in order to reflect our diverse
audience's stories with more wisdom and impact. As many of us
have discovered, it's a long, hard, confusing, and complex path. It
involves far more than simply announcing that we're looking for
African American or Hispanic or Native American performers. It
requires us to look hard and unblinkingly at our own histories in
relation to race and class, to tell our own stories and learn from
them, to educate ourselves about the history of our country and
our region and its often hidden injustices. It requires us to have the
compassion and fortitude to work with conflicts around race and
class that will inevitably arise when we are lucky enough to find
people of color who want to join our companies. It may require
us to be flexible about the requirements of company membership, and yet to be clear about what's not negotiable. It requires

9. See social change section in Chapter 1, "A Changing Landscape."

us as companies to be fundamentally unified in our commitment to this kind of expansion and inclusiveness.

In fact, it's a very tall order. And many companies get discouraged.

The story is not over, of course. We are in a long-term process and some of our achievement so far is not as visible as having Black or brown faces in the room or in the line-up. It is a sign of success that many people are talking and writing and holding workshops about this topic. Compared to ten years ago, there are far more people worldwide whose Playback work takes place in a context of commitment to justice, inclusiveness, and change. Playback Theatre is growing vigorously in African and Asian countries, and the international Playback community is stimulated and enriched by their work.

I've been talking from the point of view of someone who's already in the Playback world, as most of us here today are. But let's think for a few minutes about the point of view of someone who's not—let's think about Jerome, whose story I began with today. Someone who came across Playback Theatre and was drawn to it, and tried it out, and liked it even more, and then found that it just didn't fit into his life, and left it behind. Jerome was different from everyone else in that company, and not just because of the color of his skin. Unlike everyone else, he'd never gone to college. The work that he could get with a high school diploma was at best moderately paid and physically taxing. What financial security he had came only from his paycheck. No one in his family could possibly help him out if he lost his job.

Katherine, the director, sometimes complimented the company on the way that money seemed to be unimportant to them—people often forgot even to ask if a new gig was paid. The performers were delighted to get a check, of course, but as they often reminded each other, they were not doing Playback for the money. In the beginning it never occurred to Jerome, either, to do Playback Theatre for the money. He found it rewarding in exactly the same ways as the rest of the company, and he loved the idea of simply offering a service to the community. It reminded him of the way his mother did volunteer work with her church. But with the company growing and getting more invitations to perform, the gulf widened between him and everyone else. On the rare occasions that he could take part in a contracted show, it did make a difference to him if he got paid or not. Most uncomfortable of all was just the way that the others took certain things for granted—having time and money for training; having families and savings accounts and investments and houses that were a bulwark against poverty.

As I said earlier, our stories are always part of much larger stories, the great tides of history. If we take another step back to look at why things were so different for Jerome, we see the history of our society: we see hundreds of years where Jerome's forebears worked without pay, without the possibility of accumulating property and wealth to pass on to their descendants, instead building wealth for white people. We see repressive forces in post-slavery times that used (and still use) more covert means of preventing African Americans from becoming fully and equally rewarded citizens—discrimination, intimidation, red-lining, and the pernicious stresses of racism that can erode a person's health, will, and ambition.

This is not the place for a full discussion of race and privilege. There is far more to be said, far more complexity and history that we need to explore. What I am concerned to do here is to look as honestly as I can at how our treasured and well-merited place in the gift economy may work against our goal of increasing access and diversity. If Playback Theatre is still significantly a volunteer activity, is it possible to include people whose economic reality makes volunteerism on this scale out of reach?

To explore these questions, I sent a short survey to all the companies in the US and Canada that were listed in the IPTN directory. For simplicity's sake I limited this inquiry to North America. Much of what I'm saying here applies, more or less, to the other western countries. (In nonwestern countries, the story is often quite different and I'll say a bit more about that later.) I contacted about thirty groups and received responses from sixteen.

My questions were aimed at discovering where a company was positioned in relation to the gift and market economies, and how this might relate to the question of diversity within their company. Here's a summary of the responses I received:

Company age ranged from two and a half years to twenty years. Average company age was eight and a half years.

Six companies were nonprofits, four operated under a non-profit umbrella, two were considering becoming nonprofit, one operated within a nonprofit institution. Three said they had no plans to become nonprofit.

One company had done thirty-two shows in 2004, one had done thirty-five, and one had done sixty. For the remaining thirteen companies the average number of shows was twelve.

Yearly budgets varied greatly, from $400 to $85,000. Six companies had budgets of $10K or less. Two companies did not know their yearly budget. Four companies had budgets of $25K or more. Budget did not necessarily correlate to the number of shows per year.

The average number of company members was nine and a half. The smallest group, in transition at the time of responding, had only three members. The largest group was fifteen.

I asked about payment—who gets paid and for what. The responses ranged from one of the new companies where no one gets paid for anything to a 20-year-old company in which all performances, rehearsals, and administration are paid. The degree to which people are paid did not always correlate to age of the company. Most companies paid performers for contracted gigs, and minimally or not at all for administration. Except for the groups at either end of the spectrum, either fully volunteer or fully paid, most responders indicated some discontent with the lack of money to pay performers and administrators adequately, at the same time emphasizing that rewards came in other forms beside money.

The next question asked about the composition of the company in terms of gender, race, age, and class, followed by a question about the degree to which the company's diversity matched that of their region. Two groups were all women. In fourteen of the other groups, women outnumbered men, in some cases substantially. One group was evenly divided and one group had more men. Five groups were all white. Six groups had one person of color. The other five groups had between two and five members of color. Only two of the companies felt that their racial/cultural mix matched that of their local region. Ages varied widely, often within companies, with the overall majority between late thirties and fifties. One company which is itself white, middle class, and middle aged has engendered four younger companies which are 50% Hispanic and 50% white.

I asked about leadership in terms of gender, race, age, and class. Nine companies were led by a white woman, or by a team of two white women, all but one self-described as middle or upper class, and mostly middle aged. Two companies were led by white middle-class men, one young, one early 40s. Several others were led by teams of men and women. One team of three women included an African American, the only person of color in a leadership role among all the responders. One group said that all company members shared leadership.

The tenth question was "How important is diversity to your company's vision? What kinds of diversity?" Eleven companies said emphatically that diversity was extremely important. Some mentioned diversity of ability and sexual orientation as well as race, age, gender, and class. Several spoke of the importance of diversity but said that not everyone in the company was in agreement about this.

Question eleven asked "What is your company's attitude and vision in relation to monetary payment?" Eight companies were clear that they would like to be able to pay better for performing and administration. Others were more at peace with their status quo, either earning and paying very little, or using any money earned by the company for training, or, in one case, being able to pay fully for all work. Two mature companies said they had pulled back from trying to earn money as a group.

The last question invited any further comments about diversity and/or compensation. Here are some of the responses:

"There are those in the company that are artists first and foremost and want to grow the company and make as much of a living from it as possible. There are others who have another livelihood and see playback as a fun, extra thing—they are dedicated but don't need it to grow for their livelihood. We need to empower those new and old members who want it to grow to do networking, marketing and curriculum building and become leaders in the company."

"We feel that the homogeneity that we have as a group has been a strength as well as having limitations on our outreach capacity. We are very tight as a group, the keepers of one another's stories, and we are able to take personal risks in our company life but the issue of new members is difficult as we do not want to increase in size or leave a certain comfort level that we have attained."

"Not needing money is a privilege that limits who can join the company."

"Pursuing ethnic diversity seems a luxury at this point; we don't have enough income to pay members."

"It is difficult to draw an interest from the groups of population that we want to diversify with for our history has been playing to a predominately Caucasian audience. We must diversify who we perform for as well. We visit compensation on and off, lightly touching it for we haven't made serious money to pay members. It is also a difficult topic to explore."

"Although everyone seems very enthusiastic about the form, it is a simple matter of hand to mouth survival—living expenses are high and most people have to work very hard to make ends meet. It's an issue especially for the people of color and those with less income in the company (the last two often linked). But also, we hope that new people will stick around long enough to feel the other, non-monetary rewards, which they have so far."

"Ideally I would like to see all the company members paid for performances and workshops. I think it is a way in which people feel value. Currently the company in existence is willing to work for no money as the value of Playback in itself is enough. We meet weekly whether or not we have a gig and the deepening in that process is priceless."

"It is often educated Caucasians who have the luxury of doing volunteer work. The actors appear compensated by the reward of hearing a patient say; 'That's it! You got it!' The community provided by troupe life is also a compensation." [A group that works within a hospital]

Three members of a company:

A: "We have had to talk about issues around diversity as a company as they come up—in stories; in recruitment; with groups that we work with and with themes that we have. It is crucial to having an open, loving and respectful group. We have laughed, cried and gotten angry and hurt but we are committed to continuing the discussion whenever it is needed. Telling each other our stories so we understand who we are, where we came from and what matters to us is fundamental."

B: "The more diverse (in all areas) a playback theater group is, the easier it will be for the group to serve our diverse world."

C: "Although we like to hassle our artistic director about getting a raise, I feel we are gracious for what we do receive in terms of compensation."

A: "Regarding [racial] diversity, I believe we value it and make sure the group is diverse not just because it's the p.c. thing to do or to get more grants or look good, but because our core values are about respect, listening, honoring, and knowing we don't grow as humans without diversity. It's important to be clear about that, and unfortunately pressure can get put on the people of color in our group. If we're doing a gig on 'diversity' then a couple of people in the group know they especially are going to be asked to be there. It's kind of a double-edged sword, on the one hand we want to be diverse because we're going to do stories about diversity, on the other hand it's not fair to subliminally put the pressure on people of color that they somehow 'represent' diversity—just how one African American or Native American does not represent their entire race. So it's a delicate dance that requires much nurturing, attention, clear communication, and openness to learning. But the benefits of understanding, compassion, advocacy and camaraderie are well worth it."

"We are trying to build a sustainable organization, which means we can't run on good will forever. Thus, I aspire to gradually increase the degree to which we can compensate ourselves. That said, up until now we have been successful because of the intrinsic value of the work to our own personal and professional growth. The challenge is to maintain the inspiring nature of the work for everyone involved."

I imagine that as you listen, you recognize your own experience in some of these responses.

What are the red threads here? A few things emerge for me: most of the groups struggle with questions about compensation, about where they are and where they want to be in relation to the gift and market economies. Most of the groups seek to serve the diversity of their community by having diversity among their own membership, and most are not satisfied with the degree to which they've fulfilled this goal. Some are very aware of the contradictions between the goal of diversity and the implications of operating significantly as volunteers. (Three responders referred to doing Playback as a luxury or privilege which is less accessible to people of color, while another person referred to *seeking* diversity as a luxury—an interesting difference.)

The picture that emerges is of a network of mostly middle-class people, two-thirds of them women, 95% white, devoted to each other and to Playback Theatre, trying without a lot of success to bring in people of different backgrounds, and searching for a foothold in the world of paid work in order to grow but most often working for non-monetary rewards like satisfaction and companionship. The majority of the sixteen groups operate on low or very low budgets; and most carry out relatively few performances per year.

There's food for thought here. I would have said, and I think many of you would concur, that Playback Theatre is fundamentally about serving our communities through our art. In any town or city, even small ones, there are hundreds or thousands of people with stories to tell and in need of a place to tell them. How many of them will have this chance if their local Playback group performs only six or eight or twelve times a year? Of course, in some cases this figure has to do with being relatively new. For others it is the result of a conscious and valid choice to remain very small. But

what does it mean if the *majority* of Playback Theatre groups operate at this level? If Playback Theatre is an act of service, who are
we really serving? Could it be that, as a network of people, we are
primarily serving ourselves? For me that is a disturbing thought.

THIS YEAR, 2005, Playback Theatre itself is thirty years old.
We've come a long, long way since the pioneering days: we've
deepened and refined our understanding of Playback Theatre,
we've developed our skills and our training resources, we've
extended our outreach to all parts of the world, we've continued to polish our work as a dynamic and beautiful theatre
form. Perhaps where we grow next, for the next thirty years, or
the next ten, is toward becoming an active, valued, recognized
player in the life of our local communities.

As the artistic and executive director of a busy company committed to paying performers and administrators, I know all too well
what this path entails and how extraordinarily difficult it is. Even
with a gifted and committed ensemble, with great support and
encouragement from our community, and with all my own years of
experience, I wonder if it's possible.

I know of another well-established and extremely active company—not one of the 16 responders—whose work is carried out
on a fully professional basis and has been from the outset because
of the founder-director's conviction that artists should not work for
nothing. This group could teach us a lot about being viable in the
market economy. But, like other less-professional groups, its success
has also depended to a significant degree on the personal sacrifices
of the director, who for years worked 80 to 100 hours a week before
scaling back the group's operations.

I am beginning to think that the challenge of truly fulfilling
Playback's potential role is not something that a company can
or should meet alone. What can we do as a collective? What
changes can we consider, what steps can we take? We may have
to re-examine our relationship to the gift economy; those of us
who are trainers may have to begin teaching the practical skills
and knowledge needed to build viable companies; we may need to

become more stringent about standards so that there is, at least to some degree, a recognizable consistency of practice between one company and another; we may have to develop further systems of communication and accountability amongst ourselves.

And we will need to do all this without leaving the gift economy behind. We are artists, healers, activists. We need to pay our rent and buy our food but our work will always spring from the impulse of gift.

In other countries, it is perhaps an easier task than here. In the US, unless we perform for private corporations, our audiences or clients can't support us. We need funding for our projects and for our general operations as well. The United States gives less money to the arts, proportionately, than any other industrialized country. As many of us know to our chagrin, even after thirty years we are still likely to be denied funding by arts councils because they don't recognize our work as art; and by social services funders because we're too arts-oriented.

The recent growth of Playback in nonwestern countries has often taken a different path, in part because it's simply not an option to use the mixed-economy model that we're used to. Training, rehearsing, and performing without guaranteed pay in Burundi, for example, is out of the question because of pervasive poverty.[10] There is no volunteer viability point. So the Playback Theatre company there has been on a paid basis from the beginning, with funds from several NGOs. In their first 18 months they did over 70 performances, and the spirit of gift seemed to thrive alongside the compensation. In India and other Asian countries some groups are part of larger social institutions: employees do Playback as part of their regular work.

Those of you who are "company partners" with the School of Playback Theatre recently received Jonathan's article[11] inspired by a Rockefeller Foundation report on their PACT program: Partnerships Affirming Community Transformation.[12] This report

10. See Chapter 19, "Burundi Journal," and Chapter 21, "Playback Theatre in Burundi."
11. Jonathan Fox, "Your PT Identity." In *Company Partnership*, February 2005.
12. Don Adams and Arlene Goldbard, *Creative Community: The Art of Community Development*. Rockefeller Foundation, 2001.

has a couple of very interesting implications for Playback Theatre. One is the concept of what the authors call "community cultural-development workers," meaning, in fact, people just like us: artists who offer their vision and skills and labors for the wellbeing of their communities. Not art-for-art's-sake artists; not arts therapists; not arts-in-education specialists, but a category all our own, with its own long traditions and values. When I read the Rockefeller report I felt relieved and affirmed. The idea that there is a place for us, that we may not have to endlessly rationalize our work in the terms of other fields, was tremendously validating. The other point which had a strong impact on me was the authors' blunt assessment of the completely inadequate funding available for community cultural development. Whereas this field of the arts is well-recognized and supported in other countries, here it is not. And so we compete for scarce funds with all the other kinds of arts, and we often lose.

WELL, HERE WE ARE, looking back and looking ahead, exploring the paradox that Playback Theatre's inherent generosity may limit the scope of its gift and may restrict the inclusion of people from different racial, cultural, and class backgrounds. How many Jeromes will come and go before we solve these dilemmas?

We need new creativity, new dreams, and ideas from many voices before we can discern the directions we might take. But if, as a field, we succeed in creating a more professionally based and fairly compensated practice, we may at last find ourselves with the diversity we have longed for. We may at last become an active network of dynamic and diverse community cultural-development teams, securely funded so that we can serve our communities regardless of our personal wealth, making places for stories every day.

8

What We Mean by "Dialogue" in Playback Theatre[1]

Jo Salas (2006)

THESE DAYS WE OFTEN describe Playback Theatre as community dialogue, but without further explanation it may be a misleading description. The kind of dialogue that we are referring to is not a cognitive dialogue. It is not the same as hearing someone speak their thoughts and feelings and reasons, then responding with your own thoughts, feelings, and reasons. It is not a process of discussion, of thought and logic.

Instead, it is a dialogue in the realm of story, image, emotion, and physical action; an embodied, imaginative dialogue. We call it a dialogue because, in the unfolding of a show, the stories are summoned and prompted by each other. No one knows ahead of time which voices will be heard, which stories enacted. An audience member hears a story and watches it enacted, then finds herself recalling an event from her own life. It may or may not have any apparent connection with the story she's just seen. She remembers a moment from her life, and thinks yes, she'd like to tell about it. The conductor asks for another story and she raises her hand.

Whether the connection is apparent or not, her story is most likely a response to what has just happened, or perhaps to something that happened earlier in the show.[2] But it is not a logical or dialectical response. In Playback Theatre, every statement, every story is conveyed, comprehended, and responded to on kinesthetic

1. An earlier version of this article has been circulated and translated but not previously published.
2. See Chapter 13, "The Theory of Narrative Reticulation."

and imaginative levels. The dialogue proceeds through association and inspiration in relation to any aspect of what the teller has said and how the performers have brought it to life on stage. To the degree that they are able to listen with full openness and attention, the enactment will reflect the story's constellation of meanings for the teller and convey those meanings to the audience by embodying them in aesthetic form. The teller will know she has been heard. The stories that follow will respond with authenticity.

After a Playback event—particularly one that has addressed a social issue—in which different voices have spoken and their stories enacted, audience members, including tellers, are *affected*, in a lasting way, by what they have witnessed. It's not that opinions have necessarily been changed. It's that each person's comprehension of the shared reality has been altered and expanded, however subtly.

In a non-Playback gathering dealing with a pressing and con-troversial topic, a more traditional dialogue may take place where many people speak their minds, often in direct response to others. Arguments are presented and either supported or refuted. The conversation moves fast. Many words are spoken.

The limitation of this kind of dialogue—even when it is facilitated with care for maximum access and involvement—is that it is easy to resist in any way being changed by what you hear. It is easy to simply reiterate, louder and louder, what you knew and felt before you came into the room.

In Playback it's the opposite. The process moves slowly, "at the speed of trust," in Adrienne Maree Brown's phrase.[3] Words alternate with action. Fewer voices may be heard, though they are likely—if the conductor is attentive and skillful—to represent all the diversity in the room. Audience members express their points of view through highly personal testimony and narrative. Performers listen attentively and transform what they hear into theatre, witnessed by the rest of the audience without any demand to comment, judge, analyze, or approve. A teller's point of view may be unwelcome, even anathema, to others listening, but after

3. Adrienne Maree Brown, *Emergent Strategy: Shaping Change, Changing Worlds*. Chico, CA: AK Press. 2017.

hearing the human voice of the teller and seeing the story, there is a little more space inside any audience member (and performer) to accommodate the humanity of that person and his or her opinions. And there is the immediate opportunity to tell one's own story or feelings in response.[4]

A Playback show which addresses a contentious topic (whether intentionally or because audience members raise it) is unlikely to result in "reconciliation" in the sense of agreements and understanding reached—though it could well be part of a longer, more complex process in that direction. But it *is* likely to build a realm of openness in which people become less walled off by their views and experiences, more receptive to each other as people. This more expansive place is an essential to any kind of long-term mutual learning or reconciliation.

In 2004, prior to George W. Bush's second election, Hudson River Playback Theatre carried out a series of shows, mostly on college campuses, called "Play Back the Vote." Prompted by the low voter turnouts in the US especially among 18–24 year olds, we wanted to explore voting itself—why people vote or don't. We hoped to encourage some nonvoters to register, and we arranged for voter registration to be available after each show. One of the shows took place at a local community college where the student body included a wide range of age, class, and race. Prior to the performance, I taught basic Playback skills in a drama class and several of those students joined our team for the performance so that our performing team was more congruent with our audience.

At the show we heard markedly different and often heated points of view. Although our explicit focus was voting itself, many spoke about the candidates and the issues as well. Our tellers included a student who was vehemently pro-Bush, pro-Bible, and anti-gay; a faculty member who said she would vote "to stop the killing" in Iraq; another student who was fed up with the main political parties and wanted to vote for a controversial third-party candidate. Someone

---

4. See Chapter 6, "The Wider World," on stories that convey not just a different viewpoint but disrespect or intolerance. In those cases the performing team has an ethical imperative to communicate their values.

spoke of alternating between hope and disgust; another was committed to voting as a responsibility of citizenship; a student said she refused to vote because she found the whole process meaningless; a teacher was incensed by reports of voters being intimidated by election officials who assumed they would vote the "wrong" way. Hands flew up each time we asked a question or invited the next teller. The audience of about 120 seemed thoroughly engaged. Afterwards, people gathered around the voter registration tables in the hallway.

As the performers stood together in a circle backstage after the show, a young man—who'd spoken up several times during the performance—approached us to tell us that in his opinion Playback Theatre is not a good vehicle for dialogue, because we have to make everything so simple. He said that it became like television, just soundbites.

It was not the right moment for us to engage in a critical discussion, especially for our young guest actors, vulnerable after performing. We thanked him and went back to our own sharing. But afterwards I thought a lot about his critique. I think he was reacting in a valid way to the word "dialogue" which I'd used in opening the show. But in fact, Playback Theatre is the opposite of soundbites: more than most other vehicles of communication, it has the capacity to hold complexity without forcing resolution. It embraces the multifaceted nature of reality and subjective experience.

As I said above, a Playback show is not a dialogue, or not an effective dialogue, in the way we usually use the word. But what he overlooked was the other level of dialogue where people were exchanging their deeply felt statements and stories; the fact that so many voices and opinions were indeed heard aloud and honored by being transformed into theatre; the fact that everyone, audience and performers alike, heard and felt a range of feelings and points of view much broader than the range most of us are likely to expose ourselves to in our chosen circles. Through the medium of theatre we could listen to those otherwise-uncomfortable opinions without inwardly clenching and then quickly dismissing them.

I myself usually feel so wounded and enraged by extreme right-wing views, or by the scourge of apathy and ignorance, that I insulate myself from hearing those voices. I turn off the radio, I put down the newspaper, I avoid talking politics except with those whose views are like mine. It's just too personally painful to do anything else. But from the Playback stage I can find room in myself for any point of view. I can listen to them, engage with the teller, take care that we respect and capture this person's experience, without shutting down or becoming distressed. And even after the show is over, I notice a difference within myself, a space that has expanded. It becomes easier for me not to lose sight of the fact that people with radically different points of view are still fellow-beings, not alien from myself. They are people with stories.

If we can't bear to listen to each other, no connection, no dialogue, no reconciliation is possible. It is only from this expanded inner space that change of any kind can come. This is the kind of dialogue that Playback Theatre can achieve.[5]

5. Tragically, the Trump era has widened the gulf until it is all but impossible to bridge, with US society now so polarized that there appears to be no shared ground on which to stand and speak about our differences.

9

Searching for Beyond: Belschner's Model of Consciousness Research[1]

Jonathan Fox (2009)

Introduction

IT WAS A GREAT PLEASURE to hear Prof. Wilfried Belschner himself explain his theory of consciousness at the conference on Playback Theatre at the University of Kassel in 2008. He gave spirit and energy to his theory of a spectrum of mental agility, from rationality to empathy to what he calls the "nondualistic" domain. Prof. Belschner reports that practitioners from various disciplines (mainly in health and clinical services) have empirically confirmed both the existence of his three postulated states of consciousness and their importance to professional life (Belschner, p. 70). What follows is the subjective account of a practitioner from a different profession who finds this model of consciousness research a helpful explanatory theory.

Playback Theatre conforms to the general objectives of artistic forms that promote community cultural development; its practitioners perform for school children, seniors, the incarcerated, and general community audiences including members of organizations. Yet it is distinct from other kinds of community-based interactive theatre, such as Boal's Theatre of the Oppressed, in that it has no didactic agenda and is not solution-oriented.

Before detailing how Playback Theatre embodies many aspects of Belschner's theory in training, rehearsal, and performance, let me

---

1. First published in *Transpersonale Psychologie und Psychotherapie*, Germany 1/2009.

briefly set the intellectual context of its discovery. I had no training in psychology. My background was in literature and the arts. Moreover what inspired Playback Theatre was an artistic vision, not a set of ideas. Yet such discoveries are never made in a vacuum. At the time I was an ardent practitioner of what was called in the United States "experimental theatre," and while I most certainly would not have thought of it this way myself at the time, I cannot disagree with the assertion of Heinrich Dauber that Playback Theatre is the brainchild of an urban, Jewish American of the Vietnam generation indirectly influenced by the "Berlin-Vienna-Frankfurt magical triangle of the twenties and thirties" (Dauber, p. 45). I took a critical stance towards institutions of power and believed in social justice. I had a humanistic orientation, although I mistrusted the American humanistic psychology movement and its popular New Age manifestations with their overly insular and positive life view. I could not accept any approach oblivious to historical injustice and the oppression of population groups. I could not accept any approach that privileged what Bellah, et al. term "entrepreneurial individualism," that me-first attitude that shows scant concern for the betterment of society (Bellah, p. 51).

However after an introduction to psychodrama, I found myself drawn to the philosophy of J.L. Moreno, a transplant from that Germanic center of humanistic culture Dauber references. Moreno advocated spontaneity, the unmediated person-to-person encounter, and the possibility of transcendence. His approach did not whitewash history. I resonated with the following:

> My position was threefold: first, the hypothesis of spontaneity-creativity as a propelling force in human progress...; second, the hypothesis of having faith in our fellowman's intentions... the hypothesis of love and mutual sharing as a powerful, indispensable working principle in group life; and third, the hypothesis of a superdynamic community based upon these principles..." (Moreno, p. xv)

As an American, I inherited an unconscious legacy of the pantheism of Emerson, trusting in a generalized spirituality. I found resonance in what I later learned was personalism and its focus on the spiritual value of each person. The contention of Jacques Maritain that human beings were "transversed by the solicitations of actual grace" (Maritain, p. 10) was not incompatible with Moreno's concept of Godhead.

Perhaps because I had also spent two years in a pre-industrial Asian village, giving me firsthand experience of some of the cultural expressions that I had pursued in my academic study of oral traditional composition, I found myself also drawn to eastern approaches, where the deepest feelings might reside in "the evocation of an emotion beyond expression, of thoughts that do often lie too deep for tears" (Fox, p. 155).

Such background predisposed me to the search for an artistic form that went "beyond art," both in terms of its purpose and its definition.

Belschner's theory

Gregory Bateson called the artist's experience, with its "paradoxes of play" (Bateson, p. 191), a practice of mind for which his metaphor was cybernetic transformation, but which nevertheless is congruent with Belschner's concept of modulation. Bateson's theory included the nondualistic concept: "The cybernetic epistemology which I have offered you would suggest a new approach. The individual mind is immanent but not only in the body. It is immanent also in the pathways and messages outside the body; and there is a larger Mind of which the individual mind is only a subsystem" (ibid, p. 461).

Belschner's theory has not yet been empirically tested among artists, but we can recognize that for the artist nondualistic consciousness is a frequent state of mind. "Every great dancer or actor passes in performance into a state referred to as the 'other thought,'" writes the specialist in dance Beryl de Zoete (p. 24). "You try to cross over," says the jazz pianist Dwike Mitchell (Zinsser, p. 144). The writer of a widely known book on drawing, Betty Edwards, reveals of her own process: "I could either talk or draw, but I couldn't do both at once" (Edwards, p. 4). The artist needs to expand everyday consciousness in order to connect with his or her inspiration and to gain powers of expression.

Thus while the broader consciousness of artists may be assumed, Belschner's theory nevertheless has specific explanatory power for the practice of Playback Theatre artists.

In today's fast-paced world, with much of our communication through electronic media, Playback Theatre serves as a humanistic antidote. During the Playback Theatre event, the people present must speak to each other; listen to each other; bear witness to each other. Since all material for dramatization comes from the audience in the moment, the performance will break down without a will towards active participation. That the performance succeeds is a tribute to principles of engagement that in many ways can be explained by Belschner's theory. As Jo Salas writes: "Part of the... job is to entrance, to induct audience and teller into an altered state for the duration of the enactment" (Dauber & Fox, p. 31).

In the next section I will give some specific examples.

Development of the form

The premise for Playback Theatre is to enact improvisationally the personal narratives of audience members. At the outset, we approached the challenge by focusing on artistic issues, such as the demands of spontaneous staging, accepting actors' offers onstage, and creating effective music on the spot. To this end we practiced theatre games and exercises from the experimental theatre.

However we also played other kinds of "games." I remember spending time on an exercise in which one person, as the "teller," sent telepathically a personal experience to the other members of the troupe, who tried to "receive" the information through wordless exchange. At the time we did not take this activity very seriously and could not have defended it, but in retrospect we were attempting to develop skills in communicating beyond language, a hallmark of the right side of Belschner's spectrum. Without realizing it we were working to develop skills in what we now refer to informally as "deep listening." This is the skill that Belschner himself mentions when in recording his response to witnessing Playback Theatre for the first time, he marveled at the manner in which the performers were able to make "perceivable, visible, audible, and perceptible" the experience of a teller that was expressed with no more than a mere, "Hm, well" (Belschner, p. 59).

More significant was the attention we began to pay to a specific nonartistic element. We called it "presence," and by this term we meant how we comported ourselves on stage—not during the enactments, but in between (in a performance of Playback Theatre the performers are visible the entire time and sit facing the audience in between audience narratives). We learned empirically that if we sat with a certain serious demeanor; if we entered into the enactments with a certain measured pace; if we concluded the enactments with a look of acknowledgment to the teller, this ritual of presence had a positive impact on the audience. It provided a vital and neutral framework that enclosed enactments that might in themselves be funny, happy, or very sad.

Many years later we refer to this shamanic element as the "ritual" of Playback Theatre. Most practitioners know it is a vital nonfictive aspect of our performances. They also know that it is very difficult to maintain this ritual presence regardless of the emotionality of the stories and the vicissitudes of a spontaneous process.

At the time we did not have a cognitive understanding of our ritual; we only knew that it worked. The tellers' stories are quotidian, located in individual personal experience. Developing the ritual gave the performance a transpersonal dimension. It provided safety, for every story told and enacted was enclosed in a framework that was "beyond personal." Music played an important role in the establishment of this other level: "Music, especially at moments of beginning, ending, and transition, will strongly enhance the ritual dimension. At such times, the musician, like the conductor, is consciously fulfilling a shaman-like role" (Salas, p. 106).

Another major area of learning during the development period for Playback Theatre might be called "reducing ego." As improvisers seeking to capture the emotional core of a person's story and render it artistically onstage we needed to be in a very open whole-body communication with each other, giving and accepting dramatic offers fluidly. True teamwork was essential; an actor with a need to be the star of the show only got in the way.

Furthermore we found that this principle of open collective communication extended to our group discussions. Over time we learned to give space for the quiet ones to speak; the inequities of participation balanced out. Thus we were constantly reaching for an approach to communication that valued the mood of the group, assessed in verbal and nonverbal ways. In short, we learned to extend our empathic skills.

Because the capacities required to become more empathic and to develop the ritual aspect of our work were strikingly ignored in our formal education, which of course heavily favored what Belschner calls algorithmic thinking, we painstakingly pursued this alternative education. We discovered the learning curve was long. One could not pick up these skills overnight. In fact, it takes a minimum of a year of constant practice for a new Playback performer to acquire the basic skill set, and these skills only deepen with extensive practice. Despite its difficulty, this study is necessary to fulfill the potential of the Playback Theatre idea.

The performance process

Performances of Playback Theatre are improvisational. The task is to enact whatever the members of the audience chose to tell. An intermediary, whom we call the conductor, interacts directly with the audience, asking them questions. As can be easily imagined, audience members find themselves at the start of the performance in varying degrees of distraction, unease, even fear. In a 2004 dissertation entitled "Public Performance, Personal Story: A Study of Playback Theatre,"[2] Rea Dennis found that many audience members undergo a rite of passage from reluctance to eagerness to participate. "What is depicted through the stories and enactments draws audience members into the ritual in such a way that some have felt compelled to tell," Dennis writes (p. 170).

This "loss of reflective distance," to use Dennis's words, would

2. See "Crossing the Threshold" by Rea Dennis, first published in *Journal of Interactive Drama*, Vol. 2.1, January 2007 and on www.PlaybackTheatreReflects.net, March 2017.

seem congruent with Belschner's theory if we consider the audience experience at a performance of Playback Theatre as a passage from everyday to altered consciousness. Exactly what kind of emotion and thought are unleashed has not yet been studied, but judged by the growth of Playback Theatre, the experience is positive for most. We have many anecdotal accounts of the transforming effect of the performance on tellers and witnesses. In fact, from his own experience with Playback Theatre, Belschner himself comments that "unanticipated healing processes may be triggered" (p. 15).[3]

Audience members familiar with this process in performances become used to it and participate with gusto. Thus audiences often split—the old-timers eager, the newcomers reluctant, posing a knotty challenge to the performers, whose task, in Belschner's terms, is to guide the entire audience on a unified journey towards the nondualistic state.

The Playback performers know that they have a task to "warm up" the audience, and have developed a many-part process for doing this. The outcome is variable, of course. Yet often enough, audience members are enlivened by the end and afterwards exhibit a reluctance to leave. As Playback practitioner John Stevenson has written:

> The difference between Playback and all other theatre that I'd seen or participated in can be illustrated by the fact that people generally come to other theatres, have their theatre experience and go away.... But after every Playback performance I've ever seen people have stayed and talked to each other. I start to explain Playback to people who have never seen it by asking them, "What do you think it would take to make that happen?" (Stevenson, p. 4)

Inspired by Belschner we might answer that audience members are savoring their moment of nondualistic consciousness, feeling empathic, and taking time before they head out into the everyday world.

3. Traditional societies practice ecstatic rituals for similar healing purposes. See Fox and Turner.

Belschner gives us a way to comprehend the arc of the performance as a process of opening up the audience to the full spectrum of consciousness. In other words, the performance becomes a journey towards nonduality. As audience members become caught up in the stories of successive tellers and the enactments of these stories; as they listen to the musician playing both within the scenes and framing them; as they see the actors maintain a ritual presence on stage at all times, they often become transfigured and are left with a feeling of wholeness:

> Very important for this process to happen is the trance I was talking about earlier, the images and story trance. This slight change in the state of consciousness allows a dreamlike connection and logic. Stories answer each other and communicate like parts of a dream or like the dream and the actual life of the dreamer. There is an opportunity for the inherent tendency for wholeness. (Hoesch, p. 49)

The Playback Theatre performers (musician, actors, conductor) are the guides for this rite of passage. The outcome is never certain, but Playback performers have succeeded often enough that Playback Theatre has survived and grown over its more than thirty-year history.

Of course to some extent all theatre and many other kinds of performance are trance-inducing. But most involve a level of manipulation that limits the transpersonal possibility. To use the words of Richard Schechner, such performances may accomplish a state of transportation, but not transformation (Schechner, p. 126).

An overview of articles in *Interplay*, newsletter of the International Playback Theatre Network, reveals a significant number of contributions attesting to the "miracle" or "magic" of Playback Theatre (see, for example, the June 2008 issue). While at one level such reports smack of naïveté or self-promotion, from another perspective, however, these practitioners are attesting to an outcome they do not fully comprehend—the experience of nonduality. What are not so fully documented are the many instances when the performers, despite their best intentions, fail to achieve the goal, when the energy drops mid-show, when the tellers hesitate to raise their hands, when audience members sneak a look at their watches. Years of practice have taught us that a successful Playback Theatre performance depends on many interlocking factors, including some that are out of the control of the performers.

For example, there must be a certain level of intimacy; Playback Theatre will not work as it is meant to with too-large audiences. There must be an equivalent intimacy in the performance space, giving a sense of performers and audience in a single social field (in contrast to traditional theatre, which places the performers apart on a raised stage). The performance must be a certain duration; this journey cannot be accomplished in the fast-food rhythms of modern life. Most important, perhaps, the space must be private. For instance: with its community focus, Playback Theatre teams often perform in schools (so often driven by algorithmic-oriented demands of all kinds). Classrooms are liable to be interrupted at any time; cafeterias are often surrounded by other students and invasive noise. The Playback Theatre team must anticipate these factors and insist on appropriate conditions.

THE SUCCESS OF A PLAYBACK THEATRE performance can be thwarted if the individuals in the audience mistrust each other. For though Playback Theatre builds empathy, it must encounter a minimum of empathy for the process to work. Occasionally an institution is so riddled with hate and mistrust that no one dares participate. Playback Theatre does have promise as a promoter of dialogue among conflicted subgroups, but only once there is a base of goodwill. In other words, the conflicted parties must be at first willing to enter a shared space of viewing and listening.

Very often the individuals who act as institutional liaison in arranging a performance of Playback Theatre have no concept of the vulnerability of Playback Theatre to context. Even the Playback teams themselves frequently find themselves too polite— or eager for an engagement—to make clear their performance prerequisites. Yet even when the playbackers are totally insistent on the necessary conditions, liaison personnel will frequently either ignore or just not hear these requests about performance conditions. We often arrive at a venue to find our demand for an intimate space or a limited audience size ignored, and we are confronted with the challenge of deciding whether the Playback performance arc can succeed in the given conditions.

If Belschner's theory is an implicit plea for greater understanding of the value of the nondualistic domain, three decades of Playback Theatre performances attest to a general ignorance in society at large regarding conditions for its achievement.

Belschner himself would most likely not be surprised to find that time and again the concept and purpose of Playback Theatre has met with puzzlement. By modern definition, art is a product; therefore a process-oriented theatre like Playback Theatre strikes many as something other than art. To many, the idea of a teller invited to tell *any* story, even the highly personal, suggests it must be a therapy. Yet unlike contemporary forms of therapy, it is not private. Nor does it seek to cure (Rowe, p. 181). Thus for the same reason that we as practitioners needed to spend years learning to access alternative skills that society did not care to teach us, representatives of social institutions, like arts councils and community organizations, dismiss or look askance at a modality they have no framework for understanding.

Playback practitioners themselves are often tongue-tied trying to find language to mediate the comprehension gap, ultimately, giving up with a "You just have to see it yourself to get what it is."

The performers

I would like to make a few speculative remarks about performers in performance. First, the musician(s). Music has a primal appeal. The musician's role as a keeper of the ritual (framing the enactments) is as important as her/his role as an artistic embellisher. In Playback Theatre considerable time is spent in social interaction when the musician is silent, such as when the conductor is talking to the audience or interviewing a teller. Thus the musician must be willing *not* to play, which takes uncommon humility.

Likewise, the actors during these in-between moments sit facing the audience, simply being present and listening. In order to be successful in performing Playback Theatre, the actors, as has been suggested above, must be empathic with each other and with the audience. They must also be engaged in a kind of attunement that will facilitate attaining a nondualistic state. Thus most Playback performers warm up for one and a half to two hours before each performance. It is not only artistic readiness they seek, but something more.

Because the Playback performance is unplanned, the unexpected often happens. Inexperienced actors sometime lose their ritual presence at such moments. Even experienced actors, at moments of great risk, such as when a teller tells a particularly serious story, can lose focus. The goal is to remain in a guiding role no matter what, shepherding the audience into and out of the altered state. Success often requires a courage and strength of purpose that has nothing to do with artistic talent.

A final comment about the actors: with the challenge of taking anyone's personal narrative and giving it form on stage, part of the actors' challenge is algorithmic; they must choose the particular dramatic form they will use from a menu of available choices; they must enact that form, keeping to its particular demands. If they become lost or stuck on the right side of the spectrum, they will fail. In this sense, they need to modulate between all states of consciousness—algorithmic, empathic, nondualistic.

For the conductor, modulation is even more critical. The conductor is a talker, speaking to the audience, interviewing tellers, and giving occasional instructions to the actors. The conductor follows a schedule of performance elements designed to create an effective arc from start to finish. Yet the conductor must also be at all times empathic. The conductor also plays a vital role in leading the audience towards a liminal experience. We have empirically found the conductor's role an extremely challenging one, and Belschner's concept of modulation is useful in explaining why. In fact, Playback Theatre conducting can almost be defined as a public performance of modulating consciousness, and as such raises intriguing possibilities for research and training.

Rehearsal process

Playback Theatre performers cannot learn the dramatic and nondramatic skills to guide their audiences to a state of oneness if they cannot—or do not seek—to achieve nondualistic consciousness in their rehearsals. By now we can look to the experience of hundreds of Playback groups and begin to understand why some Playback Theatre companies fail. For instance, there have been groups with a dominantly artistic focus. They are made up of working actors used to a traditional kind of theatre rehearsal. Such individuals do not see the value of nondramatic practices, such as those exercises that might be necessary to bring the members into attunement with each other. Moreover, under pressures from other work, they often minimize the need for being together. As a result, while they might have good actorly skills, they fail to achieve nondualistic (and occasionally even empathic) dimensions of consciousness in their practices—thereby making them inadequate guides for Playback Theatre performances. Such groups often complain, "Why don't we get deeper stories in our shows?!" The answer, unfortunately, lies in themselves.

Even for those practitioners who sense that the rehearsal is a crucial opportunity to experience the full modulation of consciousness, the task is not infrequently beyond their reach, owing to many factors. Many Playback company leaders lack the vision and skill to guide the process; and often their group members are not sufficiently clear about the goal to support it. A group's diversity can become an issue, as well as its history. If the members as a whole are not interested in their own development as learners of a little understood process, then the group will fail. Or if the members are not united in their fundamental purpose, then the group will fail.

Then there is the time problem: most groups meet for an evening's practice—three hours at the most. They must shuck off their everyday preoccupations, deal with organizational business, practice their craft, connect to each other. All of this is challenging enough, but reaching experientially the altered state of mind that lies at the heart of their purpose is even a greater challenge. It is an unhappy irony that many Playback

Theatre practitioners have experienced heartache and suffering in their theatre company due to struggles of their group on the learning path towards oneness.

Many groups have muddled through, however, slowly building a culture where members open up to each other and to larger fields of mind. In these groups the turnover is extremely slow. Members belong for five years, ten years and longer. For them, Playback Theatre may be an instrumental association, but it is also a practice that gives them a very deep satisfaction that extends beyond the performance moment. It has become a way of life.

Conclusion

In his essay "Playback Theatre from the Vantage Point of Consciousness Research," Prof. Belschner hypothesizes that "Playback Theatre builds on the ability of the actors to enter all three conscious waking states." He goes on to make two more statements: Playback Theatre performers "must be able to modulate the three conscious waking states," and "Playback Theatre may have a healing effect" (p. 73). My experience confirms these observations.

Playback Theatre in performance moves in the direction of transpersonal space, and at its best, can offer audiences an exhilarating transformational experience. The particular skill set required to perform this approach makes it of interest as research in the attempt to learn more about how people expand their capacities of consciousness. I am also left with curiosity whether the Playback Theatre approach might be a useful method for teaching skills in developing the skill of modulation for individuals from all walks of life. Thus Playback Theatre might be used as a training vehicle for people with no interest in theatre or performance as such, but as a way to increase their understanding of the spectrum of consciousness.

Belschner has offered a most intriguing theory that helps explain our three decades of work developing Playback Theatre to bring healing to communities.

References

Bateson, Gregory. (1972). *Steps to an Ecology of Mind*. San Francisco: Chandler.

Bellah, Robert N.; Madsen, Richard; Sullivan, William M.; Swindler, Ann; & Tipton, Steven M. (1985). *Habits of the Heart: Individualism and Commitment in American Life*. New York: Harper & Row.

Belschner, Wilfried. (2008). "The Playback Theatre—From the Vantage Point of Consciousness Research." Conference papers, University of Kassel, March,

Dauber, Heinrich & Jonathan Fox, eds. (1999). *Gathering Voices: Essays on Playback Theatre*. New Paltz, NY: Tusitala.

Dennis, Rea. (2004). "Public Performance, Personal Story: A Study of Playback Theatre." Doctoral Dissertation, Griffith University, Australia.

de Zoete, Beryl & Spies, Walter. (1938). *Dance and Drama in Bali*. London: Faber & Faber.

Edwards, Betty. (1979). *Drawing on the Right Side of the Brain*. Los Angeles: J.P. Tarcher.

Fox, Jonathan. (1994). *Acts of Service: Spontaneity, Commitment, Tradition in the Nonscripted Theatre*. New Paltz, NY: Tusitala.

Hoesch, Folma. (1999). "The Red Thread." In *Gathering Voices: Essays on Playback Theatre*. New Paltz, NY: Tusitala Publishing.

Hoover, Thomas. (1977). *Zen Culture*. New York: Random House.

Interplay, newsletter of International Playback Theatre Network. www.iptn.info.

Moreno, J. L., ed. (1953). *Who Shall Survive*. Beacon, NY: Beacon House,

Rowe, Nick. (2007). *Playing the Other: Dramatizing Personal Narratives in Playback Theatre*. London: Jessica Kingsley.

Salas, Jo. (1993). *Personal Stories in Playback Theatre*. Dubuque, IA: Kendall/Hunt. 3rd edition 1999, New Paltz, NY: Tusitala.

Schechner, Richard. (1985). *Between Theater and Anthropology*. Philadelphia: University of Pennsylvania Press.

Stevenson, John. (1995). "The Fourth Wall and the Third Space." Essay, School of Playback Theatre.

Turner, Victor. (1981). *From Ritual to Theatre*. New York: Performing Arts Journal Publications.

Zinssner, William. *Willie and Dwike: An American Profile*. New York: Harper and Row.

10

IS PLAYBACK FEMALE?[1]

Jo Salas (2010)

IT'S A MATTER OF DEBATE as to whether there are inherent differences between the nature of women and men, or not. Are women inclined to be receptive, nurturing, empathetic, collaborative, intuitive, supportive, protective of nature and human life? Are we innately inclined to value relationship more than achievement and power? You can undoubtedly think of women who do not fit these descriptions, and men who do. You may say that gender can no longer be thought of as a polarity but rather a spectrum. And yet many women, across history, generations, and cultures, do share these traditionally female characteristics. Is it the result of how we are raised and acculturated? Or is it something deeper—something arising from our physiology, our hormones, our genes? Our archetypal nature?

I live a woman's life in a woman's body. Two-thirds of that life have been as a mother and a wife, all of it as a sister, a daughter. I don't know how much of my own way of being comes from something innate or ineffable and to what degree I've been shaped by the pressures and expectations of others—sometimes explicit, often covert—from my earliest days. I acknowledge, though, that I, along with the majority of the women I know, embody many of the characteristics that are thought of as traditionally female. Caring for others is central in our private and professional lives; we put committed energy into weaving a resilient web of connections throughout our years; our life decisions are often made on criteria other than

---

1. First published in *Interplay*, December 2010, in an issue focusing on Playback Theatre and women.

monetary or worldly success, such as considerations for others' needs and preferences, and our own satisfactions.

As a result, our professional lives may not resemble what is usually meant by a "career"—forthright identification with a particular field, a coherent, committed path from training to success and recognition. As Mary Catherine Bateson wrote in *Composing a Life*, women's lives are often "an improvisatory art," combining "familiar and unfamiliar components in response to new situations, following an underlying grammar and an evolving aesthetic."[2] These "new situations" often include bearing and raising children, for most mothers a significant vector in the trajectory of their lives.

As I said, I do not claim that these qualities and modes of being are inherent to women, common to all women, and not to be found in men. That is clearly not the case! What interests me is that this constellation of supposedly feminine characteristics also describes Playback Theatre.

We, the practitioners of Playback Theatre, are enormously varied in our interest, our commitment, our expertise, our backgrounds. And yet we are all are engaged in a practice that devotes itself to listening to others, attends to the needs of the individual and the group, and is inherently collaborative. Bateson's description of life as an improvisatory art could apply directly to Playback itself.

Playback Theatre places art in service to purposes beyond art. It values creativity, satisfaction, and service over ambition. Many playbackers operate mostly in the gift economy, earning little or nothing for their work. Those who are paid earn a fraction of the income that our peers in other professions may earn. Playback requires endless humility and flexibility—as an actor, you must be constantly prepared to take on a lead role, a supporting role, multiple roles, or no role at all. And how many times have you begun a performance or a workshop by picking up a broom or moving furniture around? How many times have you adapted to conditions that might have made another kind of theatre artist walk out?

Our work is predicated on collaboration. You can't do solo Playback. Co-creativity with the teller is irreducible: our art form

2. Bateson, Mary Catherine. *Composing a Life*. New York: Penguin, 1990, p. 3.

requires that person and her story, at the very least. Without it we are mute. And of course our collaboration always goes beyond the teller: we perform in close-knit teams, responsive to each other's inspirations, cues, and occasional lapses. We need one another, and we embrace this interdependence as part of the delight and magic of what we do. A performer who yearns for individual glory may find Playback unsatisfying: it is not a rewarding place for a star. Stars shine and dazzle, they may shoot across the sky, but they are not so good at collectivity.

The substance of our work is the stories themselves. Here, too, Playback embraces the feminine. In her essay "The Carrier Bag Theory of Fiction" Ursula Le Guin, the fiction writer and essayist, imagines the lives of our prehistoric ancestors, spending their days gathering seeds, berries, roots, and so on. Once in a while a few of the males go off and hunt a huge animal, coming back with not only an impressive amount of food, but also a story of quest, danger, blood, courage, and victory. The plant gatherers can't begin to compete with such a narrative. "It is hard to tell a really gripping tale of how I wrested a wild-oat seed from its husk, and then another, and then another..." says Le Guin's imaginary Paleolithic woman. In contrast, the hunter's story "not only has action, it has a hero. Heroes are powerful. Before you know it, men and women in the wild-oat patch and their kids and the ... songs of the singers are all part of it, have all been pressed into service in the tale of the Hero. But it isn't their story. It's his."[3] Le Guin talks about how this action story, the Hero story, the killer story, has overshadowed the quotidian stories that have all kinds of shapes and are not necessarily about conflict. Like a sack or a net—the cultural invention, according to some theorists—a story can be a container for all kinds of things. A carrier bag.

Le Guin is talking about novels, but what she says is also true of the kind of stories that people tell in Playback. In a Playback show we are less likely to hear a hero's story than we are to hear about a surprising or disturbing encounter, or a realization, or an

3. Le Guin, Ursula K. "The Carrier Bag Theory of Fiction." *Dancing at the Edge of the World: Thoughts on Words, Women, Places.* New York: Harper & Row, 1989, pp. 165–166

enigmatic dream; a story about loss, or injustice, or love. A story that contains a constellation of meanings, which our enactment strives to embody without reducing it to a straight line.

In the stories we listen carefully for the emotions that give color and movement. Sometimes we enact the emotions themselves, in short forms like fluid sculptures. Portraying those feelings requires empathy from the performers, and fosters empathy in the audience. Foregrounding emotion makes sense to anyone who understands how it drives human life for all of us, men and women alike, whether acknowledged or not (even the hyper-masculine stock market rises and falls on pure emotion— "Stock prices declined today as consumer confidence fell."). But some people—usually, in my experience, a man—may query this emphasis. "It's not professional to talk about feelings," said a new manager by way of explaining why he would not hire my company, as his predecessor had, to give his stressed-out employees a chance to tell their stories.

Le Guin goes further: she claims that the future of human existence depends on finally telling the seed gatherer's story instead of the killer story, as she refers to it. "Lest there be no more telling of stories at all, some of us out here in the wild oats, in the alien corn, think that we'd better start telling another one, which maybe people can go on with when the old one's finished. Maybe. The trouble is, we've all let ourselves become part of the killer story, and so we may get finished along with it. Hence it is with a certain feeling of urgency that I seek the nature, subject, words of the other story, the untold one, the life story."[4]

Playback's femaleness is evident as well in the way that it has evolved over its 36 years of existence. Playback Theatre has grown slowly, very slowly, and still has not ventured far beyond its grass roots. We are diffuse, horizontal. As a field, we have evolved story by story, relationship by relationship. We have grown in multiple directions, anarchically, led by a dream that we dream together. There is no overall structural control. Playback is not vertically organized or mono-directional. You could not shoot an arrow

4. Le Guin, ibid, p. 168.

through our history: it would become immediately entangled in orchards where peaches grow alongside pineapples. Our strength is not worldly power, influence, wealth, or fame. It is our relationships: within companies, within networks, with our tellers and audiences, our communities. It is our belief in what we do. It is our ability to listen and connect. It is our willingness to do so in any setting, with any group of people, any stories.

The female nature of Playback Theatre is, in my opinion, something to embrace and celebrate. But I'm also aware of three ways in which it's a liability.

Firstly, it means that Playback Theatre's values and practices make more intuitive sense to women than to men, which is why so many Playback ensembles struggle to find and keep male performers. If we are going to perform convincingly for audiences of both men and women, we need men in our line-ups—just as we need to reflect other kinds of diversity.

Secondly, we live in a primarily patriarchal world in which female difference is historically equated with inferiority. Even in cultures where women are no longer treated with outright contempt or cruelty, an approach that embodies femaleness may find it difficult to gain respect. From this standpoint, Playback Theatre can be dismissed as being soft-edged, unpredictable, too much about feelings and hopelessly unspecialized.

Thirdly, there are ways in which our female diffuseness is indeed a weakness and has impeded our effectiveness so far. Considering how long and how widely Playback Theatre has been in existence, our work overall lacks consistency and impact, in spite of many wonderful performers and successful projects. The enthusiastic "anyone can do it" attitude with which we in the original company sent Playback out into the world now seems naïve and oversimplified. The citizen actor and especially the citizen conductor have a more complicated task than we understood back then. Anyone can indeed tell a story and almost anyone can act in a story told in a workshop. But *leading* that workshop, or performing for the public, or carrying out community projects requires talent, time, training, substantial practice, and competent organization, without which the work of Playback Theatre cannot fulfill its promise.

I do see signs of a new chapter in our history taking form. We will see what happens when the work is approached more systematically, with more alignment between Playback entities, and with other organizations as well. Perhaps we will succeed in bringing in the elements we are lacking, without compromising the fundamental strength of our femaleness.

And—more idealistically—perhaps Playback Theatre will help to create a world where empathy, resilience, humility, the give-and-take of collaboration, and the seed gatherer's story will take their rightful and respected place.

11

Is There More?
Theatre, Work, Play,
and the Gift Economy

Jo Salas (2012)

"ARE YOU TRAVELING FOR WORK OR PLAY?" asks my fellow passenger in the shuttle bus from Denver International Airport. In my jet-lagged state I simply do not know how to answer. I've just come from teaching improvisational theatre workshops in Germany and Switzerland and I'm about to lead another in Colorado before returning home to New York. This teaching is indeed my work. But it's also, integrally, play: play that enables the ultimately serious purpose of this theatre. My companion on the bus is a sales manager. On her business trips she meets with clients and sales teams in big hotels. When she travels for pleasure, she tells me, she likes to go to beach resorts or skiing at Aspen. For her, as for most people in our western culture, the distinction between business and pleasure, work and play, is self-evident. Work is serious, adult, a central part of one's identity. It may also be burdensome, something you wouldn't do if you didn't have to, whereas play is freely chosen, pleasurable, without responsibility, the domain either of children or of adults seeking escape from the adult world.

The assumptions implicit in her question to me are both familiar and problematic for most theatre artists. My own particular realm of theatre is even harder to explain than most. It is not scripted; most of the time it does not take place in theatres; it is not a potential stepping stone to Broadway, as even the most humble production of a traditional play can be in the dreams of its cast members. And yet it fulfills theatre's fundamental nature and intent: it brings human experience into aesthetic form in order to embody and reveal its meaning. Playback Theatre, as it's called, invites audience members to tell their true stories and then watch them enacted on the spot. Since the mid-seventies people have been performing Playback Theatre in cities and towns around the world, in theatres, schools, refugee camps, prisons, clinics, conferences, and so on, seeking to create dialogue and connection through the medium of art.

Playback Theatre requires actors to have considerable personal courage, maturity, and social awareness in addition to acting skills. Between stories, they sit on stage undisguised by a role. They listen to strangers tell experiences from their lives—memories, dreams, epics or fragments, sometimes historical or political events that have personal resonance, infused with discovery, pain, delight, remorse, love, conflict, anger, longing, confusion, indignation. Then, without discussion, relying only on the completeness of their attention and their openness to their fellow actors and musician, they create a piece of theatre, with dialogue, movement, and music. When it's done skillfully it is stunning. Teller and audience alike are often moved, even changed by what they've seen. Each successive story adds to a mosaic depicting the themes of importance to this particular group of people.

It's only possible to do this kind of acting by investing one's whole being, one's body, mind, heart and soul; by venturing into realms of adventure, expressiveness, connection, and emotion that are seldom called upon in most professional pursuits. One of the paving stones of the path to whole-self artistic expression is playfulness. It's a paradox that in our work, play is integral, the doorway to the profound. If you can't release the constraints on your body and spirit placed there by age, education, and convention, if you can't enjoy the flight into uncharted co-creativity with your fellow-players, you will not be able to transform an audience member's story into the work of art it deserves to be.[1]

When I teach Playback, easing through the barriers to playfulness is one of the first steps. One of the theatre games I sometimes use in the early stages of a workshop is called "Is there more?" (It originated with the pioneering improvisation teacher Keith Johnstone, who might not recognize it in the version I'm about

---

1. See section on Spontaneity in Chapter 13, "The Theory of Narrative Reticulation."

to describe.) This is how it goes: in partners, one person begins a simple, repeatable physical action such as scratching her nose or wiggling her shoulders. The other person praises warmly. "That's good! That's very, very good! I had no idea you could do this!" etc. After a minute or so of this, the praiser says: "Is there more?" at which the other person says: "Oh, *yes!*" and immediately steps up the action, exaggerating the original gesture as much as she possibly can while her partner praises her ever more lavishly. The game builds for another step or two, then ends, and the partners switch roles. As each pair finishes they join in the praising of others so that the game culminates with everyone calling out extravagant praise to one thrilled and blushing person.

Almost invariably, the effect of this game is that the recipients of the praise feel tremendously flattered and take a large leap toward expressiveness, in spite of being fully aware of the set-up. This expressiveness will be essential in the Playback work that is to follow, in which the actors will be called upon to reflect other people's personal experience in action and words. The less you are hamstrung by inhibition, the more access you will have to spontaneous, in-the-moment receptivity and responsiveness to another's story, no matter what it is. If, later in the training, you are chosen by a teller to play his ailing grandfather, or a young apple tree ravaged by deer, or the teller himself at the age of nine, you'll be ready. Your adventurousness will be there, your readiness to serve the role no matter what it asks of you. The wild hilarity of "Is there more?" and other games will not usually be apparent in enacted stories: Playback is not comedy improv where all input from the audience becomes grist for a comic mill. But the spontaneity fostered by playfulness allows an actor to enter a character with depth and sensitivity, in the space of seconds, which is all the time we have to prepare.

So the apparent silliness of "Is there more?" and many other activities has a deeply serious purpose: to return us to the state of playfulness which contains in it readiness, openness, receptivity, inspiration, and the generative power of creativity—a state we have by rights as children and which few of us retain as we grow up. When we are fortunate enough to rediscover it, there is a sense of both revelation and recognition. Play is the freedom and delight of the creative, the interactive, the inspirationally inventive; it is a place where human beings inhabit the present moment with an intensity that opens horizons of possibility. In an impassioned response to the question "Why play?" posed in the German theatre magazine *Theater Heute*, the director Thomas Brasch wrote a list of 40 reasons, the first and last being "to render this question superfluous."[2]

It is worth noting that of the multiple meanings of the word "play" in English, the other most familiar meaning is explicitly theatrical: "play" as a piece of writing meant to be acted by characters upon a stage. These two meanings, along with all the other applications of this small and nimble word, share a common past in the Old English *plegian* (verb) and *plega* (noun), referring to recreation, frolic, exercise, and performance. And, according to etymologists, "play" has been opposed to "work" since 1377.

Money is a significant part of the conventional distinction between work and play: work is what you do to support yourself, to generate a paycheck. Play is respite from work and not productive monetarily or otherwise—indeed, it's likely to require spending, on equipment, clothes, and travel. Interwoven with this conventional polarity is the opposition between professional and amateur. Broadly accepted as they are, such divisions ill fit those who work seriously at their art regardless of recompense, including myself and my Playback compatriots.

The polarity of paid work and unpaid play leaves out the notion of calling, or vocation—work that you do because you are called to it. If you are both lucky and deeply committed, your calling may indeed support you financially. Or it may not. If you do it anyway, for other, more compelling reasons, you are an amateur. In contrast to the most immediate connotation of "amateur"— someone who is not professional, not the real thing—the word's root reminds us of the possibility of love as a motivation for action. (In traditional Chinese painting, it is amateurs, not professionals,

2. Thomas Brasch, "Warum spielen?" *Theater Heute*, 1983.

who earn the greatest honor, because their art arises solely from the inner urgency to convey their vision, not from the need to satisfy a customer's requirements. The amateur artist can be pure, free from the compromises of the marketplace.)

In his book *The Gift*, Lewis Hyde speaks of the "gift economy" which exists in contrast to the market economy.[3] The essence of a gift is that it is neither demanded nor paid for. Even in western culture, where the market economy prevails in almost every corner, the idea of gift exchange persists. We retain, as Hyde points out, a more or less consensual understanding about what belongs in the gift economy—for example, we generally agree that things like kidneys or blood should be given, not sold. Most people willingly give free housing to their dependent children and elders. Art, too, belongs in the gift economy, at least in its origin and purpose: an artist's motivation is the drive to embody a perception of truth, of experience, not the money to be made from selling it. Artists may want and need to get paid for their work, and some artists earn a great deal, but making their art comes first: it is their calling. Even if the work is subsequently sold, it remains a gift if it came into existence as an offer of meaning. The artist's reward may include money, but more fundamentally it is the satisfaction of knowing that her or his vision has been received and valued. The gift has moved, as the gift must always move.[4]

Playback ensembles tend to grow in the direction of "professionalism"—from operating on an informal and volunteer basis to becoming organized in a more business-like way and earning fees for performances necessitated by the simple equation of economic survival: the hours and days we spend doing Playback Theatre must generate the income that we would otherwise earn during that time. But sometimes we do a show just because we want to do it, because we're invited by a worthy organization with no money, or because the theme or occasion feels important.

3. Lewis Hyde, *The Gift: Imagination and the Erotic Life of Property*. New York: Vintage Books, 1979. See also Chapter 7, "Playback Theatre, Diversity, and the Two Economies."
4. Lewis Hyde, "The Gift Must Always Move." *CoEvolution Quarterly*, No. 35, Fall 1982.

LAST DECEMBER my company did a public show for Human Rights Day, honoring the signing of the International Declaration of Human Rights in 1948. We heard and enacted personal experiences of persecution as well as stories of witness and historical remembrance. Performers and audience members alike were stirred by seeing these painful and triumphant incidents brought to life on the stage, with each teller sitting to the side, their responses visible as they watched. As usual there was a palpable here-and-now dialogue going on: a man tells of being targeted as an African American in high school, and after his story is enacted a white man recalls being a passive witness to racist violence in his own school. Later in the show the first man speaks again, this time about standing up for the free speech rights of a white student in the school where he now works.

We began the show with actors and volunteers from the audience reading some of the key articles from the Declaration. A six-year-old girl in the front row challenged us: "I heard a lot of 'he' and 'him' but no 'she,'" she said—a salutary reminder that human rights are an evolving issue and the equality of women is not reflected in the Declaration's old-fashioned language. We enacted her passionate comment.

There was no funding for this show. Audience members made a small donation at the door, which went toward our expenses. Performers were not paid for their time, travel, expertise, and hours of preparation—we couldn't rehearse the stories because we had no idea what they would be, but we had immersed ourselves in the topic of human rights and told our own stories in rehearsal. Had we been funded, the show would have been exactly the same. Our compensation came in other forms: the bracing richness of the stories themselves; the knowledge that we had made space for a rare public exchange on a vital topic; the audience's evident appreciation; the artist's satisfaction at making theatre; the exhilaration of trying something risky and worthwhile and seeing that it had worked; the pleasure of our teamwork. We would have liked a paycheck too but its absence did not diminish our sense of reward.

I imagine trying to explain all this to the skeptics I meet so often. "Well, it sounds great," they might say. "But you can't call it work if you weren't paid." Could I help them understand? Would they, no matter what I said, frame this event as somehow less adult, less important, less professional than the activities of their own work day?

The majority of theatre artists in this country, including Playback performers, are "amateurs"—devoted, talented, well trained, hard-working, and unpaid or barely paid. What they do earn—except for those few who've make the great leap to commercial success—is not enough, in monetary terms, to recompense the time they've put into rehearsals and travel as well as the event itself. My company, with 70 to 80 performances per year, still straddles the gift and market economies: we cannot generate enough income to pay fully for our real costs. We debate about this sometimes: if the miraculous happened and we suddenly had enough money, would we lose something intangible if everything we did was compensated at "market value"? Would our creative work, so firmly rooted in a collective voluntary commitment, start to feel like a job—just a job? We're unlikely to find out. Instead, we'll continue to appreciate the non-monetary rewards that supplement our modest earnings.

So how should I answer the woman in Denver who wants to know whether I am engaged in work or play? I could tell her that on my trip I have been hosted by people who have become dear friends as well as colleagues and students, that they invited me for the purpose of teaching them how to act out true stories, that at times during the workshops we cavorted like baby seals and enacted fairy tales in drag, and that this led to the telling of deepest personal truth and its transformation into theatre, to an exchange of true gifts among those who told, those who acted, and those who witnessed. I could tell her that the reason I travel is neither simply work nor play but something beyond, a right livelihood that brings rewards indeed.

"Is there more?"

"Oh, *yes!*"

The Theory of Narrative Reticulation: A Brief Description[1]

Jonathan Fox (2018)

Introduction

THE PURPOSE OF THIS CHAPTER is to provide a short explanation of the theory of narrative reticulation (NR). The theory is still in construction, and aspects may still be revised. In order to keep the essay brief, I will for the most part omit examples (please provide illustrations from your own experience). The theory of narrative reticulation, conceived as a comprehensive theory for Playback Theatre, describes the dynamic balance of four attributes—story, atmosphere, spontaneity, and guidance—allowing a flow of interconnected stories.

The word "reticulation" comes from biology and can be used to describe the veins of a leaf or the lines of the palm. In our context the name evokes the interrelationship of the personal stories told by a community group in Playback Theatre. Narrative reticulation constitutes a spontaneous, face-to-face mode of communication that stands in contrast to reason-based, planned approaches. It is a tool for assessing effectiveness in Playback Theatre work, and it may also explain a general approach to reducing social alienation in modern life. The four attributes do not exist in hierarchy, but I will begin with story.

---

1. Previously published in *Playback NR Workbook* by Jonathan Fox. New Paltz, NY: Tusitala, 2019.

Story

We all know what a *story* is, whether it is a "true story," a "newspaper story," a "short story" in a magazine, a novel, or an actual lie, as in, "a likely story." However, the kind of story we ask for in Playback Theatre is different from all of these everyday uses of the word. We seek a personal true experience articulated on the spot. This kind of story appears within a spectrum of conscious awareness, bounded by an obscure unknowing at one extreme ("I have no story") and a stubborn rigidity on the other ("I need seven characters and three scenes in my story.") We are hoping that the teller's story will emerge from a zone of discoverable truth that lies within this spectrum.

The teller's story may be rough, its details unclear, the meaning not at once graspable. But if it is authentically emergent, then most of the time the actors will have something substantial to work with, and most important, the story will say something important about the teller. Even everyday stories about ordinary events will contain an intended meaning that reveals who that teller is. In this sense, our stories are key to our identity. Because the Playback performing team are "completing" the story, giving it clarity and meaning, they need basic skills in the quick apprehension and dramatic portrayal of stories, including fleshing them out thematically, in space, in character, and in plot (these are abilities we do not learn in school and university, where even the study of literature is determinedly cerebral and far from the sensualized experience of live narrative).

What is true about an individual teller is also true about a community (I am using the word "community" here to mean the people present, the audience). When the stories are truly emergent, and the narrative reticulation is strong, one teller's story sparks another through a web of association, and there are complex connections between narratives. The sequence of stories, considered as a whole, will reveal important aspects of the identity of a community. If the NR is weak, on the other hand, then the connections will be shallow, the meanings thin. A strong NR leads to augmentation of meaning—a deepening of the stories as the event proceeds—and a vigorous exchange of various perspectives. For instance, a story of triumph will be followed by one that does not end happily, as if the second teller is responding by saying, "Life is not always this way;" the story by a parent will be followed by a story from the perspective of a child. In this way, NR promotes dialogue.

It is a very dynamic process. For the most part, the community responds unconsciously, and the performers focus on the challenges of enactment story by story. ("Reticulation" as a name for the theory is a compromise, for while it highlights the connections between stories, the name does not suggest the importance of an emergent, energetic process.)

In the early days of Playback Theatre we often redid a story, if the teller was not satisfied. We called these additional scenes "corrections." However, an intuitive appreciation of NR at work led us to drop corrections; we learned to trust that what was uncaptured or unexpressed in any particular story would come to the fore in the next one. In other words, the NR creates a kind of tapestry with a unified design and a sense of the whole, and it is not necessary to provide a sense of completion for each element. Of course, even though we rarely redo a scene these days, we always give the teller the last word about her story.

The same awareness helps us relax about a sequence of grim or heavy stories. We learned to trust that the NR, with its tendency to produce different points of view, will produce a teller with a story of resilience and hope. It is only a conductor ignorant of NR who will ask the community, "Let's have a happy story now." Of course, the opposite is also true. Communities often need to balance positive experiences with a more complicated version of the truth, one that includes suffering and disappointment.

Atmosphere

One distinguishing feature about a Playback Theatre event is attention paid to *atmosphere*. First, the performers will do their best to create a feeling of neighborliness in the room. As much as possible, we want the community to relax and be ready to open up in front of each other. There is no one way to promote neighborliness, and of course each setting is different. The conductor's manner is so important, as well as the presence of the actors and musician. The team usually introduces themselves and at some point invites individuals in the audience to introduce themselves to their neighbors. There is a distinct warm up phase to the performance, beginning with the most nonthreatening questions from the conductor, such as "How was your day today?" or "How do you feel about this weather?" If the event is a workshop, then this process is drawn out and may involve a prolonged sequence of steps.

What is essential is that a community, who will often come to the event stressed from the pressures of daily life, be skillfully led up to and across a threshold of engagement, so that they will find themselves ready to share personal experiences. Community members need to let go of their critical minds, both toward others and themselves, sufficiently to dare to raise their hands. For if no one reaches this state of readiness, then there will be no performance.

Playback Theatre depends on the revelation of individual experience in a public setting. If the group exists in a milieu where it is impossible to create a mood of neighborliness—if there is such mistrust or fear that no one will want to expose themselves in front of the others—then Playback Theatre cannot function as designed. Thus a Playback leader must make a careful assessment of the milieu and often negotiate conditions before an event.

Relaxation is a crucial element. The Playback team wants the community to begin to open up their minds, thus deepening their field of associations. For the more active the memory and imagi-nation of the community, the greater is the potential for a strong narrative reticulation. That the environment feel protected from harsh judgment is also important; otherwise tellers will not dare to expose the subjective truth that is the key to their identity narrative. It is easier to achieve this kind of space with a small community, rather than a large one; thus Playback audiences will most often be intimate ones.

A second aspect of atmosphere contrasts with the first. A dis-tinguishing feature of Playback is the *theatrical retelling* of each story.

In this way, the experience becomes a heightened dramatic event that, like all theatre, is inherently exciting. In fact while a neighborly atmosphere may help someone feel sufficiently at ease to raise their hand, the dramatic atmosphere will, paradoxically, also inspire them to do so. The movement, the music, the colors, the lights, and the dramatizations elevate the community into a kind of trance state in which individuals are likely to surprise themselves and jump into the fire, as it were, perhaps telling a story they have not thought about for years or ever dared to voice aloud.

The dramatic intensity of the atmosphere helps with another aspect: what we familiarly term the ritual—a structure for the event that envelopes all the action and provides the community with the security that each revelation is containable and will be handled in the same fashion. A teller will be invited to the chair; there will be a short interview, at the end of which the conductor will say, "Let's watch!"; music will mark a brief scene-setting phase; then follows the enactment, ended by the actors' look of acknowledgment to the teller; finally, the conductor invites the teller to have the final word. The ritual also includes other elements, including structured moments of music and silence.

The demands on the conductor will vary. At one moment, she will want to be warm, friendly, and good-humored to put people at their ease, while at another she will turn shamanistic, even fierce, in her determination to establish and hold the ritual framework.

A core value of Playback Theatre is the belief that everyone has the right to tell their story. Unfortunately, however, our societies rarely share this conviction, even if modern concepts of democracy and human rights pay lip service to it. The reality is that in many contexts some people have great access to public attention, while others are silenced. In this way the practice of Playback Theatre becomes an act of social change, as we encourage communities to be willing to listen to *everybody*.[2] Inclusivity relates to the challenge of building a positive atmosphere, because we all feel it when one person, or type of person, dominates the narrative; such bias negatively affects the narrative reticulation.

2. See section on social change in Chapter 1, "A Changing Landscape."

Where inclusivity prevails, however, and there is a sense that anyone is welcomed to speak up, there occasionally occurs a state of resonance among the community, where standard dualisms, such as self and other, fade, replaced by sense of oneness that is akin to spiritual experience.[3] While Playback Theatre may rarely achieve this state, most practitioners will recognize it. Playback Theatre, caught up in the energy of NR, moves toward resonance.

In a traditional society that lacks the benefits of modern technology, cultural events occur in attunement with nature. The dance cannot be danced if the wind is too strong and kicking up too much dust, for example, forcing either a change of venue or postponement. In a similar way, the Playback Theatre team is making constant adjustments, depending on the "weather" of the community, which at different times will be reluctant, or eager. One moment may call for good-humored tomfoolery, another for inviting a particularly quiet member to be teller, another for an unplanned moment of music, and another for strict adherence to the ritual. Because it is spontaneous, we might say that the Playback Theatre process follows natural rhythms. This is very different from literary theatre, which takes place in an artificial, unchanging environment.

The overall goal is a relaxed community, listening closely to their fellow citizens, open to deep associations of memory, and ready to raise a hand to tell a story.

Spontaneity

Without script or audience plants, Playback is an uncompromising form of improvisation. Spontaneity is its catchword. The term embraces several meanings, however.

The first is sheer playfulness and joy. It is no accident that the word for acting and playing in many languages is the same.[4] Even serious scenes are created upon a bedrock of improvisational play based on give and take between actors. They use the unplanned interaction of their bodies, their emotion, and their language

3. See Chapter 9, "Searching for Beyond."
4. See Chapter 11, "Is There More?"

to create vivid and meaningful action. It would appear that as human beings we are made to enjoy such play. It brings us joy.

The second is the ability to react on the spot to sense information. We need super-alive receptors to take in all aspects of the teller's narrative. Thinking too much gets in the way (there is an aspect of spontaneity that relates to thinking; we will discuss that in the next section).

The third is the ability to draw on creativity and imagination. A story that may be incomplete or unclear needs to be shaped and given all the attributes of drama. The performers let impulses for action lead them to the stage—impulses that often come from preconscious sources that consist of an image, a shape, an emotion, a thought—and then meld their different "ideas" into one coherent scene. In this practice, summoning the imagination, finding action that expresses it, and shaping inspiration into meaning, all in the unspoken moment, proficiency can take years to acquire. The performers' gradual increase in capacity, and the satisfaction that comes from it, is one reason members of Playback Theatre groups often stay involved for a decade or more.

A key area for training is movement, which unlocks the imaginative mind. Again, the difficulty of developing the necessary performing skills for this kind of spontaneous story enactment is made greater by the lack of training available in general education; we are not taught to pretend (be imaginative), to dance, to collaborate. In fact, we are often taught to drop the natural play and role play of our early years for sedentary, rational, distinctly antiplay, narrowly imaginative learning.

The fourth is role flexibility; the ability of an actor, for example, to play whatever role is called for in the story presented, whether it be a fierce employer at one instance and a cute puppy dog, the next. Most of us find some roles much easier to play than others, and in the sense of expanding our role flexibility, spontaneity can be trained. We practice by enacting our own stories. We also perform a wide variety of exercises designed to expand our readiness and range, so that we are ready to fulfill any story that comes up.

A fifth is collaboration. A Playback Theatre group, like a sports team, learns to cooperate with each other to a high degree. The task of creating improvisational scenes before audiences demands it. Communities are as often impressed by the teamwork of the performers as by the stories themselves. The members of a Playback group must remain in positive relationship with each other, or else it will be prohibitively difficult, even impossible, to achieve spontaneous teamwork on the stage. This is a tall order, requiring that groups take valuable time away from skill-building in order to talk things out with each other.

Lior Noy and colleagues at the Weizmann Institute in Israel, which has featured its own Playback Theatre team, have conducted an interesting experiment. Noy created a device he calls the Mirror Game, in which the movements of two players are precisely measured by sliding a counter along a two-dimensional axis as they try to synchronize with each other. The scientists found that random individuals lead and follow each other in jerky motions, while practiced improvisors, by seeming to be able to anticipate each other's movements, can actually achieve a "no-leader" state, creating a smooth line on the graph.[5]

Inherent in the idea of spontaneity is a core of integrity. A performer needs to have a sense of her own boundaries—not so much in a psychological sense, although this also is true, but in an imaginative sense. Otherwise, how can she know that an image for embodiment is inspired by the teller's story rather than her own? In other words, meaningfully "retelling" a story means not being triggered by it, keeping one's artistic distance from it, adding to and subtracting from it—in short, making art from it. For this reason, an individual who has a very incomplete or fuzzy sense of her- or himself will find it very difficult to perform Playback Theatre, because it will often be impossible to evaluate impulses. It may seem paradoxical, but a story can only be successfully "retold" by

5. See Noy, Lior. "The Mirror Game: A Natural Science Study of Togetherness." In *Performance Studies in Motion: International Perspectives and Practices in the Twenty-First Century*. Editors: Atay, Citron, D. Bloomsbury Methuen Drama, 2014. Also see the Theater Lab of Noy's colleague and collaborator at the Weizmann Institute, Uri Alon: https://www.weizmann.ac.il/mcb/UriAlon/research/theatre-lab.

performers who find their own unique manner of embodying the teller's intended meaning. This license to be creative is what makes Playback Theatre so full of vitality and brings depth and beauty to an often commonplace-seeming story.

Spontaneity lies at the heart of the art in Playback Theatre. Clearly the Playback approach does not fit in to the conventional definition of art as "product." It does not embrace the common "art for art's sake" disregard for the welfare of both audience and performers. Nevertheless the challenge of reenacting personal narratives on the spot, drawing on movement, spoken language, music, and other theatrical elements, allows for impressive artistic achievement.[6] Narrative reticulation allows for Playback Theatre to be effective at many levels, including a high artistic standard. Some would argue that of course the highest artistic standard represents the pinnacle of potential achievement in Playback Theatre. I am not sure about that. While it stands to reason that the most artistic performers, so long as they are also skilled in the other attributes of narrative reticulation, will be able to succeed in the widest number of milieus, I am convinced, however, that the allegiance of Playback Theatre to spontaneity allows for all sorts of practitioners to draw on the artist in themselves and find necessary sources of creativity.

Guidance

The four attributes that make up the cornerstones of narrative reticulation pertain to every aspect of the Playback Theatre process, but for reasons of brevity, this essay has focused on the teller in discussing story, the group in discussing atmosphere, and the performers in discussing spontaneity. In the same vein, this section, on the last attribute, *guidance*, will primarily concentrate on the role of the conductor.

The conductor leads the audience throughout the Playback performance as an emcee. She welcomes them at the start and explains the nature of the event. She prompts the audience for narratives by asking questions. She interviews tellers. Most of the time, she chooses what specific forms the actors use in their

6. See Chapter 4, "What is 'Good' Playback Theatre?"

enactments. She monitors the arc of the performance, deciding when is just the right time to invite the first story, and when will be the last. She conducts the ritual, making clear what are its rules and keeping them honored. Finally, she is responsible for choosing the next teller, encouraging the audience when no hand is raised and selecting when there are many raised at once. These leadership tasks take a variety of skills, ensuring that the conductor is a complex role that takes considerable time to learn.

In the unfolding of a Playback event, there are many moments when the attributes converge. The emergence of just the right story for the moment represents a convergence of story and atmosphere. Or a particularly satisfying enactment, for instance, will be the result of story and spontaneity coming together in a synergistic fashion.

Often, however, the attributes will not converge, but will pull in opposition to each other. At such moments it will be the conductor, more than anyone, who must make an intervention. A typical example is the long-winded teller. The demands of spontaneity will argue to let the person's story unfold naturally, while the demands of atmosphere will argue for an interruption to prevent the community from growing bored. Another example occurs when interviewing a very sad teller, who might find herself wordless with grief during the narrative. The demands of atmosphere call for the conductor to provide comfort to the teller, but again, the demands of story will be to hear the details of what happened. The conductor in this situation will need to encourage the perhaps weeping teller to get the words out, while in the previous example, the conductor needs to contain the flood of words. In these and many such situations the conductor must decide exactly when and how to intervene (or not).

It is important to note that the actors will also need to make such discriminations. For instance, in the case of a story containing violence experienced by the teller, the actors need to weigh the demands of story, which may involve cataclysmic events, with those of atmosphere, since they know that if they retraumatize the teller in front of the community (by enacting the story too literally), the flow of the narrative reticulation may suffer irreparable harm.

Thus even though the Playback event unfolds in an unplanned manner, the team is constantly making on-the-spot decisions, guiding the progress of the event in response to challenges presented by opposing attribute demands. In one sense this control is the opposite of spontaneity. But on another level, this thinking constitutes another order of spontaneity.

Balance is key. In the unfolding of the Playback Theatre event, the interplay of the attributes often becomes unbalanced (or threatens to become unbalanced). It is the job of the team, especially the conductor, to sense this and make an intervention that will restore an equilibrium that fosters the flow of stories.

There is an ethical imperative that underpins Playback Theatre, and maintaining it constitutes another major area of guidance. The conductor must see that no one gets harmed during the event; this includes other community members and actors, as well as tellers. In listening to a narrative, the conductor must balance respect for the teller with fairness to others. For instance, the conductor should not allow a teller to tell a malicious story about another person present; the conductor should not allow a teller to insult an actor. This precept has its distinct complications, such as in instances where the teller's story contains clear prejudice of some kind.[7]

That part of atmosphere which calls for inclusivity will need guidance to make the ideal a reality, often consisting of a direct invitation to a specific community member, framed in just the right manner and occurring at just the right moment.

Guidance is an essential component to every Playback Theatre event. However, when the event has a special purpose, such as staff development (a private company introducing a new management concept), healing (a performance for residents of a women's shelter), or dialogue (a village community divided by participation in civil war), then the conductor will need to exercise additional guidance to make sure that event keeps to its intended purpose.

Human beings seem to have a primal urge to relate stories to each other, and I imagine that it is not particularly difficult to achieve some degree of narrative reticulation in any social group,

7. See Chapter 6, "The Wider World."

provided the members get a chance to talk openly and leisurely with one another. Nevertheless, years of experience have shown that the presence of performers as artistic retellers can make a huge difference to the resonance of the stories shared, and guidance can provide a major catalyst to an increased level of narrative reticulation.

Discussion

Narrative reticulation theory is designed to elaborate both the red thread concept and the three-circle theory that have been useful for Playback Theatre practitioners over many years. The four attributes of narrative reticulation operate in a similar way to a complex system (like the human body). Each attribute is a very different world of its own, but they ultimately must work in synergy for narrative reticulation to take place. Many factors bear on this, including the skill of the performers, the openness of the audience, and the milieu.

Let's look briefly at negative outcomes. If the conductor or actors mis-hear or fail to understand the intended meaning of the teller, or if they fail to have an adequate grasp of how stories work, then the theme of the enactments will head off in an unintended direction, and the community may feel uneasy, since they sense that a key element about the narrated experience was missed. We could call this an example of misplaced guidance, since the team takes the story off on a tangent not intended by the teller. If the conductor is too unassertive, failing to intervene when needed, the ritual may be loosened to a fatal extent; or in the opposite case, if the conductor is manipulative, the atmosphere will be poisoned by unempathic leadership. If the conductor sticks too rigidly to a pre-event plan of which forms to use when and cannot adjust to the circumstances as they unfold, then the performance will feel over-structured and the necessary dynamism of the NR process will be throttled.

When the integrity of an individual attribute is not maintained (some PT groups are too unskilled in one area or another), or the interplay of the four attributes becomes unbalanced, then the narrative reticulation will be weak. Tellers will hesitate to come forward. The energy will diminish. The emotions will be flat. The overall meaning will feel superficial.

When each of the four attributes thrives, in contrast, and the Playback team nimbly maintains them in balance with each other, then the energy will grow as the event proceeds. Hands will start to rise as tellers feel compelled to share. Emotions will be strong, including a sense of connection among the community. The narrative reticulation—the connection between the stories them-selves—will be deep and complex.

Outcomes

Finally, let's look briefly at how narrative reticulation theory might be useful. For Playback Theatre practitioners, the theory can be applied to structuring training and rehearsals, as well as assessing performance. What are an actor's and conductor's strong and weak points in terms of the theory? What areas need strengthening? Where did the performance become unbalanced? At what junctures? What other action might have kept the NR strong?

It might also be possible that the theory has relevance outside the world of Playback Theatre.[8] NR provides a rationale for dia-logue through personal story. It emphasizes the power of listening and community engagement. It charts a method of on-the-spot decision-making that may be useful for other areas of work. Finally, NR presents a concept of modulated consciousness that is an alter-native to logic-driven concepts of thinking.

Narrative reticulation means connection, perceived meaning, energy for communication. More of it in our social contexts will lead, one can hope, to more cohesive and civil communities.

8. See Chapter 18, "The Listening Hour."

TELLING STORIES IN PUBLIC

Jo Salas (2020)

PLAYBACK THEATRE is not the only contemporary performance practice built on a belief in the importance of personal stories, nor is it the best known. Since our work is often compared to other popular forms of story-sharing, I want to look at the ways in which they are distinct.

After practicing and teaching Playback Theatre for so long I've learned to be philosophical when a new acquaintance asks me about my work and then says flatly, "I've never heard of it." Or they might say, "It sounds like The Moth." In the US and some other English-speaking countries, the radio show The Moth is a weekly broadcast of a live stand-up event where both ordinary people and celebrities recount their own personal stories. The stories, rehearsed and memorized, are often very funny, sometimes shocking or moving. The Moth has published three print collections of selected stories.

Our new friend might also mention StoryCorps, another approach that's well known in the US where one person interviews another, often a family member, about his or her life. They audio-record the conversation in a booth provided by the organization, in the presence of a StoryCorps staff member. Stories may then be shared publicly, or published in print. In our upstate New York region we also hear comparisons to the locally created TMI project ("too much information"): personal narratives of struggle refined in workshops and presented in front of a live audience and online.

These personal storytelling forms, and others, have sprung up in the last 25 years—The Moth in 1997, StoryCorps in 2003, TMI in 2010—to meet a hunger that human beings share. We have stories and we long to tell them. We are endlessly curious about each other's lives, and we seek to be touched by them. It is the same yearning that Playback Theatre seeks to fulfill. It can be met in any number of forms and formats, with or without a performance element, and with varying degrees of public-ness. The confessional storytelling popularized on television talk shows, as well as deliberate self-exposure on social media, exploit the same desire.

Compared to the 1970s when Playback originated, the power of personal story as a vehicle for meaning and connection, as well as for entertainment, is now far more widely recognized. Personal story has long been the basis of the structured sharing in 12-step programs like Alcoholics Anonymous and some kinds of therapy groups. Devised theatre such as *The Vagina Monologues* or *The Exonerated* is typically distilled from personal stories previously written or told by participants. I'm most concerned here to look at Playback in relation to the storytelling performance forms—The Moth and so on—that have attracted wide public attention, and with which Playback is often compared. Despite apparent similarities, there are three fundamental differences between any of these forms and Playback Theatre: the fact that Playback Theatre embodies stories in action, not just narration; the role of emergence; and the atmosphere that is necessary for emergence to take place.

How stories are generated

Those of us who are immersed in Playback can take for granted what is perhaps the most extraordinary thing about it: how stories emerge. They are neither planned nor selected ahead of time. They have not been curated or crafted. They have not been rehearsed. The audience and performers hear the story for the first time as the teller is telling it. In most cases, it's even new for the teller: typically, she or he has not told this story before. It has arisen in her mind during the performance, perhaps in that very moment before she raises her hand, in response, consciously or unconsciously, to a previous story. Somehow, it's just there—a memory, an experience, a sudden synthesis of impressions.

The teller may have come to the event with no story in mind, with no intention to tell—or even a firm intention not to tell.

She senses a call from somewhere within herself, often coming as a surprise—"I haven't thought of that moment for years!" Sometimes there is a resistance, the "tension of participation" as Rea Dennis refers to it: an inner debate about to whether to offer one's story.[1] No matter how timely or pressing the story might be, telling it involves exposure and can feel risky.

Even those who walk in with a story in mind are likely to wait for an intuitive sense that yes, this is the moment for my story—or they find themselves telling something else altogether. (There are occasional exceptions: a person who comes with a story that they're determined to tell, oblivious of the mood or emerging theme. Or a teller who offers a much-told anecdote. A skilled conductor can sometimes ease the story off its well-worn tracks, allowing something more authentic to emerge.)

Playback shows, whether public or commissioned, often have a declared theme. A "hard" theme in a commissioned show has to be adhered to because of the agreement with the host organization. The conductor may need to repeat a warm-up to the theme if the stories move in a different direction. A "soft" theme in a public show is a more flexible scaffolding that can comfortably accommodate stories on other topics. Regardless of how hard or soft a theme might be, it does not dictate the actual stories. They are summoned by the here-and-now events of the show. A detail or character or interaction in one story sparks a link to another. The echoes that a story creates—of myth or archetype, of history or politics—may prompt a memory or vision in a listener. As the stories emerge they create a deep dialogue, of image, allusion, perception, and perspective, not a cognitive dialogue of argument and counter-argument.[2]

In the Playback community we've long talked about this dialogue with reference to the "red thread,"[3] the response of one story to another. One story might seem to be saying, for example, "Life

---

1. See Dennis, "Crossing the Threshold," www.PlaybackTheatreReflects.net, March 2017.

2. See Chapter 8, "What We Mean by 'Dialogue' in Playback Theatre."

3. See Hoesch, "The Red Thread: Storytelling as a Healing Process," in *Gathering Voices: Essays on Playback Theatre*, Eds Dauber and Fox. New Paltz, NY: Tusitala, 1999.

is disappointing." A later story, told with no conscious intent to address the earlier one, carries a different message: sometimes life gives you a lovely surprise. As we're now realizing, the red thread is neither singular nor linear. Instead there are many threads, weaving a dense and complex network. The weaving is multidirectional and multilayered. A story told toward the end of a show may cast a new light on a story told at the beginning. The connections between stories reach out in different ways, in different directions, on different levels, sometimes not fully apprehended until after the show.

This is the process of narrative reticulation that Jonathan Fox and now others have been exploring: the idea that emergent stories, told in a genuinely inclusive atmosphere, connect to each other to create a rich network of associations and meanings.[4] The effect, by the end of the event, is that the connections among a group of people have grown stronger. There is a respite from the pervasive, subterranean fear of chaos and pointlessness. We may feel a sense of reassurance that yes, we do mean something to each other: your story matters to me, my story matters to you. On its microcosmic scale, a fulfilled Playback Theatre event is a counterforce to the crushing pressures of isolation and alienation that are our daily experience in our late-capitalist, deeply unjust and racist world.

THE DEPTH OF THIS IMPACT depends largely on the phenomenon of emergence in a Playback show. Stories emerge in the moment, enabled by a purposefully and expertly created atmosphere of connection, inclusiveness, trust, respect, and the shared willingness to step into the unknown—performers and audience members alike. The commitment to genuine inclusiveness is critical: without the engagement of everyone in the room (whether expressed in sharing stories or simply listening) spontaneity is dampened and the pool of inspiration remains shallow, resulting in stories that are either merely anecdotal or attention-seeking. So the conductor must use all possible skill to acknowledge and reach out to all who are present, to remember them and constantly, though unobtrusively, invite and welcome their participation. The other performers

4. See Chapter 12, "The Theory of Narrative Reticulation."

onstage contribute to this inclusiveness by the quality of their listening and by their respectful and empathetic portrayal of every story that is told.

There can be no Playback Theatre show without active audience participation. In a literal, not figurative sense, it is a co-creation of everyone present. The experience of shared creativity engenders a kind of aliveness, a particular delight: we did this together! It is quite distinct from the experience of being stirred or inspired by the creativity of others, and it may be unique to Playback.

The scope and goals of other storytelling performance forms are different. In The Moth and TMI, stories are selected ahead of time and highly crafted before being read or recounted in public. StoryCorps stories selected for broadcast or publication "favor highly emotional and predictable narrative arcs."[5] If there is a thematic connection between stories in these settings, it is curated, not spontaneous. The performance does not depend on or embrace the responses of the audience. Applause, laughter, or tears will certainly be noticed and felt by the storytellers but it is a one-way process: whatever is aroused within those watching will not affect the shape, direction, or outcome of the event. There is neither the intent nor the possibility to listen to the audience members' own stories evoked by what's happening onstage, any more than there would be at a Broadway play. The audience's emotional energy may be rewarding for the performers but it is not the matrix of the stories, as it is in Playback Theatre.

The role of enactment

Stories in Playback are enacted, not simply told. Playback Theatre is theatre, with movement, interaction, music, and un-scripted dialogue created on the spot by actors and musicians, who summon an artistic sensibility to embody the essential meanings of the story they've just heard. The more creative and sensitive they are, the deeper will be the resonance of the story and its connections to other stories told.

5. Nancy Abelmann, Susan Davis, Cara Finnegan, Peggy Miller, et al. "What is StoryCorps, Anyway?" *Oral History Review* 36, no. 2 (2009): 258.

The embodied artistry of live improvisation adds a different dimension to performed storytelling. The stories are not only heard but sensed in the watcher-listener's body as she witnesses the bodies of the actors as they move and interact, opening pathways for complex associations.

Storytelling without enactment is of course a noble and ancient art form in itself, whose traditions are part of Playback's origins.[6] In the modern personal story-based forms that I'm discussing, considerable artistry is brought to bear. In TMI, stories are selected in workshops prior to a performance, where participants are coached to edit and perform their monologues with as much impact as possible. The Moth invites would-be storytellers to "wow us with a 2-minute pitch of your story." Those whose stories are chosen are asked to practice until they can tell them fluently, without notes, with expert timing and heightened drama. StoryCorps is not a performance form in itself, but stories are recorded, and, with participants' permission, may be excerpted, edited, and presented in audio segments and in written form.

Why tell personal stories in public?

Some years ago I attended a performance by a Playback group whom I did not know. It took place in a beautiful theatre, with a large audience. The performing team was experienced and artistic. The music was outstanding. And yet I found the performance disappointing. There was no arc, no weaving together of stories and voices, no sense of a group of strangers drawing closer. The conductor did nothing to acknowledge or include the different subgroups in the audience, such as those who had or had not seen Playback, or those who were visiting from far away—an omission likely to leave some people feeling marginalized and reluctant to offer stories. Each time he invited a story he took the first one offered rather than sometimes waiting for someone who might be a little slower to raise a hand. Sitting in the almost-dark (the

6. The new "Listening Hour" form, launched during the Covid-19 pandemic when face-to face performance was not possible, brings Playback back to those particular roots: stories told without enactment. See Chapter 18, "The Listening Hour."

houselights were dim and the conductor could barely have seen faces) I felt increasingly distant, and out of touch with my own stories. But other hands were flying up. There was, in fact, a torrent of stories, each more emotional than the last, told quickly, enacted quickly, one weeping teller quickly replaced by another.

I found it difficult to witness. But I learned something. Even in the absence of the careful, conscious building of trust and inclusiveness in the audience, stories might come, including high-stakes stories of love and loss. But they will not emerge from the deep place of sincerity and spontaneity that Playback seeks to reach. They will not add up to a whole that links and enriches all who are present. This performance had the outward form of Playback Theatre. But it lacked its essential heart.[7]

People tell personal stories publicly for all kinds of reasons, not always constructive. Telling a story of incest or betrayal on a television talk show might feed the gossipy curiosity of viewers, and might be welcomed by the show's ratings-hungry sponsors, who are happy to commodify personal stories for profit. Such attention could indeed be gratifying for the teller. But a story coming from such motivation does nothing to deepen our sense of shared humanity. The teller is unlikely to walk away with a sense of dignity, of being understood and accepted, their bonds with society strengthened.

Members of Playback audiences are of course as susceptible as anyone else to the full range of motivations to offer a story, from the exhibitionistic to the altruistic or didactic, from the revelatory to the humbly self-explorative. Our task and our goal as performers are to create an atmosphere where our audience members can speak in a spirit of genuineness and the desire to connect. Only then—if their sincerity is met with receptiveness and artistry—will we see the fruitful possibilities of Playback fulfilled.

The same spectrum of motivations is evident in other storytelling performance forms. The way in which stories are solicited is informative. The Moth's stated mission is to "promote the art and

---

7. To their great credit, the performing team later sought out my feedback, genuinely wanting to learn.

craft of storytelling" while also honoring the "diversity and commonality of human experience." Their guidelines bear this out, with advice about craft (beginnings, endings, "stakes" that will make the story compelling). Stories are also expected to be true, and to adhere to the stated theme of a live event. Consequently, the stories told on The Moth, reflecting all kinds of lives, all kinds of experiences and emotional range, are expertly shaped, told with basic respect for others, and true to the storyteller's experience. The Moth's mission and guidelines do not rule out stories told in order to be sensational, but if that's the teller's wish, it's mediated by the insistence on craft, sincerity, and respect for others.

StoryCorps's mission is "to preserve and share humanity's stories in order to build connections between people and create a more just and compassionate world." Their guidelines seek to help participants hold a meaningful conversation with another person, suggesting questions such as "Can you tell me about someone you'll always remember?" The content is open-ended, though stories selected for further sharing tend to be well-shaped stories that follow a familiar arc of hardship and redemption.

TMI is explicit about what kind of stories they're looking for. Their mission statement refers to focusing on "the 'too much information' parts of a story, the parts typically left out because of shame or stigma." The emphasis on shame is repeated in TMI's workshop guidelines, encouraging participants to focus on stories that you "keep shrouded in secrecy because of fear, shame or embarrassment." In the workshop you will be "gently nudged" to "tell the parts of your stories you usually leave out."

TMI's success indicates that there are many who have such stories and want to share them in public, and many who enjoy listening—though others find the emphasis on stories of shame to be somewhat uncomfortable. TMI leaders have also used their method to address community concerns including racism and mental health, with considerable effectiveness.

Painful or shameful stories may emerge organically in a Playback show. When they do, it's because of the sense of safety, trust, and spontaneity that has developed (or, extremely rarely, where the atmosphere resembles a talk show, as in the show I described above). The teller offers her story out of an intuitive recognition that it is the right story to come next—not because she's edited and rehearsed this story and she's next on the program. The teller maintains her own agency. She senses that the audience is ready to hold her story's revelations in respect and compassion. Her story will become part of the co-created network of stories, inspiring others in response.

There is no personal story that is inherently too shocking or too sad to be told publicly. It is always a matter of how it is generated and how it is received.

"Oh, it's like Playback Theatre!"

Playback Theatre has been in existence since 1975, far longer than the storytelling forms that I've mentioned. With performing groups in 70 countries, it involves the direct participation of a very large number of individuals. So why is it not better known? Why doesn't it get compared to StoryCorps or The Moth instead of the other way around?

I can only hypothesize. Unlike the other personal storytelling forms, Playback cannot be packaged and broadcast. It is live, ephemeral, and unpredictable. The atmosphere, so crucial for Playback's effectiveness, is almost impossible to capture on video, let alone audio. One can record and transcribe stories, but they tend to fall flat on the page: it is the creative interpretation of the performers that adds grace and resonance to the bare details shared by the teller. So Playback's worldwide following is limited to those who actually attend shows or participate in workshops—many people by now, certainly, but far short of the large radio audiences for both StoryCorps and The Moth, and the wide readership for their publications.

Another reason is the greater demands of a theatre performance compared to non-enacted storytelling. We need physical space, and a set-up that's more than just a microphone and a stool. We need a team of committed performers, and that means ensembles that take years to develop teamwork and skills. And our audiences need to be small for Playback to work. There's no limit to the number of people who can watch a performance of TMI, but Playback does best in the intimacy of an audience of 50 or 60 at most.

These constraints make what we do all the more precious. Each time we participate in a show, whether as a performer or an audience member, whether or not we tell a story, we are in a charmed circle of listening and openness which may engender stories of great meaning, reverberating far into our lives and our communities.

Citizen Actor

Jonathan Fox (2020)

"CITIZEN ACTOR" was a term I used from the start of our work in the 70s, but I never elaborated on it until I held a workshop on the topic in Germany early in 2020. At the very end of the workshop, a participant politely asked me to once and for all define the term. This was my response.

Citizen actor is an evocative term, perhaps uniquely suited to the English language. It denotes "actor" in the standard meaning of a theatrical role player, and at the same time a suggestion of "activist." There is a long-standing debate in our theatre community around this question of activism, but whatever your view, Playback Theatre practice is committed to general principles of human rights, which includes the possibility of everyone having the chance to articulate their story in a public forum. Because of the ongoing suppression of certain groups in our societies, not to speak of the widespread skepticism about the idea of inalienable rights, any Playback Theatre actor will also be an activist if she is to live up to this credo of all humans deserving a voice, including women, children, and minorities.

"Citizen" implies is a sense of community responsibility, in the sense of the image of Benjamin Franklin founding the first lending library. This is congruent with the community focus of applied theatre and stands opposed to an art for art's sake philosophy, where the artist has principle allegiance to her own creation. The citizen actor will espouse an ethics that strives for a theatre event benefiting everyone involved.

Citizen also connotes a "common man." Even though the Playback actor has developed a high degree of skill, she does not hold herself apart, but melds into the social fabric when not on stage. This integration—the Playback actor as common citizen—requires humility, an absence of ego in social standing that mirrors the egolessness of our stage work, with its emphasis on collective creation. One can assume that the time spent by the Playback actor as an ordinary member of the community will help her grasp the stories of ordinary people as they are narrated on the Playback Theatre stage.

The meaning of contemporary experience is often not visible without a sense of context that includes historical and political knowledge. Nor are the emotions of tellers and audiences manageable in a constructive manner without psychological knowledge. The citizen actor should educate herself in both these kinds of awareness.

Because those holding political power tend to write history to their own advantage, we are all indoctrinated during our formative years, especially perhaps if we benefit from social and economic privilege. It is also incumbent upon the citizen actor to interrogate herself regarding social stereotypes and prejudice that might contaminate understanding and enacting others' stories.

In summary, the citizen actor fulfills an artistic calling and more. We can encapsulate these meanings into a brief definition: A citizen actor is a creative artist dedicated to the betterment of self and society.

Playback Theatre for a Planetary Crisis

Jo Salas (2020)

AT THE INTERNATIONAL PLAYBACK THEATRE CONFERENCE in Bangalore, India in December 2019, a pick-up group of Australian playbackers offered a performance called "The World is Burning." Other shows were offered that evening but for me this title was irresistible. It spoke to my own sense of urgent danger. At that time much of Australia was literally on fire, with worse to come over the next couple of months. We did not know then that a climate-linked global catastrophe was about to descend on us all.

About fifty people streamed into a small lecture hall on the top floor. The Australian performers introduced themselves with their own strong feelings: "We are deaf to the wisdom of the old-est culture in the world!" said one actor. "My dream is that fires of anger might create change in the world, and fresh hope grow from the burned places," said another. Responses flowed from the audience members. After a while I raised my hand. Tears threat-ened to overwhelm me. Someone put a comforting hand on my shoulder. I am terrified, I said, scared to death, of the world that awaits my beloved small grandchildren—that awaits all the chil-dren. Watching the actors' fluid sculpture in response, sensing the sympathetic understanding of the audience, knowing that some of them, like me, had young children in their lives whom they adored and felt impelled to protect, I felt—not relief, exactly, but an easing, a strengthening, as the burden of my grief was shared.

A couple of days later Pontus Holmgren from Sweden and I held an ad hoc workshop on the climate crisis: a chance to share further and also to generate ideas about how we, as a Playback community, might play a constructive role in the existential crisis facing every soul on the planet. We sat in a circle, eighteen people from eight or nine countries, and reported to each other what was happening with climate in our own corners of the world. We hear every day in the media about the effects of climate change. But listening to these voices and seeing these faces felt different, and critically important—a kind of people's council. A woman from India described the deforestation taking place outside her town and the exhilaration of joining a protest against it. Another woman from Germany spoke of her teenage daughter's involvement in the school strikes. Most striking of all were the voices of two participants from Bangladesh. One man described the permanent loss to floodwaters of his four-centuries-old family home on an "evergreen heavenly island." They told us about a proposed coal-fired power plant adjacent to the largest mangrove forest on earth, a UNESCO World Heritage site, that will threaten not only the ecosystem and biodiversity but also the lives of fifty million Bangladeshis who live in the area. Environmental activists have fought hard, with some success, but now they're being violently suppressed.

We listened to each other's reports, with the fully attentive, whole-body listening that is sometimes the only thing we can offer in the face of horror. It was utterly sobering, and yet the fact itself of our being together in that circle, our direct sharing, our attuned and creative embodiment of the feelings expressed had an impact that is strongly with me six months later.

I AM WRITING IN THE MIDDLE OF the Covid-19 pandemic, or perhaps it's still the beginning. At this moment, in early May of 2020, we do not know. There are some signs that it is diminishing. It is also likely to surge again. The pandemic will come to an end, eventually, or at least a pause. But looming behind this crisis is a far larger threat, the catastrophe to end all catastrophes. As everyone who is not swallowed up in denial or ignorance now knows, we are on the brink of unstoppable global warming which could lead to the extinction of most living creatures including ourselves, bringing human civilization to an end.

It is very hard to hold that reality in the front of one's consciousness. The mind skitters away to the thousand and one exigencies of the moment. Our intuitive conviction, as biological beings, is that our extinction as a species is not possible. How could it be? Here we are, here we have always been, here we always will be.

But when we summon the courage to look at the voluminous scientific evidence from the past fifty years, there's no escape from what it means. We either resign ourselves to despair, or we sink back into denial, or we face the question: what do we do? And this: if the world is profoundly changing, or ending, how do we, as individuals and as a society, choose to be in this time? The existential choice that underlies every moment in our lives is suddenly stark: will we live in fear, selfishness, cruelty, greed? Or will we fulfill our more loving, generous, resilient selves?

Some Playback Theatre practitioners have been paying attention to climate change for a long time, during which the nature and the perception of this threat have changed markedly. We don't even talk about climate change any more. We talk about the climate emergency, or climate breakdown, or climate chaos. As the crisis has escalated, public attitudes have shifted as well. Ten or twelve years ago only a small minority of people were interested and concerned. The challenge in Playback shows on climate was to bring the dangers of future ice melt and sea level rise and desertification and displacement to the immediacy of personal story. Audience members often had strong feelings, certainly, but they were prompted by looking far into the future or to the other side of the world. It was hard to find experiences in their own lives that they could tell and that we could enact.

That has changed. There is now scarcely a place on earth that has not been pummeled by floods, fires, droughts, hurricanes, seasonal anomalies, extreme temperatures. Bird and insect populations are decimated, including our precious pollinators: we are approaching the "silent spring" that Rachel Carson warned us of sixty years ago, not just because of pesticides but because climate

change and over-consumption have destroyed habitats and migra-
tion patterns.[1] Deforestation to meet insatiable demands for meat
and metals has forced wild creatures into dangerous proximity to
humans, bringing their viruses with them. Covid-19 is the first zoo-
notic infection in our lifetimes to become a full-fledged pandemic.
It will not be the last.

So what do we citizen actors do in a time like this?[2] What
is our responsibility, what are our tools, what impact could we
possibly have?

My own conclusion, having participated in climate-themed
Playback shows since 2009, is that there are two ways that we
can use our practice to contribute in this moment. And, further,
that we must make a change in our own carbon behavior as a
community.

Playback to inspire action

Our practice is centered on personal stories: eliciting them,
enacting them, being changed by them. Shared stories have the
power to inspire and encourage fellow community members to
take action to mitigate the danger, and I mean "encourage" in the
original sense of the word, to give heart.

The scientific consensus is that radical alteration of the earth's
climate is now inevitable, with dire implications for agriculture,
health, habitable land, and global geopolitics. We can never return
to the stable climate that allowed human civilization to flourish for
the past 10,000 years, a stability that we assumed was permanent.
But while we cannot turn back the clock, we can take actions
that will steer us to a world that is livable, if different and far less
comfortable. The alternative is a world that cannot support human
life.[3] As all the experts have been telling us—pleading with us—this
is the moment to take such actions. Right now. This year. This
month. Today. Time is running out.

1. Rachel Carson, *Silent Spring*. New York: Houghton Mifflin, 1962.

2. See Chapter 14, "Citizen Actor."

3. Numerous recent books elaborate on this point, including *The Future We Choose* by
Christiana Figueres and Tom Rivett-Carnac. New York: Penguin-Random House, 2020.

The actions needed are simple in concept but, so far, beyond our apparent capacity, at least in terms of our collective will: end the use of fossil fuels in order to stop putting carbon and other greenhouse gases into the atmosphere, and end our addiction to mindless consumption. A world order predicated on endless growth is not sustainable.

What could motivate an ordinary person to stand up in the face of such gargantuan challenges? There is only one thing: our human emotions. As we see all too clearly, information alone will not prompt action. Scientifically sound warnings by the truckload have been available for decades. They're not enough. We need to be moved. We need our human empathy and vulnerability and indignation to be engaged. We need our hearts to pound, tears to sting our eyes, adrenaline to rush through our bodies, making us leap to our feet and demand that we *do* something.[4]

And what arouses our emotions? Stories.

Playback Theatre is, obviously, only one of countless ways that people can encounter the stories that will galvanize them. There are brilliant books, films, television programs, TED talks, plays, and more. But for those of us who have made this work central to our lives, it's the tool at hand. We can bring people together and provide a resilient framework where stories and emotions can be shared and felt and metabolized. And we can take care to link our stories to factual information and practical ways of taking action in our communities.

By now there is some knowledge and experience in the wider Playback world about how to set up a show on the climate crisis—how to lead audiences into the topic without either falling into a pit of despair, on the one hand, or sidestepping the deadly seriousness of the issue, on the other. As I discussed in a talk delivered by Skype to a Swedish-Russian Playback gathering on sustainability,[5] it has proved very helpful to use a structure based on Joanna Macy's

4. The Australian climate scientist Joëlle Gergis writes: "There is great power and wisdom in our emotional response to our world. Until we are prepared to be moved by the profoundly tragic ways we treat the planet and each other, our behaviour will never change." "The Great Unraveling." *The Guardian*, October 14, 2020.

5. Later published on www.PlaybackTheatreReflects.net.

spiral model.[6] Macy, a long-time activist for social justice and the environment, developed this model as she witnessed the trap of despair and paralysis in herself and others who try to confront harm. In her beautifully simple but profound concept, we can face the hardest truths if we first of all open ourselves to gratitude and make our way step by step toward vision and action. As new thresholds of danger emerge, we enter the spiral again. In this way it is a tool for ongoing resilience and impact.

A Playback performance on the climate crisis is different in significant ways from most other kinds of performance. Audience members have come to together to face an immediate and looming urgent threat. That is our shared desire and need. But we risk being overwhelmed by fear and sadness, on the one hand, and, on the other, being distracted from the topic. The Macy spiral is a roadmap that keeps us gently focused in the direction we want and need to go. As in most other shows, we begin with performers sharing their own brief stories that might spark stories later on. Then, the first part of the spiral: we invite audience members to reflect with a partner on their love and gratitude for the natural world. This brief conversation is followed wider sharing, with each statement then expressed in a short form. The partners talk again, this time about the pain of climate breakdown. The gift of the spiral is that attuning to gratitude makes it possible to "go there"—to let ourselves feel the true depth of our pain. Some of those moments are shared with the audience, reflected again in short forms.

The next stage on the spiral is "seeing with new eyes." In the Playback show we ask: "What has allowed you to see with new eyes?" It might be a book, a conversation, a wilderness experience, the birth of a baby. We enact audience members' responses, in short- or long-form stories depending on the arc of the show. The final step is "Going forth," invoking stories of vision, inspiration, intention, determination—next steps, whether large or small, followed by a closure in action or music. There may be other elements in the show: brief scripted plays,

6. *Active Hope: How to Face the Mess We're in without Going Crazy* by Joanna Macy and Chris Johnstone. Novato, CA: New World Library, 2012.

as in Climate Change Theatre Action[7] events, or a short talk by a climate activist, or announcements about upcoming events.

In this way audience members, whether new to climate action or seasoned environmentalists, are able to face the unbearable, as we must, and as I as an audience member was able to do in Bangalore, thanks to the actors' creative reflection and the audience's empathy. By the time many voices have been heard and the performance comes to an end, participants are often eager to take action— whether signing a mailing list or a petition, committing to driving less, or protesting at a fracked-gas power plant. We encourage concrete action steps by providing up-to-date factual information and by having representatives of climate organizations on hand to answer questions.

Even with this careful structure we have often sensed that there is far more to be said. More time is needed. The conversations with one or two other audience members are essential and would benefit from more time than the four or five minutes that a 90-minute performance permits. An ideal framework might be a half-day workshop with ample interaction, as well as the opportunity for everyone to embody stories in simple Playback action.

Playback to strengthen community bonds

There is a second gift that Playback Theatre can offer in the looming crisis. The Covid-19 pandemic is revealing the fragility of social institutions and patterns that we have taken for granted. Global responses vary greatly: some governments have quickly established science-driven rules for safety and recovery, supported by the general public, with good health results. Others, notably the US, have lapsed into lethal confusion and chaos. Particularly in the countries with the least internal cooperation, we are seeing the breakdown of social norms, outbreaks of selfishness, entitlement, and aggression, often with racist undertones, and weaknesses in the essential supply chains of equipment and food. We are also seeing an extraordinary flowering of kindness, resilience, grassroots

---

7. Climate Change Theatre Action is a worldwide initiative held in conjunction with the biennial United Nations COP talks. http://www.climatechangetheatreaction.com/

organizing, and inventiveness. And this is where our practice can play a role: it teaches us how to bring people together in spaces of trust, inclusiveness, and creativity. A Playback show on any topic is (or certainly should be) an experience of cohesion and respect. It is also a place where any story can be held, including trauma stories, even when, as will be the case, the trauma is shared by audience and performers alike as we grieve the loss of a way of life that will never return.[8]

These aspects of our knowledge transcend Playback contexts. For example, the unobtrusive sociometry that is integral to a successful show or workshop is also applicable in any non-Playback group or gathering: acknowledging who's new, recognizing sub-groups, steering the discussion back to inclusiveness if there are lapses into unconscious dominance, so that all voices are represented, not just those who are accustomed to being heard. The element of ritual that is second nature for playbackers will serve any event that seeks to bring people together, even something as simple as a go-round to hear each person's voice at the opening of a meeting—which invariably leads to more balanced participation later on. The attention we pay in training and practice to patterns of oppression can enable to us to address them when they arise.

Using Playback to strengthen community resilience is different from devoting Playback performances to the topic of climate change and generating action: it is about consciously using the inherent qualities of Playback to foster compassion, empathy, and connection in order to counter the forces that threaten to drive us apart. It is also recognizing that a Playback event on any topic is an opportunity to feel the strength and the importance of the group—of the collective good. The individual's story is vital, but it does not stand alone, any more than any of us can stand alone. Our lives and our stories exist in relationship, a reality all too often occluded in our relentlessly individualistic western culture. A major factor in the contrast between the effective response of many Asian countries to the pandemic compared to that of most non-Asian countries has been the fatal insistence, in countries like the US, on

8. See Chapter 17, "Enacting Testimony: Trauma Stories in Playback Theatre."

individual rights and wellbeing—even the rallying cry of "freedom" (in this case, the freedom to recklessly infect oneself and others). The pandemic has shown us beyond any doubt that our wellbeing is inseparable from that of others. "No man is an island, entire of itself," wrote John Donne in the seventeenth century, "every man is a piece of the continent, a part of the main."[9]

A particular tension that has been escalating for years is the worldwide phenomenon of people displaced directly or indirectly by climate change. Their desperation is all too often met with intolerance, scapegoating, and exclusion. As climate disasters multiply and as vast swaths of land become unlivable, this stress will grow exponentially. Some will migrate mostly within their own countries, as they do now. Millions of others will cross borders, seeking survival. There could be 150 to 250 million climate refugees by 2050.[10] If privileged societies do not learn to accommodate fellow humans who are forced to leave their homes, then we are facing a future not only of insecurity and deprivation but also soul-corroding inhumanity. And no one is immune: any of us, privileged or not, could find ourselves displaced, seeking safety in a strange land.

In the future that awaits us we will need each other more than ever. And we will need whatever resources of wisdom and skill we can find. For many of us, that points to Playback Theatre. As the authors of a recent article wrote about choosing to use Playback to address a different crisis, "Playback is what we do well together."[11]

There is a third action available to the Playback community and that is to look at our own carbon behavior, particularly in terms of travel. The pandemic is already forcing us to do so. Training workshops and gatherings have been postponed or canceled because getting together in groups is not safe and most air travel is not possible. Organizers and trainers are scrambling to create online

9. John Donne, "Meditation XVII, Devotions upon Emergent Occasions," 1623. In Donne, *Donne's Devotions*. Cambridge University Press, 1923.

10. As estimated by Friends of the Earth, Greenpeace Germany (Jakobeit and Methmann 2007), the Council of Europe, UNESCO, and UNHCR among others.

11. See "Bilal Bagh: Playback Theatre at a Historic Protest by Muslim Women" by Kavya Srinivasan, Laxmi Priya S.N. and Rashmi Ravikumar. www.PlaybackTheatreReflects.net, July 2020.

equivalents. But this forced pause is also a chance to look at long-term alternatives. It may no longer be acceptable for hundreds of people to take long plane flights to attend an international or regional conference. The cost in carbon emissions is too high. Even a single trainer traveling between continents becomes increasingly hard to justify as the planet suffers.

I don't have answers or solutions. The time may come when we can again be with our own Playback companies and audiences face to face. But we are in a crucible at this moment of discovering what's necessary and what's possible, when we cannot be physically with far-away students and colleagues. Will our international community become a scattered constellation of groups that never meet, sharing ideas, experiences, and learning only online and in writing? Will Playback Theatre exist only in its localized form, like our sources of food and energy?

The world is changing rapidly and inexorably. We are called upon to adapt, and I hope we will, because in the daunting future that we're heading toward, our work will be needed.

16

Unexpected Resilience of the Participant Performance Model for Playback Theatre[1]

Jonathan Fox (2020)

CONTRARY TO EXPECTATIONS, recent findings suggest that Playback Theatre performances using minimally trained actors can create positive theatre experiences, even in challenging social contexts of civil and natural disruption where the level of civilian trauma is high. An approach called the Participant Performance Model has accelerated this development. In this chapter, I will describe the model and some of its applications.[2]

Two-sided start

Playback Theatre is an interactive approach in which actors dramatize personal stories of others present. It originated in 1975, founded by me and Jo Salas. From the start, Playback Theatre adopted a somewhat double-headed format. Inspired by the work of contemporary experimental theatre ensembles in the USA, such as the Open Theatre and the Performance Group, it aspired to a level of dramatic art that demanded intensive skill building and theatrical values. Following the work of the original Playback Theatre company, which was located in upstate New York, today long-term groups practice and perform in this spirit in cities and towns in over 70 countries, see for example Melbourne Playback Theatre and Houston Playback Theatre.

1. First published in *The Applied Theatre Reader*, eds. Tim Prentki and Nicola Abraham. 2nd Edition. London: Routledge, forthcoming 2021.

2. Jo Salas's concept of the Participant Performance Model, inherent in our earliest work, has only grown in importance for me over the years. This essay is my assessment of its continuing usefulness today. See also Chapter 22, "Stories in the Moment."

At the same time, influenced by the creative dramatics movement in the UK, Playback Theatre often took the form of a workshop format, in which participants, without any training, improvised enactments of their own stories. Creative dramatics also demanded that the experience be constructive for all concerned. Over the years, the performance format and the workshop format continue to be vibrant forms for the practice of Playback Theatre. Other guiding practices at the outset, in addition to experimental theatre and creative dramatics, were psychodrama, with its emphasis on spontaneity and an inclusive group process, and the student-centered pedagogy of Paulo Freire (Augusto Boal was also an influence, but his book, *Theatre of the Oppressed*, did not appear in English until 1978, three years after the start of Playback Theatre).

The original vision entailed the simple idea of acting out the real stories of the community. Unlike Boal and his followers, who focus on scenarios of oppression, we did not have a narrative agenda. Instead, we espoused an idealistic vision of the value of each person's story, no matter how ordinary. We offered "an empty space, where personal stories are mirrored with emotional resonance" (Dirnstorfer & Saud 2017: 2). However, while we did not seek intensely dramatic stories, at the same time, we knew we did not want to avoid them. We wanted to offer a forum for *any* story, including those that many people chose not to hear, either because the stories were harrowing or their tellers were not normally given space. The exposure to psychodrama on the part of myself and many of the early performers of Playback Theatre helped convince us that people could reveal and see dramatized even the most painful experiences and emerge with a burden lightened.

AS PLAYBACK THEATRE slowly spread from the original group outwards through a combination of word of mouth and trainings we offered, audience tellers began to offer their most serious stories, even though we did not explicitly seek them. One explanation was the respectful atmosphere the Playback Theatre groups engendered; it was clear that the requested audience narratives were not primarily mere stimuli to showcase the artistry of the actors, but rather as elements of a genuine community discourse. Another was the evident interest of the performers in listening. A third was the careful structure of each event, which we term the "ritual," which offered a framework of safety. A fourth was Playback Theatre's "gentle" approach. We enacted just what the teller said and had no need, in contrast to many therapeutic approaches of the time, or indeed Artaud-inspired experimental ensembles, to go to the "bone," enacting in all its dramatic detail what might be barely hinted-at violence. Thus, we learned to be not surprised, even in a public setting, about stories of the death of a child, an accident, a shooting, or a fire.

Meeting the crisis

The interest in big, life-changing stories was not just a one-way process. As Playback Theatre practitioners, many of whom were socially and politically-minded, became used to enacting very serious stories, they began to express interest in "emergency" Playback Theatre. In 1999 at a global Playback Theatre conference, one participant suggested a kind of flying theatre squad that could travel to communities in crisis, such as the Balkan Wars dominating the news at the time. In an article written in 2000 about bringing Playback Theatre to communities ravaged by forest fires in the Northwest USA, William Layman wrote of the "interest in Italy, Hungary and Washington D.C. for some form of a Playback Emergency Response Team to address community needs during a period of crisis" (2000: 4). Despite this growing interest, however, for a long time there was little progress. The practical obstacles were formidable. Performers would have to be ready to drop everything at a moment's notice to travel to the site of the crisis. They would need to make onsite arrangements in contexts where basic communications were usually disrupted, and food and shelter was often scarce. Most decisively, such interventions would take considerable funds that would be needed immediately.

Intermittently, Playback Theatre practitioners, helped by the Centre for Playback Theatre, did mount occasional interventions, such as trips to Angola and Burundi in the early 2000's, funded by Search for Common Ground, a large conflict-resolution NGO, as well as to hurricane-ravaged New Orleans in 2006. During this time, there was a general assumption among Playback Theatre leaders, including myself, that performing for audiences who were facing or had faced traumatic upheaval in their lives, required a high level of skill and experience. Such stories tended to be complex as well as emotionally charged, posing an intense challenge for the improvisers.[3]

Underlying this assumption was an ethical concern. As Susan Evans, a mental health professional involved in Playback Theatre wrote: "It is not difficult to see that performances/events of this nature would place a great weight and responsibility on conductors and actors alike as energies involved within an audience were likely to be considerable" (2002: 2). Following a major community crisis, the personal story often mirrored the societal story, leading to highly emotional audiences as well as tellers. Performers who were shaken by what they were hearing and the intensity of feeling in the room could get overwhelmed and frozen; or the opposite could happen. They could lose sight of their own boundaries and overdo the enactment. Tellers could indeed, to mention a concern often voiced by health professionals, become reawakened to their ordeal in a psychologically damaging way—retraumatization.

In addition, there was another ethical issue. Theatre artists from a faraway place swooping in to "serve" suffering local inhabitants faced an issue of congruence. The visiting performers did not know the local culture, customs, or the deep background to the stories. They often spoke a different language. Most critically, they were sometimes white-skinned and from the global North, who could not avoid the shadow of colonialism when traveling the global South. Who was benefiting most in such cases was a valid question. As I admitted after a teaching trip to Burundi: "Personally, I get a trip to Africa, a tremendously stimulating new experience, and a new item for my resume. I even get paid" (Fox 2003: 13).

3. See Chapter 17, "Enacting Testimony: Trauma Stories in Playback Theatre."

For the visiting artists, the experience could also be profoundly unsettling. Researching visiting Playback Theatre trainers who undertook an intervention in post-conflict Sri Lanka, McCormick and Henry identified a significant "loss of self." "Good intent" and the "itch" of an altruistic calling was not enough to overcome the "challenges of a naïve understanding of the inherent complexities of working within other cultures when individuals position self as 'expert' in an environment that has a colonial past" (2017: 11).

The Participant Performance Model

In 1999 Hudson River Playback Theatre, a skilled group headed by cofounder Jo Salas, initiated a program in schools called No More Bullying![4] Inside of an hour, the team delivered to school children a presentation on the power of bystanders to curtail bullying, enacted stories from students using Playback Theatre, and role-played solutions. The role-plays involved audience participants, in the manner of Forum Theatre. Highly isolated individuals often took the opportunity to tell some part of their story. Perpetrators occasionally also told. The group provided teachers with suggestions for pre-and post-visit lessons. The program was sought after by schools (Salas 2005: 79). In nineteen years, Hudson River Playback Theatre performed for over 35,000 kids.

As a development to the No More Bullying! program, the group established an 8-week program involving 15–20 students who undertook a weekly training session in Playback Theatre, then at the end performed Playback Theatre along with the adults for other students. Salas, who was naming an approach practiced by Playback Theatre practitioners in different configurations since the first workshops in the 70's, defined this configuration as the Participant Performance Model (PPM). It was based on "training a small number of members (ten to twenty) of a particular interest or population group to carry out performances *for other members of that same group*." Salas was encouraged by the result, writing "For the audience members,

4. See Chapter 22, "Stories in the Moment."

seeing their peers onstage increases the impact of the content" (Salas 2011: 106).

The PPM idea also appealed to adult Playback Theatre practitioners who did not aspire to high artistic achievement based on extensive ensemble training. An example is the work initiated by Yuen Chun Chan in Toronto. Toronto was home to Toronto Playback Theatre, a professionally oriented group. In a new initiative in 2013, Chan and a colleague invited "our friends and their friends," all Chinese-speaking immigrants to Canada, to a four-week evening class to experience Playback Theatre. After the class, enough wished to continue and became a group with no name, which nevertheless espoused the mission to "serve the people in the community where we came from" (Chan 2014: 7). This is an example of citizen actors, just one step away from their audiences, making themselves available to act out the stories of their own demographic community. Despite their self-professed lack of experience, they manifested the courage to take their work into the public sphere in order to reach individuals in their community in need of being heard, including "single mothers, empty nesters, unemployed people, and new immigrants." Other instances of the PPM for Playback Theatre began to crop up around the world, including a group of mothers in Japan, with a mission of providing relief to the isolation of their own demographic and a group of asylum refugees in the Netherlands, who performed for other immigrants.

In these examples, the PPM performers played for audiences whose readiness to share deep stories varied on a wide spectrum. For the most part, the performances had open themes (unlike the original No More Bullying! program, which was sharply focused) and welcomed everyday as well as momentous narratives. Nor did they benefit from the onstage support of the professionals, as took place in the No More Bullying! program.

Even so, the big stories came. An ambitious project in post-insurgency Nepal called EnActing Dialogue offers an instance of PPM in a context where most of the stories recalled the time of conflict. Supported with German funds and administered by a

German NGO in partnership with Pro Public, a Nepali organization, the project trained twelve theatre professionals from
Kathmandu in Playback Theatre, who in turn trained forty-eight
volunteer "dialogue facilitators" from areas still feeling the effects
of the Nepali Maoist insurgency. Although the insurgency had
ended, there was lingering social devastation, even a decade later.
The six teams, comprised of ex-combatants and villagers of
diverse representation, each in a different district of the country,
performed 186 times in 2015–6 (Dirnstorfer & Saud 2017: 10).
The experiences lived through by many audience members, so
many unheard and unacknowledged, quickly rose to the surface
in the Playback Theatre format, with the result that dialogue
facilitators were often faced with the challenge of extremely
intense stories. Consulting with this project in 2016 and 2017,
I observed many such narratives, including being wounded in
battle and being sold as a young child to be an indentured servant
to a violent master.[5]

To ask the dialogue facilitators, previously untrained in theatre
and themselves having lived through traumatic times, to perform
Playback Theatre in public might seem like a recipe for theatrical
disaster. One might expect frequent artistic failure and psychologically overwhelmed performers, leaving tellers and audiences either
dissatisfied from stereotypical, shallow enactments or plunged
back into their trauma. However, this is not what resulted. The
performances, even upon a revisit to a specific location were "well-
attended" and received "positive feedback" from the audiences
(Dirnstorfer & Saud 2017: 10). According to an external evaluation
commissioned by the funder, the overall impact was "significant":
"When people sat together and engaged in the story of their
own community member, their attitude toward the storyteller
had changed.[6] Through this process, audiences in many districts
changed their previous antagonistic perspective and started sharing goods, foods and information" (IPRAD report 2016: 10).

5. See Chapter 24, "Garland of Flowers."

6. See also Chapter 8, "What We Mean by 'Dialogue' in Playback Theatre," and the
section on Kiribati in Chapter 22, "Stories in the Moment."

The assumption was that "the actors' open hearts and listening skills are conditions that make the telling for conflict-related stories *likely*. At the same time, the performers do also deepen their skills in listening and enacting with every process of theatre-facilitated dialogue. So, the more they perform and reflect on their learning to refine their skills, the deeper the dialogue processes can become" (Dirnstorfer & Saud 2017: 8).

An additional outcome concerned the growth of the dialogue facilitators, many of whom had previously lived socially isolated lives as ex-combatants in the conflict. At the conclusion of the initial 3-year funding cycle for the project, the originator of EnActing Dialogue, Anne Dirnstorfer, wrote: "[…] the most radical changes could be observed at personal level for those who were intensely engaged in the project for the period of three years. … Initially, some of the ex-combatants that joined the project were afraid of rejections from the audience while being on stage. However, the opposite held true: in their role as 'artists' who engage their community, they were increasingly accepted" (2018: 1).

Narrative reticulation[7]

Another approach to assessing the effectiveness of any Playback Theatre performance, including those using the PPM approach, is to note the level of narrative reticulation—the extent to which the individually emergent narratives are linked. According to narrative reticulation theory, a successful event will feature a spontaneous sequence of intricately connected stories that add up to more than a sum of its parts, whereas an unsuccessful event will not. One might suppose that a performance of less-trained actors, especially in a context where complex and emotionally charged stories are told, would inevitably lead to a weak narrative reticulation. Dirnstorfer described this process further, noting that stories holding shared themes such as loss of trust and meaning create subconscious connections that lead participants to offer similar stories to the space creating a relationship between narratives (Dirnstorfer & Saud 2017:12).

7. See Chapter 12, "The Theory of Narrative Reticulation."

Vulnerabilities

The formal evaluation of the EnActing Dialogue project, as well as confirmation arising from my own observation of the level of narrative reticulation in observed performances, suggest that the PPM approach can deliver effective theatre in a post-conflict setting. Using PPM is practically easier, since the performers are local, and it will be congruent, since they are of the same culture as their audiences. Arguably, despite lower levels of skills than more trained Playback Theatre performers elsewhere, their performances are more impactful than if a team of strangers had flown in to act out their stories. We can be cautiously optimistic that PPM offers a way for Playback Theatre to expand farther in the world in every kind of circumstance. Salas suggests that "[t]he participant performance model—a reiteration of the original idea of the citizen actor—may prove a more portable model for Playback in the future [than the experienced ensemble concept]" (2011: 123). For this to happen the trained experts in Playback Theatre need to identify as teachers rather than performing artists; they need to be content to be sowers of seeds rather than bright sunflowers waving in the field.

For PPM to work, especially in settings of social disruption, special attention must be paid to a few vulnerable areas. One is the training of the conductors, that intermediary who acts as an MC during the performance, inviting tellers and holding with them a very brief interview before saying, "Let's watch!" and turning the focus over to the actors and musicians. The conductor is mainly responsible for guiding the dramatic ceremony, listening effectively to the tellers and helping the performers get just enough information, and intervening appropriately in order to contain emotions. "The Conductor requires sophisticated skills in any context," writes Salas (2011: 98). How to teach those skills in a minimal time frame will remain a challenge for those designing PPM programs. Despite the special demands on the conductor, however, most of the same advantages that apply to actors and musicians apply here, too. For instance, in one of the PPM performances I witnessed in Nepal, the conductor was able to speak to the audience and interview tellers in the regional language; in a country with dozens of local languages, this is a distinct benefit.

PPM performers in post-conflict settings need special training in how to enact violence, because it is a frequent presence in audience stories. Clumsy, often excessively graphic embodiments have the power to retraumatize. The performers need to learn to find the "right level" (Saud 13). This task is a delicate one when the performers themselves, as members of the community, have experienced identity-shattering violence and may need psychosocial support along with their training. To be avoided is the kind of outcome where audience members run from the room, as happened once in Burundi (Fox 2003: 13), or an actor faints onstage, as occurred during a performance in Afghanistan (Salas 2011: 117).

Finally, the practical challenges of bringing Playback Theatre to remote regions and disrupted communities, while perhaps logistically easier and cheaper than sending a touring theatre company from far away, remain formidable. There is the need for effective administrative support under often-difficult conditions, and there is the ever-present issue of long-term stability, for while the PPM approach does not have the same pressure for continuity as a self-identified artistic ensemble, the PPM project itself needs ongoing support to survive. As Dirnstorfer writes about EnActing Dialogue, "in the case of Playback Theatre work it seems especially difficult as the structures of the Nepali government seem yet too rigid and too little supportive to nourish such a demanding project in a fruitful way" (2018: 5). Even a self-started group like WTCPT in Toronto faces the challenges of recruitment (attracting community members to something so different from their everyday cultural experience), continuity (members are constantly dropping out because of the economic and social pressures), and finance (members cannot afford even minimal training and do not have the leisure for it) (Chan 2014: 12).

Conclusion

Undoubtedly, some concerns about applying PPM in social contexts of civil and natural upheaval stem from the pervasive reach of the trauma concept, which emerged from a Western model of therapy that privileges the individual and private space. The contention that a PPM Playback Theatre performance is "risky," in a context like a Nepali village, a Toronto neighborhood, or a school classroom undervalues the positive potential of communal discourse in the public sphere. It ignores what Salas terms the "unique potency of the arts, which invoke creativity, synthesis, vision, and imagination" (2011: 105). In fact, a community may—by using an applied theatre approach that features telling and embodying their own stories—uncover sources of healing and resilience themselves.

References

Chan, Yuen Chun. (2014). "Participant Performance Model: Exploration by a Toronto-based Chinese Playbacker." Centre for Playback Theatre (Essay for Leadership course).

Dirnstorfer, Anne. (2016). "EnActing Dialogue: Community Level Reconciliation through Theatre-Facilitated Dialogue: Final Report. Institute for Policy Research and Development (IPRAD)." Kalimati, Kathmandu, Nepal.

Dirnstorfer, Anne & Saud, N.B. (2017). "A Stage for the Unknown? What Theatre Art Can Bring to Peacebuilding." Paper presented at the International Conference on Political Transition, Non-Violence and Communication in Conflict Transformation in Pattani, Southern Thailand.

Dirnstorfer, Anne. (2018). Coda to the Paper, "A Stage for the Unknown." Centre for Playback Theatre.

Evans, Susan. (2002) Personal communication.

Fox, Jonathan. (May 2003). "Burundi Journal." *Interplay*, newsletter of the International Playback Theatre Network, XIII (3), 12–14.

Layman, William D. (2000). "Playback Theatre and the Landscape of Disaster." http://playbacktheatre.org/wp-content/uploads/2010/05/Layman_Disaster.pdf

McCormack, Lynne & Henry, Evelyn. (2017). "The 'lived' Experience of Playback Theatre Practitioners in Post-War Sri Lanka: Naivety, Altruism, Reciprocal Caring, and Psychological Growth." *Arts & Health*, 9(3), 224–237. https://doi.org/10.1080/17533015.2016.1262879

Salas, Jo. (2011). "Stories in the Moment." In *Acting Together: Performance and the Creative Transformation of Conflict*. (Eds C. Cohen, R. Varea Gutierrez, & P. O. Walker.) (Vol. 2). Oakland, CA: New Village Press.

Salas, Jo. (2005). "Using Theater to Address Bullying." *Educational Leadership*. September 2005, Vol. 63 (1), 78–82.

17

Enacting Testimony: Trauma Stories in Playback Theatre[1]

Jo Salas (2020)

TRAUMA IS THE EXPERIENCE of dreadful terror and helplessness in the face of a threat that is beyond the capacity of the individual to cope with, and from which she or he is unable to escape. "The essence of trauma is that it is overwhelming, unbelievable, and unbearable" (Van der Kolk, 2015, p. 195). It may result from a single incident—an accident, an episode in war, a natural disaster—or from experiences that continue over years, like domestic abuse. It may occur at any age from infancy on, or even earlier, in cases of transgenerational trauma. It may be consciously remembered, or not. For some people the immediate impact of the trauma fades over time, without clinical help. Painful echoes may remain permanently, to be stirred up from time to time by new stresses or life changes. For other trauma sufferers, because of the severity or duration of the trauma or other complicating factors, normal life becomes impossible in the face of horror and its damage to the soul.

Recovery from trauma, whether spontaneous or assisted by clinical treatment, is generally acknowledged to require a sequence of stages, described by Judith Herman (1992, p. 155) as "a gradual shift from unpredictable danger to reliable safety, from dissociated trauma to acknowledged memory, and from stigmatized trauma to restored social connection." She and other theorists of trauma (e.g. Van der Kolk, 2015; White and Epston, 1990) emphasize the central role of storytelling after the essential first phase of establishing safety. At first, storytelling is likely to be a private narration, however

---

1. First published in *Trauma in the Creative and Embodied Therapies: When Words Are Not Enough*, eds. Chesner and Iykou, Routledge UK, 2020.

incomplete or disorganized, of what happened. Later comes a more public storytelling that can restore the traumatized person's sense of meaning and connection to society. "In the telling, the trauma story becomes a testimony," Herman writes. "Testimony has both a private dimension, which is confessional and spiritual, and a public aspect, which is political and judicial" (1992, p. 181).

For Van der Kolk (2015), Herman's stages of storytelling represent only one "avenue" of trauma healing. Another avenue is the use of pharmaceuticals or other technologies. And a third is "allowing the body to have experiences that deeply and viscerally contradict the helplessness, rage, or collapse that result from trauma" (Van der Kolk, 2015, p. 3). While primarily exploring methods that can address the physiological effects of traumatic stress—muscle tension, breath, heart rate, brain functioning—Van der Kolk also acknowledges that most people need some combination of these approaches. Levine's approach also emphasizes somatic experience: "[T]rauma is something that happens in the body. We become scared stiff or, alternately, we collapse, overwhelmed and defeated with helpless dread. Either way, trauma defeats life" (2010, p. 31).

Playback Theatre and trauma

This chapter is about how Playback Theatre, a mostly non-clinical resource, can contribute to the integration of trauma both individually and societally through stories, artistic embodiment, and the call to imagination—another key element in trauma healing, according to Van der Kolk: "Without imagination there is no hope, no chance to envision a better future, no place to go, no goal to reach" (2015, p. 17). Although adaptable for use in therapeutic settings, Playback Theatre is not primarily a therapeutic modality. Its main use is in the wider community with participants who are not diagnosed with mental illness or disorders. Based on the universal desire to tell one's story, the need to know beyond doubt that it has been heard, and the yearning to hear the stories of others, Playback Theatre has been adopted worldwide in contexts that include theatres, classrooms, refugee camps, staff retreats, and prisons, as well as in therapeutic treatment.

The basic format of Playback Theatre is this: a volunteer relates a personal experience and others act it out on the spot. Other stories follow, building a dialogue of images and themes. In performances, stories are told by audience members and enacted by a team of trained improvisers including a musician, with the facilitation of a "conductor." A performance typically includes short dramatized reflections of brief statements from audience members as part of a warm-up process, followed by three or four longer stories and a closure. In this unscripted theatre the artistry lies in the performing team's ability to transform raw experience into aesthetically coherent, emotionally meaningful theatre, with distilled language and expressive movement—all based on their empathic comprehension of the teller's story.

Playback also frequently takes place in groups such as training workshops, professional development sessions, or therapy groups, without a designated performing team. Instead, one or two leaders guide participants in enacting stories for each other, using the same basic format. A heightened ritual atmosphere prevails even in the most informal or intimate settings, with a distinct arrangement of the space, a consistent sequence in time, and the attentive, authentic demeanor of the conductor and actors. This ritual aspect is fundamental in Playback Theatre, creating a strong and flexible container for whatever stories may come.

Playback is a theatre of everyday life. It seeks to lift up the stories of ordinary people by embodying them in aesthetic form. It welcomes stories of joy, delight, discovery, and humor as much as stories of sorrow and struggle. At the heart of Playback Theatre is the rich complexity of real lives, along with the conviction that as social beings we long to know and learn from each other's life experiences. Fulfilling this longing is healing in itself, not in a clinical sense, but in the wider sense of affording insight, ontological meaning, affirmation, a sense of belonging, and community cohesion. A performance or workshop is fundamentally a collective event. Although the utmost attention is paid to each individual voice, the overall meaning comes from the interwoven story of the group and the sense of connectedness that it engenders.

Playback Theatre's effectiveness in addressing trauma belongs mostly to the third stage of Herman's formulation, when trauma sufferers are ready to give "testimony" in order to rebuild their sense of belonging to the community, to gain validation, and to claim their right to justice in cases where they were wronged. When this testimony is embodied in creative action the teller sees her story from the outside, perhaps for the first time. She and other watchers respond kinesthetically to the movements, voices, and interactions of the actors. The teller knows *with her body* that she has been heard. She, as well as audience members, may be "moved" in a literal sense, as they respond to the action onstage and are drawn imaginatively into the teller's story—breath changes, bodies lean forward, laughter or tears may come.

The recognition of these integral elements—storytelling, embodiment, artistry, and imagination—has led to Playback's use with communities coping with collective and individual trauma in the wake of a natural disaster, political or personal victimization, and other significant hardships.

In a women's prison

The other members of Hudson River Playback Theatre and I are in the yellow-painted recreation room of a medium-security women's prison, two hours north of New York City on the Hudson River. It is World AIDS Day. About 60 women troop in wearing dark green prison garb—young, middle-aged, a few elderly. Most are African American, with others who appear to be Latina or white. This day is a somber anniversary for people whose lives have been shadowed by HIV/AIDS. We are prepared for stories of grief, loss, shame. M, the social worker who is our liaison, is a necessary presence: the women know and trust her, and we trust her too. She will be available for whatever follow-up might be needed. This is our fourth visit for AIDS Day. Some of the women remember us from previous times and they greet us warmly. Others, sentenced in the past year, keep their distance.

We start with a song. The women join in, the newcomers' reserve melting quickly. In response to our warm-up questions they tell us about missing their loved ones—far away children, family members who have died.

I invite a volunteer to come to the teller's chair onstage and tell a longer story from her life. Hands go up immediately. I choose a woman who spoke up earlier. The others call encouragement as she makes her way to the stage area. "Brianna, right?" I say as she sits down beside me. "Where does your story begin?" Brianna was in the audience the year before and she knows the ritual. Perhaps she decided ahead of time to tell her story tonight. She launches into it with a bold statement: "I got AIDS." Brianna looks at the audience as if in defiance. Although HIV/AIDS has touched almost everyone's life one way or another, having the virus oneself carries stigma here and is normally kept secret. The audience is now silent except for a murmur or two of support. Brianna continues. Her story is about how she became infected as a teenager. It is a horrendous story of rape, incest, violence, and abandonment. Her defiance evaporates and her voice becomes almost inaudible. I have to repeat her words so that others can hear. To my right, the social worker draws her chair nearer. Brianna chooses one of the three actors to play herself in the story. The actors and I know that we need to be very careful in this enactment—to embody her story accurately enough that it is meaningful to the teller, without overwhelming her. Brianna has chosen to tell her story tonight. She has judged that this is a safe place and time to reveal not only her AIDS status but also how she was desperately wronged by her brother and her family. Despite her agency, however, she is still vulnerable and fragile.

Accompanied by quiet keyboard chords, the actors begin the enactment. They depict the violence with the slightest of movements, a far from literal portrayal. Even so, it's too much for the teller. She lowers her head, unable to watch. I call out for the actors to pause so that I can check in with her. Would she like us to stop? No, Brianna says, she wants to see her story. But it's hard. With her agreement we decide to continue with a series of short forms embodying feelings, not characters or events. Brianna watches this time, tears falling, her hand gripping mine, but nodding in assent. The actors pause and look toward her, as they always do at the completion of a scene. Brianna nods again and lets out a breath. Then she faces the women in the audience, several of whom are also in tears. "But I want to say, look, here I am, they didn't kill me," she says. The audience breaks into loud applause and cheers. Brianna goes back to her chair. The women sitting on each side of her hug her, one after the other.

Brianna had lived with her terrible memories and their life-threatening consequences for some years. Time, if not therapeutic help, had allowed her to metabolize her traumatic experience to the point that she was ready to tell her story in front of peers, through the vehicle of the theatre that we offered. She received the affirmation that she hoped for: the other women, instead of rejecting her, showed their respect, empathy, and moral indignation at what had happened to her. Even so, the theatrical depiction of her story had to be carefully titrated, in Levine's term (2010), allowing Brianna to apprehend her story at the degree of intensity that she was able to tolerate. Every gesture by the actors, every interaction, would have its echo deep within her body and her brain. Too much could harm her. Too little would disappoint her. The correctly judged potency would help her to take another step in her journey of integration.

There was also an altruistic element to Brianna's story. In the prison community, other women looked up to her. By telling her story, she challenged the stigma that clung to HIV/AIDS, lightening the burden of others who were afraid to reveal they were infected.

Stories of natural disasters

Playback Theatre teams have sought to support communities coping with trauma following the 2005 tsunami in southern India, Hurricane Katrina in New Orleans, the earthquake and tsunami in Fukushima, Japan, and other natural disasters. Though each event is different, disaster-related trauma has characteristics that are distinct from other kinds of trauma, even other collective trauma. Natural disasters happen with little or no warning. They disrupt the previously normal lives of vast numbers of people, sometimes with hundreds or thousands of casualties. The immediate crisis itself is time-limited—a matter of hours or days, though chaotic and life-threatening consequences may last for years.

Playback post-disaster teams have sometimes been composed of people who are themselves part of the affected community (as was the case in India and New Orleans). In other situations the team has come from outside the disaster area but is culturally congruent (as in Japan after Fukushima). NOLA Playback Theatre—NOLA stands for New Orleans, Louisiana—was born in the aftermath of Katrina:

> A little over seven months after the "levee breaks" disaster of August 2005 and two months into the life of our com- pany, NOLA Playback Theatre performed at a popular New Orleans theatre festival…. I was still living out of our emer- gency trailer fifty miles north of our flooded home with my husband, toddler, baby, two rescued cats and the contents of our attic…. I opened the event by asking for a show of hands as to who was back in their homes and who was still living out of a FEMA trailer or somewhere else. Most of the room was still displaced…. (Juge Fox, 2013, p. 22)

When the Playback team is based elsewhere, it is necessary to develop relationships with the people in the disaster region, networking and communicating over time until there is a trusting partnership that can work together on this most sensitive of proj- ects. In the absence of such patiently developed relationships, a well-intentioned Playback team runs the risk of parachuting in on a rescue mission and possibly creating harm rather than healing, or—more likely—failing to have any impact at all when the hoped- for audience simply does not show up.

Following Fukushima, the Yokohama-based company PlaybackAZ wanted to offer Playback Theatre to survivors in the ravaged area, 700 kilometers away. They knew they needed a local partner, but months went by without finding the right connections. They gave up the idea of visiting and instead offered fundraising performances and events for volunteers returning from Tohoku (Munakata, 2013). They also used this time to educate themselves about collective trauma following a natural disaster, as well as learning the specific details of the Fukushima disaster, a complex event that included a major earthquake, a devastating tsunami, and the deadly release of radiation from the nuclear power plant.

Eventually, a man with connections to Tohoku came to one of their performances for volunteers and saw the potential for his community. Eighteen months after the earthquake, a group of four company members made their way to Tohoku. They stayed for three days and carried out four performances for volunteer helpers and local people. Kayo Munakata describes a story told by an old woman in one of the shows:

> A [childhood] story about school excursion. Mothers used to make big rice balls for their lunch. A friend of the teller dropped her rice ball and she lost all her lunch. So the teller shared her rice ball. She gave half of it.
>
> It was just a small story.
>
> But it apparently reflected their sudden tragedy and a spirit of friendship and of supporting one another. (Munakata, 2013, p. 21)

With the performers' sensitive, aesthetic reflections and their acceptance of whatever stories were offered, the atmosphere deepened. Later in the show another elderly woman told a story about her losses in the tragedy, releasing intense emotion—her own and the audience's—and a flow of further stories.

This Playback team was open to whatever stories the audience members chose to tell, whether addressing the disaster directly or in metaphor, or even recalling apparently unrelated experiences. A key principle in Playback Theatre is emergence. The stories are not curated. If we have established an atmosphere of respect, authenticity, and inclusivity, we trust that the stories offered are the stories that need to be told and will contribute organically to the overall tapestry of the event. This is the process now known as narrative reticulation where stories weave together to create meaning that transcends any individual story.[2] A story that seems slight, indirect, or even humorous—dropping one's lunch on the ground; the comical annoyance

2. See Chapter 12, "The Theory of Narrative Reticulation."

of hitting a pothole on a New Orleans street—are nevertheless playing their part in allowing a traumatized community to feel its connections, its strength of history, its pain, and its resilience.

Stories of political oppression

Political oppression inevitably creates trauma, tragically common in today's world, with millions of people affected by war, terrorism, extreme poverty, and climate change. Playback Theatre teams have sought to support groups of refugees or displaced persons in the UK, the Netherlands, Germany, Angola, and elsewhere (Glover et al, 2016; Salas, 2011). Such groups face the same responsibilities as in post-natural disaster interventions of building relationships and cultural congruence before attempting to enact stories. Political awareness and analysis become essential preparation.

Wasl, a Playback Theatre group in Lebanon, provides performances to traumatized communities including Syrian refugees (one person in four in Lebanon is a refugee), victims of human trafficking, and young men whose poverty made them vulnerable to being recruited by ISIS:

> We had a big project, 16 performances, within a closed community, more of a ghetto, that is considered the main pool of Lebanese fighters for ISIS in Syria and Iraq. [After a show where grieving mothers told their stories] a very silent guy who usually attended the shows but never shared came to us to thank us. The next day the organizer of this project from the same area gave us a call to thank us, telling that the guy who came to greet us and a few of his friends who were supposed to join the war in a few days, decided after hearing and watching the stories of the two mothers that they would rather be in prison than leave their loved ones with such pain and sadness. So they went to the military and delivered themselves. In prison their recruiters couldn't reach them so they were safe and alive. (Wardani, 2018, email communication).

This work is extremely challenging for the performers, who feel under threat because of their insistence on foregrounding the voices of victims of war rather than those of so-called martyrs and heroes. Emotional strain and vicarious traumatization are risks for any Playback ensemble working in situations of intense crisis. As well as self-education about history and context, groups must also strengthen themselves emotionally by telling their own stories in the safety of a rehearsal, giving each other generous support, finding effective ways of relieving tension, getting outside support if needed, and taking care not to commit to more performances than they can sustain.

During Hudson River Playback Theatre's eight-year series of bilingual performances for immigrants in upstate New York, stories of life-threatening danger, loss, and suffering, told with intense emotion, were common (Salas, 2008). Many audience members had fled dead-end poverty and often violence in hopes of building something better for their children. Some had come close to death crossing river and desert. Women had been raped. Children had been taken from parents, close relatives lost. Living in the United States, their hardship was not over: they now faced discrimination, isolation, separation from extended families, and the threat of deportation.

Participants seemed impelled to tell border-crossing stories and wept as they watched their stories brought to life. Often the audience wept with them. "It makes us sad to remember, but happy to see it," said one woman. Their stories were public testimonies— to each other, to their children who were often present, and to those who represented the majority culture, sometimes just the Playback team, sometimes other members of the community as well. The immigrants testified to their hardship, to their vision, courage, and resilience, and to their identity as the newest community of immigrants in a nation of immigrants.[3]

Such trauma stories, as in other contexts of political oppression, are not simply expressions of individual suffering. The teller "speaks not only for personal salvation—they speak with political intent" (Rivers, 2013, p. 15). Citing research indicating that potentially traumatizing events are far less likely to lead to PTSD when survivors "interpret their experience through a strong ideological framework"

---

3. See Chapter 20, "Immigrant Stories in the Hudson Valley."

(2013, p. 16), Rivers describes how Playback Theatre supports this kind of positive framing:

> Playback Theatre with its inbuilt potential for consciousness rais-ing, meaning-making and community mobilization, holds promis-ing possibilities for the reinforcement of certain protective factors. When a teller shares their account and sees it enacted within a communal setting, the teller is able to establish a sense of coher-ence around their experience—especially where their story is framed within the broader context of civil resistance. (2013, p. 16)

It is also essential to remember that all lives, even those of peo-ple in extreme suffering, contain love, beauty, triumph, and humor. A critic claimed that stories about "good" aspects of life showed "avoidance" behavior (Rivers, 2013, p. 16). On the contrary, such stories are a sign of resilience and a Playback performance should embrace them, for the audience's sake and for their own. Farah Wardani (2018) in Lebanon also writes about enacting joyful, affirming stories, like preparing for a traditional wedding or cel-ebrating success at school. And the ensemble often invites tellers to imagine a more hopeful future, enacting those images as well.

Trauma stories in therapeutic settings

In therapeutic settings, Playback Theatre's collective and per-formative nature lends itself best to the later stages of trauma recovery. When survivors are ready to share their story with oth-ers, the contained ritual of Playback can provide a welcoming space. For example, Playback Theatre in a residential treatment center gave traumatized children a chance to reveal some of their stories to peers, mitigating isolation and prompting empathy:

> Sharelle had been in one of the Playback therapy groups for several weeks. In the fifth session she told about a memory from when she was two years old. Finding her playing alone outside on the porch, her stepfather had picked her up and dangled her over the railings, chuckling as she screamed in terror for her mother inside. The mother didn't come, either not hearing or not caring.

I asked Prue [co-leader] to play Sharelle's stepfather. Sharelle chose waif-like Aimee to play herself and Olly to be her mother. To my surprise, Olly agreed readily to this cross-gender role. He was a quiet boy, self-conscious about a bad stammer. They acted it out. I could see Olly struggling with the desire to come and help Aimee/Sharelle as she screamed in fear. But he stayed true to the story.

"Yeah," said Sharelle when they'd finished. "Felt like that."

Watching the story was freckle-faced Herman . . . . "I wish the mom had come out and helped her," he said, his hands pressed to his throat as always when he spoke. "I felt bad for Sharelle." I hadn't heard this kind of expression of pity and identification from him before (Salas, 2007, p. 113)

Our staff team carried out both classroom performances and therapy groups, where children enacted stories for each other. The worst abuses that these children had suffered, including sexual victimization, extreme violence, even torture, did not emerge in Playback Theatre. Most could not yet speak of those horrors even in the privacy of a one-to-one session with a psychologist. They instinctively knew which stories could be told in Playback, and which could not. On one occasion, this judgment broke down. A child dealing with a very recent trauma offered it as a story in a classroom performance: his young uncle had been murdered just weeks earlier. Mayhem ensued. For other children in the room, the topic was far too raw. Thanks to quick-thinking teamwork we were able to recover the situation, but it was a lesson in the danger of trying to enact a story that is not yet ready to be a testimony, in the presence of others watching with their own traumatized eyes (Salas, 2007).

Unexpected trauma stories

Trauma is a part of life and may come up in any Playback Theatre event including public performances, though more likely in a training workshop where participants are together for several days. As practitioners, we need to recognize the signs of a trauma story, usually signaled by the content and the intensity of emotion. We need to understand that this story is being told as "a transition toward the judicial, public aspect of testimony" (Herman, 1992, p. 221). We have to attend to not only the teller's wellbeing, but also that of the audience and the performers. Advanced training in Playback Theatre now includes attention to dealing with trauma both in these occasional stories and in collective trauma situations.

Ideally, we are alert also to a wider story: even the most personal story takes place in a societal context. It may be relevant—and healing—to reflect that reality in the enactment, whether it is the prevalence of domestic abuse, the harms of racism or poverty, or the ravages of addiction. Although a teller may focus only on her family tragedy as she speaks about her addicted son, those listening, including the performing team, are also thinking of the current opioid epidemic. It is appropriate and constructive to depict that awareness in the enactment.

Conclusion

Playback Theatre's inherent aspects of collective storytelling, embodied and artistic distillation, and the call to the imagination can help transform painful, overwhelming memories into meaningful stories that survivors can tell to themselves and to others. It can allow suffering individuals and communities to reclaim their humanity and their hope.

In the public or semi-public settings that are Playback's most common context, practitioners do not need to be therapists. However, they do need to be well grounded in basic Playback skills, and to be mindful of several factors including these:

The effectiveness of a Playback show for a traumatized audience depends on relationships that have been carefully developed prior to the event, especially if the team members are not part of the affected community;

Ideally, these relationships are sustained over time, as with NOLA Playback's ongoing engagement with the New Orleans community, or a Palestinian team's practice of staying in a village for several days to help with daily tasks and exchange learning (Rivers, 2013);[4]

Offering Playback too soon in the recovery process can be harmful or ineffective: both tellers and audience members need to be ready for public testimony;

Trauma stories may convey resilience and solidarity alongside personal pain and need not be pathologized;

With an audience that has survived or is currently dealing with significant trauma, stories that might seem unrelated or "light" are in fact part of the process of asserting resilience;[5]

Using Playback's variety of forms, enactments need to be "titrated" in order not to overwhelm a teller;

Trauma stories may emerge in any Playback context.

With attention to these considerations, the Playback stage—informal, accessible, ritualized—can indeed embrace stories of trauma, contributing to individual and societal recovery.

4. See Chapter 23, "Stories by Firelight."

5. However, if a collectively traumatized audience offers no direct stories of the trauma in the course of an event, it may indicate that using Playback is premature, or that the Playback team is not sufficiently prepared to hold these stories—which the audience will unfailingly sense.

References

Glover, Kate; Mitchell, Annie; Stedmon, Jacquie; Fairlove, Alison; & Brown, Amanda. (2016). "And I felt as if I'm home you understand, with my people." *IPTN Journal*, Vol. 2 (no. 1). Retrieved from *https://www.iptn. info/?a=doc&id=362&lang=[mb_lang]*

Herman, Judith. (1992). *Trauma and Recovery: The Aftermath of Violence—from Domestic Abuse to Political Terror.* New York, NY: Basic Books.

Juge Fox, Anne-Liese. (2013). "NOLA Playback Theatre & unperforming disaster in New Orleans." In *Interplay*, Vol. 13 (no. 2), pp. 22–23.

Levine, Peter A. (2010). *In an Unspoken Voice: How the Body Releases Trauma and Restores Goodness.* Berkeley, CA: North Atlantic Books.

Munakata, Kayo. (2013). "Before You Saw a Hill Here; Now You See the Ocean: How Playback Theatre Serves Communities in Crisis." In *Interplay*, Vol. 13 (no. 2), pp. 19–21.

Rivers, Ben. (2013). "Playback Theatre, Cultural Resistance, and the Limits of Trauma Discourse." In *Interplay*, Vol. 13 (no. 2), pp. 15–18.

Salas, Jo. (2007). *Do My Story, Sing My Song: Music Therapy and Playback Theatre with Troubled Children.* New Paltz, NY: Tusitala.

Salas, Jo. (2008). "Immigrant Stories in the Hudson Valley." In Solinger, R., Fox, M., & Irani, K., (Eds), *Telling Stories to Change the World* (pp. 109–118). New York, NY: Routledge.

Salas, Jo. (2011). "Stories in the Moment: Playback Theatre for Building Community and Justice." In Cohen, C., Varea, R., & Walker, P. (Eds.), *Acting Together: Performance and the Creative Transformation of Conflict, Vol. 2* (pp. 93–123). New York, NY: New Village Press.

Van der Kolk, Bessel. (2015). *The Body Keeps the Score: Brain, Mind, and Body in the Healing of Trauma.* New York, NY: Penguin Books.

Wardani, Farah. (2018). Personal email communication.

White, Michael, & Epston, David. (1990). *Narrative Means to Therapeutic Ends.* New York, NY: W. W. Norton.

18

THE LISTENING HOUR

Jonathan Fox (2020)

EARLY IN 2020, in the midst of considering what was the best next step for the development of narrative reticulation theory,[1] Covid-19 struck. Suddenly no live Playback Theatre performances were possible. In thinking about the isolation of individuals, especially in the early days of the pandemic when most people were sheltering at home, I wondered if the experience of sharing stories, with its outcome of connection and meaning, could play a positive role in maintaining a spirit of resilience. For some time, in my thinking about the narrative reticulation (NR) theory, I had wondered how essential the Playback part was of the Playback Theatre experience—or, to put it another way, whether the outcome would be similar if personal stories were shared without artistic reflection.

Thus, as a further step in NR research, and also as a way to provide a constructive response to the deprivations of the pandemic, I created an approach called the Listening Hour, which consisted of an hour-long exchange of personal stories. The format, initially conceived especially for online experience, was very spare—five or six people telling stories for each other under the unobtrusive leadership of a guide. The guide welcomed the participants and initiated a defined but spacious structure where each person had a chance to share a personal story. There was no reflection or discussion. Each story was followed by another, until it was time to say good-bye sixty minutes later. The Listening Hour elicited immediate enthusiasm. People felt moved, connected, eased.

Although it had the feel of Playback Theatre without any

1. See Chapter 12, "The Theory of Narrative Reticulation."

enactments, it was directly based on narrative reticulation theory: it focused on *stories*, which were *emergent* and made possible by a warm, welcoming *atmosphere*, made possible and held by the *guidance* of the leader. One key feature was an artistic reprise—a selection of memorable images from the shared stories—voiced by the guide. I proposed the idea on a Playback Theatre Facebook page, to an immediately enthusiastic response. Over four hundred asked for information. Within a two-month period, after experiencing a Listening Hour as a participant, over one hundred seasoned playbackers obtained a short training in the role of the guide. These individuals immediately began to offer Listening Hours in their communities. In the first three months, guides in over forty-five countries delivered hundreds of Listening Hour sessions. Participant evaluations record an average 4.6 (out of 5) response to the question, "Did it feel worthwhile taking part?"

How to explain this response? In the pandemic crisis, Listening Hour participants reported feeling relieved. A retiree from Germany said: "I felt good and amazingly connected." An Indian program manager commented: "Yes, it was very positive and made me feel much lighter than how I had entered the session." A set designer from Russia wrote: "The Listening Hour was an entry into a dream space, where you can meet people, speak, listen and make your world reach wide." Many participants reported a feeling of excitement when from their own position of enforced isolation, they had the chance to be part of a story circle whose participants spanned the globe. Such international exchanges were only made possible by the expansion of online meeting platforms where people could hear and see each other through their computers.

Aided by the ease of online meetings, the pandemic has stimulated Playback practitioners to develop new approaches to performing, as can be seen by the many offerings publicized on Facebook. At the same time, the Listening Hour has also appealed as an alternative way for playbackers to stay in touch without the inevitable limitations of attempting ensemble theatre online when the performers are not actually in the same space.

Apart from the deprivations caused by Covid-19, the Listening

Hour offers an experience in narrative communication that may carry its own restorative power. A professor from South Africa wrote: "The method heightens our abilities to tell stories that are held by image, by descriptive word, by spoken word and silence... The relief of images, metaphors in the making of folklore was deeply felt. Something bigger could hold us; something imaged could cushion our hard realities."

Despite the absence of a theatrical enactment, it would appear that the Listening Hour provides an experience of connection and meaning similar to Playback Theatre. Investigation of the level and quality of narrative reticulation in the Listening Hour remains a study for the future and needs to be compared to research that assesses NR in Playback Theatre events. One advantage of the Listening Hour over Playback Theatre for research is that it is spatially contained and easy to record, providing ample material for analysis. At first glance it is clear that the stories shared by participants in the Listening Hour are interconnected in complex ways, and we can hypothesize that this "web" plays a part in their feeling of meaning and connection.

Two questions of immediate interest are whether the Listening Hour will appeal to those without a Playback background and whether it will take hold in live as well as virtual settings.

We have preliminary results on the first question: to date 48% of the Listening Hour participants have been without a PT background (based on information from the guides' self-evaluation question-naires), proof that guides are not hesitating to offer it to their non-PT friends and colleagues. It is too early to have an answer to the second question, although the Listening Hour has already been engaged by organizations and in at least one live setting.

The prospect of organizational interest raises the intriguing question of whether narrative reticulation theory has utility in assessing narratives of groups of tellers (where before we used it only to assess the competence of Playback performers). Could an NR analysis of stories shared and the relative strength of interconnec-tions between them reveal useful information about organizational culture? Such a prospect raises ethical questions about how the information is collected and used, especially since the stories are personal. However, from this vantage point it seems not impossible for the Listening Hour, in addition to offering the benefits of narrative communication, to become a method for identifying the character and concerns of communities.

One final thought: if the Listening Hour does succeed in taking hold in live settings beyond the Playback community, it may have the potential to be a breakthrough development, gaining acceptance for narrative communication in social institutions which would never hire a theatre company, no matter how constructive the purpose.

PART 3

STORIES FROM THE FIELD

19

BURUNDI JOURNAL[1]

Jonathan Fox (2003)

10 MARCH 2003. Departure day minus one—making last calls, transferring phone numbers into my pocket organizer, trying to decide whether to take my mobile phone (will it work in Africa?), sending a last email to my colleague, Karin, in Switzerland.[2]

Friends have urged me not to go because of the danger there. I have not been swayed. Nor am I intimidated by those who argue for staying at home because of the perilous world situation.[3]

But I am worried about the news that we will be holding the training in Ngozi, a provincial town close to the Rwandan border. A year and a half ago I worked in Bujumbura, the capital, which is protected by the army. I know nothing of Ngozi, but I know the rebel groups operate from the hills.

At Heathrow Airport Karin and I meet up, take a cappuccino before the long flight to Africa. Her Playback group is at the same moment sitting in a Zurich restaurant after their rehearsal; by telephone Karin and her colleagues exchange fond last words. We are off to teach as part of the School of Playback Theatre's Libra Project.[4]

The clouds break to reveal the green hills, a swath of Lake Tanganyika. The air on the tarmac is tropical. We see banana

1. First published in *Interplay*, newsletter of the International Playback Theatre Network, III (3): 12–13 (May 2003).

2. Karin Gisler is the founder and director of Playback Theater Zürich.

3. The US was on the brink of invading Iraq, despite worldwide opposition.

4. The Libra project sought to deliver Playback Theatre in equitable ways around the world.

trees, hear a magpie's liquid call. In the jeep, I tell the chic office manager, Nadine, in French (the colonial language of Burundi), that I am happy to be back. She answers, "Why?" I am suddenly nonplussed, not sure how to respond.

A day later in Ngozi, a one-road bustling town, we stand on a hotel terrace looking out over a lush valley. In the foreground people walk along the red-dirt road with loads on their heads. A few bicycles go by, even fewer vehicles. A solid fence, with a heavy gate that locks at night, secures the hotel. Inside the flowers are beautifully kept by three gardeners.

Pulcherine, one of my students from the initial training in '01, greets me. "Our prayers are answered," she says, enfolding me in her arms. Later, when I question the members of the Tubiyage Theatre Association I am impressed to hear how much they have done. "Many Playback Theatre performances," they say. "How many?" I ask. They are not sure. I ask Michel Ange, the leader, for a list.

Their questions are those of experienced playbackers. They tell me that their problem is too many audience members wanting to tell. That is the best kind of problem, I say. They tell me a story: In a performance a widower told about his struggle to raise his kids alone and his subsequently inviting a woman to live with them, even though she was not his wife and the arrangement was not sanctioned by the authorities. Seeing the story enacted, he broke down. How he cried! the students say. Afterwards, an audience member, who happened to be the civil administrator responsible, stood up and said he did not realize how difficult life had been for the teller and his family, and if he would come to the office, the administrator would fix everything at once.

The actors tell me that they usually perform Forum Theatre (Theatre of the Oppressed) for the first half, and Playback Theatre for the second. But they gently complain about the time needed to prepare the pieces for the Forum Theatre, and admit that not infrequently their choices miss with the audience. Playback Theatre, they say, by definition, always meets the interests of the audience.

We start the work, twenty-seven students in a cement room. Many faces at the windows looking in at us. Noise from all sides.

In the training there are two main subgroups: the experienced students from Bujumbura, most of them university educated and with acting backgrounds; and students from the Ngozi region, who have received a one-week training from Michel Ange. Most of these students do not speak French, and so we translate everything from French to Kirundi.

The sponsoring organization supplies lunch, plentiful helpings of rice, beans, fried bananas, with some meat. The meal is a necessary component of the training. Outside the fence, hungry eyes watch us eat. I am embarrassed. Each day one student or another arranges for a few to be called in and given the leftovers. How kind they are to those with less than they; and how different from our attitude in the West.

On the second day, with our encouragement, Vital brings his guitar. He plays it proudly, but it is so old and with strings so stretched that it cannot be tuned. He has brought it from his village, a two-hour walk away. We stop each day at four in the afternoon so that he and others can get home safely before dark.

During the long evenings we sit with the students, talk among ourselves, look out from our terrace at the rice-covered valley. Karin serves me slices of papaya and pineapple she has bought at the market. It is peaceful in Ngozi. Time moves like the people on the road, one slow step at a time. At night among friends, there is almost always the singing of long, freely improvised call-and-response songs.

In the first nights, sleepless from time change and excitement, I lay awake fearing the pop of rebel guns. Thoughts of Burundi's long civil war, called "la crise" by the inhabitants, mix with images of American soldiers pointing weapons towards Baghdad. The nighttime closes in on me.

During our Playback practice, the stories in the whole group feature love and marriage, but when we set exercises in small groups, we can see much violent action. It is in a group of four that Bernard tells his story of trying to escape to Rwanda during a particular difficult period, but being attacked by Burundian soldiers, who beat him so badly he was left for dead.

I work with the experienced actors on portraying violence, urging them to slow down and not fall into the almost slapstick mode that is their habit. I also give them theory about how Playback can transform traumatic memory into narrative memory, crucial to the healing process.

On my own at night I dream of war. At dawn, roosters, then the sun rising over the valley.

We have to move workspaces, make many adjustments. I do not know if I will ever get my list of Tubiyage performances: Michel Ange has said that he will type it up for me, but the office does not have much equipment, and after the first training, when I had tried to maintain email communication with Michel Ange, my messages from the US had bounced back.

We arrange four performances for the students: at the university; in a village hall; at the local office of CARE, one of the sponsoring NGO's; and for a small group of women attached to a women's center. This last performance is an effort to create an intimate enough setting for the students to tackle serious stories.

The intimate performance takes place on the day the US invades Iraq. I am very upset. The first two-thirds of the performance follows a classic pattern of tellers recounting their everyday stories: two mothers tell proud stories about the birth and raising of their children. Then one of our students, sitting in the audience, raises his hand urgently. He is called Baptiste. His story is about the death of his mother when he was twelve.

I am moved, for here is the red thread operating at its most profound: after the mother's perspective, a story from a child; after stories of endurance and joy, a story of great loss. I am also moved because I am feeling at this moment that Playback Theatre can be a source of good in the world, opposing violence and war.

But the actors do Baptiste's story as a tableau, avoiding its tragedy. They are afraid, I think. Baptiste is polite and does not express disappointment. The next teller tells a long tale about war, betrayal, and forgiveness, but it is hard to make sense of, because by not fulfilling Baptiste's story, the red thread is broken.

The next day, in the performance at CARE headquarters, Baptiste is again in the audience; again he becomes the teller, and with the same story. Again, the actors—a different set, who had not been present the day before—chose to do it as a tableau. This time Baptiste looks crestfallen.

We are coming to the end. The actors have completed their performances, marking the challenge and excitement of the first time for the Ngozi group, and the chance for feedback for the experienced group.

All that remains is evaluation and our last lunch together. And before that a final morning's work. I keep thinking of Baptiste. I invite him to tell his story once more. We coach the actors on how to do it. They perform courageously. The audience response is unexpected, however. About fifteen seconds into the interview, some people begin to cry. After two minutes, two have left the room. There is such distress that after the enactment I suggest a kind of transformation. It is not for the teller; Baptiste, finally, has that look of relaxation that comes after one has really seen one's story portrayed well. Rather the transformation ("Tell us about a happy moment between you and your mother, any moment you remember.") is for the audience. We also do a series of fluid sculptures. Many different feelings are expressed, including "I never feel a thing, including now."

I have given Baptiste during the interview my big bandana handkerchief to wipe his eyes. When the whole process is over, he returns it to me, but I push his hand back. "Keep it," I say, "on behalf of Tubiyage. Call it la Mouchoir des Larmes [handkerchief of tears], and lend it to the tellers when they tell their stories."

Michel Ange comes to me on the last day with a printed list of Tubiyage performances. The total is 72. We are all amazed. The audiences are students, staffs, the public at large. Many NGO's have hired them, including CARE, Search for Common Ground, the Norwegian Refugee Council.

The answer to Nadine's question, Why be happy to return to Burundi? is now clear to me. Of course I am glad to return just to learn this news about Playback Theatre. The idea of Playback

Theatre in Africa, especially devoted to tasks of reconciliation, had seemed "experimental" up to the time of this trip. But this list speaks of great promise for it. Furthermore, one is always glad to see again the lovely people one has once farewelled forever. Finally, I am glad to find myself again in the slow pace and human scale of traditional culture. It is a most complicated subject, of course. We cannot turn our backs on modernity. But the soul cries out for more singing and more walking, nonetheless.

Karin and I will board our plane back to Nairobi and then to our separate countries with many questions. In a county with so many wounds and such an urge to tell, can Playback actors hold the ritual event? What kind of performance is best for a place like Burundi, so factionalized by ethnicity and loss? In a world of limited time and money, exactly what support do the Playback teams need? These are questions, of course, facing not only the Tubiyage actors, but Playback Theatre actors everywhere.

On the last evening, we say our good-byes. This time, with so much Playback success behind us, we are not so afraid of never seeing each other again. So many handshakes, so many hugs. In the tumult, Baptiste approaches me. He says it soft and quick. "I'll try to keep it well," he says, "our Mouchoir des Larmes."

20

IMMIGRANT STORIES IN THE HUDSON VALLEY[1]

Jo Salas (2008)

JORGE: Every story you hear is inside of you. When you leave home, you never know what's going to happen, you don't know if you're going to make it, you don't know if you're going to see someone again. There could be a happy ending. There could be no ending.

MANUELA: I want to tell everyone that we all came here to work, but not to hurt anybody. We came here for a better life for our families.[2]

The Immigrant Stories project[3]

The Immigrant Stories project is an ongoing series of interactive, bilingual theatre performances with audiences of immigrants from Mexico, Colombia, Puerto Rico, Peru, Argentina, Ecuador, Belize, Paraguay, Guatemala, and the Dominican Republic. All live in the Mid-Hudson Valley of New York, a semi-rural region that has seen successive waves of immigration since the first Dutch and Huguenot settlers in the 1600s. Like many of their predecessors, recent immigrants have come here in desperation and hope, fleeing

1. First published in *Telling Stories to Change the World*, Eds Solinger, Fox, and Irani. New York: Routledge, 2008.
2. All names have been changed except for the three women mentioned in "Building a network."
3. Hudson River Playback Theatre carried out the Immigrant Stories project from 2006 to 2014, providing over one hundred bilingual performances for groups of immigrants in our region. The project also led to a bilingual, photo-illustrated book called *Half of My Heart/La Mitad de mi Corazón*, documenting the stories. I wrote this chapter after the first two years of the project.

poverty that is a tragic outcome of history and politics in which the United States has played a significant part—most recently, with the impact of NAFTA which has led to millions of farmers losing their land. With no way of supporting their families, it is inevitable that many people look toward the great wealth and apparent opportunities just across the border.

> OLIVIA: I came here to help my family in Mexico. In my country it was difficult, no work, nothing we could do. I came 18 years ago. This country gives me a lot and I appreciate it.

> CESAR: I wanted to come here so that I could help the ones who stayed behind.

The Playback Theatre format (used in many other contexts as well) invites audience members to tell personal stories which actors and musicians transform into theatre on the spot. It is essentially a dialogue through action—one story sparks another, directly or indirectly. The process is collaborative and co-creative: each "teller" comes to the stage to tell the story in conversation with the "conductor" or emcee, then watches as the story is enacted, giving a final comment at the end. An atmosphere of exploration and discovery develops as voices are heard and responded to in spontaneous theatre. The actors, like the tellers, step into unscripted and uncharted territory with each story.

My theatre company, Hudson River Playback Theatre, conceived the Immigrant Stories project in discussion with administrators at the local Head Start center which provides support services for a growing number of immigrant families who have children in the program. The administrators spoke of the extreme stresses that face many immigrants in our area: language barriers; poverty; isolation; distance from family of origin; the anxiety of living without legal immigration status; discrimination. As fellow community members and as an ensemble concerned with social justice, we proposed offering performances as an opportunity for public voice and as a forum in which participants could bear witness to their experience. Aware of the prevalence of stereotypes and untruths in the media, the government, and popular belief, we also hoped to foster respect and understanding on the part of non-immigrants who might attend.

Our offer was fueled by the desire to reach out to people in our midst who live in hardship, and to create change through stories. We were not at that time strongly connected to the immigrant community, nor are we ourselves Latinx—which challenged us to educate ourselves, build relationships, and find Latinx performers to join us. (In spite of developments on these fronts we continue to face such challenges, including the immediate awkwardness of writing this account without an immigrant co-author.)

With the help of Head Start staff and with funding from a local foundation, we organized twenty shows at all seven Head Start centers in Dutchess County, in playrooms, community rooms, or school gyms. Audience size ranged from ten to thirty-five. On the "stage"—not an actual stage but an open space in front of rows of folding chairs—we set up three chairs, one for the conductor, one for the translator, and one for the teller who would come to tell her story, returning to her seat in the audience after watching it enacted. Tellers told their stories in either Spanish or English, sometimes both (our team included a native Spanish speaker to translate at each show). The actors used both languages if they could (two are bilingual), as well as music, movement, and metaphor to bring the stories to life.

Non-immigrant parents and staff came to almost all the performances, listening intently and offering their own responses to the stories. Staff provided food so that people could eat and chat together before and afterwards.

Telling stories

Arriving for a show for the first time, people seemed a bit shy, a bit puzzled; and then when we explained why we were there and how this kind of theatre works, they became engaged.

Sometimes, especially with larger and Latinx-only audiences, the stories flowed. Other times there were long pauses as people decided if they wanted to speak up. Audience members laughed with recognition at some of the stories and enactments, like the time someone yelled out "Abran las fronteras!" (Open the border!) when we asked what Americans could do to make things easier for them. Often they wept over a story of danger or loss. It did not seem, as it sometimes does with other adult audiences unfamiliar with Playback, that they were wondering how to categorize this unfamiliar kind of performance. Instead, they met us directly on the terms we offered: if you want to speak, we are here to listen, and we'll do our best to reflect the meanings that are important to you. Their openness was refreshing and artistically liberating for us.

The tellers told of the complexity of their experience—the difficult choice to come, the constant weighing of whether it was worth it or not. For many immigrants the journey here is highly dangerous, even traumatic. For those who manage to get visas the expense and effort are considerable, requiring financial sacrifice and sometimes the heartbreaking decision to leave behind a child, an aging parent, or a professional identity. Once here, life is not easy, with the formidable challenges of language, low-paying jobs, anxiety about legal status, and prejudice. The routine, dispiriting suspiciousness that immigrants have traditionally encountered has been exacerbated in the post-9/11 era by attempts by the president[4] and some Congress members to foment fear about immigration, with grim consequences for undocumented immigrants. Most immigrants suffer at being far away from their extended families, especially at times of illness or death. On the other hand, people spoke frequently of their satisfaction and gratitude in overcoming obstacles and bringing dreams to fruition—in particular, the dream of education for their children.

The following fragments from different shows were each followed by improvised action and music, some brief and dance-like while others became longer scenes with characters and dialogue:

> MAYA: I left everything behind that I had worked so hard for, to come here with my husband. I now work as a cleaner. It is hard work, and it is not the work I want to be doing. I'm always thinking about the work that I did in my country, as a special ed teacher, and I hope some day to return to that kind of work.

4. The US president at the time of writing was George W. Bush.

PABLO: We were six of us crossing. During the entire night we could not do it because it was very controlled. We were waiting for dawn and were going to try it during the day, according to what the man who was helping us told us. Some policemen were watching us from a mountain, and they told us, "Come on up!" And we told them "No, you come down!" We weren't going to go up and if the policemen came down, what would happen to us?

FIDELA: When we get here the first problem is the language. All the jobs require you speak English. And we don't know how to talk with our children's teachers at school.

RENATA: I want to say that everything that happened to me back then was worth it. I'm happily married, I have my three kids, and I'm happy. At first I wanted to work in a nursing home. I went to school to become a certified nursing assistant and then I worked in a nursing home for eleven years. About six years ago I started my business. My children are teenagers. I hope they're learning from me what I learned from my parents.

BARBARA: My husband has to work at least 12 hours a day in two different jobs. He's had to endure a lot of humiliation from his bosses. I've tried to look for work in a lot of different places, but unfortunately I can't get a job because of the language.

JULIA: My son applied to all the universities. I'll never ever forget when he received the letter saying he was accepted. We are so happy now that he's actually in college. It's because of my husband, who worked so hard.

SERAFINA: I am sad because I don't see my family. Years pass without seeing them. When my father died I couldn't go.

In a Playback show, stories are received with full, respectful attention and minimal interruption, and then enacted with artistry. Tellers in all contexts frequently respond to this unusual atmosphere by telling something from their lives that is of great significance to them. The invoking of a heightened, aesthetic ritual allows stories of considerable sensitivity and pain to be told safely. Immigrant tellers spoke very openly of painful or tender memories. Other audience members, watching stories that often paralleled their own experiences, appeared riveted. We could not escape the sense that these stories constituted a new myth of immigration, as yet unintegrated into the layered national mythology of immigration, but readily recognized and embraced by the immigrant audiences.

Who were Serafina and Pablo and the other speakers telling their stories *to*? It's possible that they were addressing us, the visiting performers, as representatives of the powerful majority-culture world which, in their experience, is often uncomprehending, ignorant, and contemptuous.

It is also possible, and likely, that to some degree the tellers were addressing non-immigrant parents and staff for the same reason, although the range of content of their stories did not seem to depend on whether there were non-immigrants in the audience or not.

From what some participants have told us in later conversations, they were also telling their stories to each other, to their fellow-immigrants, friends, and family members—making use of Playback Theatre's form of public storytelling with its inherent extension of resonance and meaning, which renders it quite different from private, conversational storytelling.

Humans are storytelling beings: we make sense of our individual and collective experience by the stories we tell. So we can assume that in this sense the tellers were also telling their stories to themselves. Personal storytelling is also, for any of us, an act of claiming identity and affirming meaning by saying, "This happened to me, this is what I lived and witnessed."

Border-crossing stories

Stories of crossing the border, intensely emotional in the telling and enacting, emerged in almost every one of the Head Start shows and continue to do so in the varied settings where we now perform. We do not specifically invite stories on this topic—our questions to the audience are deliberately open-ended and non-prescriptive throughout the show. In some situations we even try to divert border-crossing stories, when we are not sure of who is in the audience and if it is wise to divulge a teller's undocumented entry to the US. The tellers' paramount urgency to tell these stories speaks of the extreme trauma they have undergone: risking life, risking violence, enduring forced separation from loved ones including children, who sometimes have to be smuggled in separately. Some tell of beloved friends or relatives who've been lost in the attempt to cross:

> CONSUELO: My brother called us when he was almost at the border. The following day the people waiting for him called to tell us he hadn't shown up. He was lost. To this day we don't know where he is or if he is dead or alive. He was my real brother, my only real sibling. For me it was very horrible not knowing. I keep thinking that I see him, but it's just people who look like him, the way they walk and their mannerisms.

Here is part of a story told by Lucia, who escaped to the US as a young teenager after being raped and becoming pregnant. Her husband and younger children were in the audience. She spoke in English, occasionally asking the translator for help.

> When I was waiting in the line to cross the border, I felt so terrible. I was one of three women with all those men, and you see the helicopters above you. We had to run and then cross the river, and pay those men, and if you don't pay those men, they force you to stay. We had to cross over farms with dogs barking and men with guns. I held my breath so I could hear if anyone was behind me. I ran and ran and tried not to breathe so no one would hear me. When at last we finished crossing I was the only woman who made it across. I went for two days without eating and I was so hungry. Looking back, I know it was because I was pregnant. Finally some men came and picked us up. They brought us two hot dogs for each person and a bottle of water, and oh god, this is what I wanted! I ate everything with one bite.
>
> They put us in a place with a lot of other people, no shower, just tortillas to eat, and we waited there, and then my brother

called. They gave me clean clothes and put me on an airplane. When I got here a taxi was waiting. It was like a dream. When I finally saw my brother, I felt so happy, I hugged him and he hugged me. I started to explain everything. I almost told him what happened with the boy in Mexico, but I was so afraid. I didn't tell anybody.

Lucia's long story was one of the most dramatic and moving I've ever heard in over thirty years of doing Playback Theatre. She seemed determined to tell it, in spite of being overwhelmed by emotion at various points. Her small daughter came to comfort her, seeing her mother's tears. The actors said later that as this delicate and detailed story unfolded they were worried about remembering all its parts, but in fact they captured it beautifully in action. Lucia nodded and smiled after it was over, still tearful but apparently content.

Almost a year after this show I asked Lucia what it had been like to tell the story, and how she has felt since then about having told it.

"I didn't plan to tell my story—it was suddenly just there," said Lucia, remembering. "There was much more that I could have told, but I didn't want to take more time. My husband was there. I hadn't told him what had happened to me—about how I came here. We don't tell each other everything. After that evening he was very quiet for about a week. Then he told me he was happy I'd told the story, he was very proud of me, and he loved me.

"I felt good that I'd told the story and I still feel good. I feel relieved now about those things that I told. The untold parts are still painful. After my children grow up I'd like to write the whole story so they can understand."

Other tellers of border-crossing stories have indicated a similar relief, consistent with the findings of trauma research that those who have undergone trauma feel a compulsion to tell their story, and that this telling is essential for healing to take place.[5]

---

5. See Chapter 17, "Enacting Testimony: Trauma Stories in Playback Theatre."

Making a book

The audience at our first show had spoken of their desire for their stories to be heard widely, which encouraged us to move ahead with the idea of a photo-illustrated book of transcribed stories. We audiotaped most of the performances. A photographer attended three shows and came with me to take photos at the homes of two families.

As we worked on the book I met with several groups of immigrant parents to find out what hopes, concerns, and suggestions they might have about it. I brought an early draft to each meeting and they passed it around with interest. Their comments emphasized, above all, their passionate desire to let non-immigrants know who they are and why they are here. Looking up from the pages in her hand, one woman said, softly and intently: "We want them to know that we are not bad people," a poignant indication of the dismissive and disrespectful attitude that she meets.

She and other parents also saw the book as a valuable means of letting their own children and their far-away families know what they have gone through. Another woman, with nods of agreement from others, stressed that the book should include success stories. They did not express concern about being identified by the stories or photos. (In the published book, *Half of My Heart/ La Mitad de Mi Corazón*, all names have been changed and photos are positioned separately from stories told by the individuals they depict. Those whose photos appear gave written permission.)

With non-immigrant readers in mind we included a section called "Myths and Facts," drawn with permission from the National Immigration Forum and challenging some of the ubiquitous untruths that bolster anti-immigrant sentiments.

I visited Renata, who had told a story about coming here as a young undocumented immigrant twenty years ago. I wanted to show her the written version of what she'd told, in Spanish and English. "I'm proud of my story," Renata said after looking it over. "Please use it, and the photos. You don't even need to change my name."

We sat for a while in the small restaurant that she owns while she talked heatedly about the ignorance she often encounters. She mentioned an Anglo customer who'd recently traveled to Mexico as a tourist. "It's so beautiful there!" the woman had gushed. "Why did you want to come here?"

"I told her that I came here for the same reason that she came back here herself when her own dollars finally ran out—because this is where the money is."

Renata's anger was shared by others I spoke to and informed their desire to make the book available to non-immigrants. We all hoped that readers would respond the way non-immigrant audience members typically responded during the shows, with increased understanding and respect:

> VALERIE: I came to a greater understanding of what immigrant life is like. It's really touched my heart and it's given me some ideas of things I can do for this community as an American, and as a deacon in my church.

> GAIL: A lot of time people don't have a chance to hear these stories—it's good to have a chance to see these stories, and it's very emotional for me.

Building a network

The asymmetry of carrying out this project as a non-Latinx ensemble has been a drawback and has no doubt felt awkward to the immigrant participants as well. We have tried to address this question in various ways. By now, the third year of the project, a growing number of immigrants are becoming involved as performers, interpreters, consultants, and creative collaborators. Local Spanish-language journalists have taken an interest in the project. Several Hispanic community leaders offer support, networking, and advice.

One of the first to be involved beyond attending shows and telling a story was Adriana, a Head Start parent from Colombia. Adriana assisted with the production of the book by transcribing stories told in Spanish and then writing a foreword:

Collaborating in this project has touched my personal life because I find myself far from my parents, my family, my best
friends, and my "other half," my daughter Natalia, who is in my
country…. These stories touch soul and heart and they give me
a lot of strength and courage to keep going forward and fulfill
all my goals.[6]

Once the book was published we began to include readings in
performances, as a warm-up to stories from our new audiences.
Adriana became a reader, as have several other participants in both
the original and subsequent series of shows. Liliana, a Peruvian
immigrant and Head Start center director, read stories in a show, as
well as consulting with me on a number of aspects of the project.
Leticia, a young woman from Mexico, came to a show and told
her story about crossing the border. Six months later, at the second
show in that venue, she told a story about recently getting her green
card, describing her pride and satisfaction but also her deep sorrow
at the fate of recent deportees. At the third she was on stage with
us as a paid performer, reading a story from the book.

The current phase of the project includes a collaboration with
the Youth Arts Group of a local advocacy and support organization, Rural and Migrant Ministry. YAG, as it is called, is composed
of Hispanic and African American teenagers who use the arts
to promote social justice. Two-thirds of them are the bilingual
children of immigrants. They learned to do Playback Theatre in
a series of training workshops and they now join us as actors in
performances. Playback Theatre as a technique has become part
of YAG's repertoire of skills: they feel empowered to use it in their
own work, separate from our project.

There is much further to go in building a broader and stronger
network with the local immigrant community. For myself, being
white and non-Spanish-speaking, it is not always easy to make
initial contact with key community members. The other HRPT
members and I share a commitment to acquiring language skills,

6. Adriana Piedrahita, Foreword to *Half of My Heart/La Mitad de Mi Corazón*. New Paltz,
NY: Tusitala Publishing, 2008.

building relationships, and continuing to educate ourselves about the complex and changing realities of immigration.

The future

As the project has evolved we have recognized both the need and the opportunity to ally the work more directly with the quest for immigrants' rights. The shows themselves are a form of activism: telling one's story is a crucial step in claiming recognition and justice, and having one's story heard and comprehended by majority-culture members is another. We hope to go further. We are now in dialogue with immigrant rights activists about linking the project with other local initiatives. We are also exploring how to bring the impact of the stories to much larger audiences without endangering undocumented tellers, perhaps by creating a scripted piece based on their stories, with the participation of immigrant collaborators and performers.

The Immigrant Stories project has deeply affected us, the members of Hudson River Playback Theatre, as individuals and as an organization. Like the non-immigrants in our audiences, meeting our immigrant neighbors and hearing their stories have changed us. We hope that the path forward is one that we walk together.

21

PLAYBACK THEATRE IN BURUNDI: CAN THEATRE TRANSCEND THE GAP?[1]

Jonathan Fox (2009)

FROM THE AIR, flying over the rolling green hills, their color so rich and uniform, it is difficult to imagine the bloodshed that has stained the earth below—over 300,000 dead in a 30-year conflict now inching towards settlement. We are flying to Ngozi, Burundi, to conduct a training in Playback Theatre sponsored by the NGO Search for Common Ground (Search). It is 2003 and my second time to this country. My face is pressed against the window in anticipation.

This article describes the hope that enticed me onto that airplane—a hope of using theatre for trauma recovery and dialogue-building, but also the profound questions the project raised, some of them ethical in nature. By mid-2006, as I write this account, it is by no means clear if our program has been a success or what the next steps will be.

The background

A white American raised in cosmopolitan New York City, I am a founder of the theatre method being introduced to pre-dominantly rural Burundi as a conflict resolution tool. Playback Theatre has theoretical roots in the oral tradition—we use no set texts on our work—but it was born of frustration with modern conditions of elitism, alienation, and art. Could such a theatre

---

1. First published in *The Applied Theatre Reader*, Sheila Preston and Tim Prentki, Eds. London: Routledge, 2009.

approach emerging out of the ferment of American experimental theatre in the '60s have any relevance for the social conditions in Burundi, where there has been so much civil disruption and where the per capita income is $700?[2]

Playback Theatre is based on a simple idea: audience members share thoughts, feelings, memories—stories—and a team of performers enact them on the spot. Nothing is prepared beforehand. The actors and musicians come before their audiences with no memorized play; they have only with their skills at improvisation, their ability to listen deeply, and their humanity. Naturally each performance of Playback Theatre is different, depending on the audience. In the course of a Playback Theatre event, a kind of tapestry is woven of stories told and embodied on the stage. The pattern on the tapestry reflects what is important for the community, made up as it is of tellers "restorying" their experience.[3]

Our sponsoring agency in Burundi was Search for Common Ground, a conflict-resolution NGO. We were invited to Burundi to train the actors of Tubiyage, a mixed Hutu-Tutsi theatre group directed by Michel Ange Nzojibwami.[4]

In the first training (2001) the Tubiyage performers received five days of instruction in Playback Theatre. They learned the most basic short and long forms, the structure of a performance, and took part in three performances. The second training (2003) consisted of 10 days. New actors received the basic training, and the experienced actors deepened their knowledge of the Playback Theatre improvisational process, including a special focus on enacting traumatic stories. The Tubiyage actors reported that in the seventeen months between the first and second trainings, they had performed Playback Theatre seventy-two times, a high number in any setting.[5] Accustomed to utilizing Theatre of the

2. Statistic from *The World Factbook* (CIA).

3. Telling one's story in Playback Theatre is an act of conscientization. "This is the challenge of restorying: It continuously requires a creative act… to live between memory and potentiality is to live permanently in a creative space." (Lederach 2005:149)

4. See Chapter 19, "Burundi Journal."

5. See "Representations en Playback par l'association 'Tubiyage'," (2003) Report on Playback Theatre training in Burundi, March, submitted to Search for Common Ground, November 21, 2005, Appendix II.

Oppressed, the actors reported that with Playback they did not have to prepare scenarios beforehand, the themes of which, they said, in any case often failed to connect with the audiences.

Similarly, if there is no rapport between actors and audience, a Playback Theatre show will fail, because no one will want to come forward as a teller. However, in the performances I witnessed in Burundi, tellers did not hesitate to raise their hands, willingly telling stories—in the public performances mostly about family issues, and in more intimate settings, such as the training workshops, about love relationships, domestic violence, and death.

Potential

Why would Playback Theatre find a positive response from audiences in war-torn Burundi? A first reason has to do with what Judith Herman calls the transformation of experience from traumatic to narrative memory. "Remembering and telling the truth about terrible events are prerequisites both for the restoration of the social order and for the healing of individual victims," she writes. (Herman 1992:1) Playback Theatre is a gentle way of lessening social amnesia in that tellers tell only what they want to when they want to.

A second reason comes from Playback Theatre's ability to avoid oversimplifying or instrumentalizing experience. Its story approach and improvisational nature allows actors, even while bringing the essentializing focus of an aesthetic sensibility to what the teller has narrated, to capture many layers of a story.[6]

A third reason has to do with the sharing of perspectives embodied in different tellers' stories. "To be in a viable culture is to be bound in a set of connecting stories, connecting even though the stories may not represent a consensus," writes Jerome Bruner. (Bruner 1990: 96) Playback Theatre inspires such divergent yet connecting stories on a very local level.

We saw many examples of this positive process at work during our time in Burundi. In groups large and small, tellers offered

6. See Cohen, Cynthia (2005), "Creative Approaches to Reconciliation," in *The Psychology of Resolving Global Conflicts: From War to Peace*, Mari Fitzduff and Christopher E. Stout Eds. Westport, CT: Greenwood Publishing Group Inc.

stories with eagerness. The Burundian actors brought them to life on the stage with commitment and were joyous at the success of the performances. My colleague Karin Gisler and I flew home full of optimism.

Yet three years later we have almost completely lost contact with the Tubiyage theatre actors. As far as we could tell—until a recent surprising communication—they had stopped using Playback Theatre. In addition, Search for Common Ground has ceased sending us to Burundi or any other of their site countries. The Playback Theatre project appears not to have been sustained. What went wrong?

Problems and learnings

Upon reflection, there were four kinds of problems, involving transmission of the method, issues of congruence, the challenge of sustainability, and cultural differences. Below is listed each problem, followed by learnings that serve as guidance for future programs.

TRANSMISSION. Developing skills in deep listening, improvisational acting, and the kind of ensemble work necessary to capture people's stories takes time. The skills of the Playback Theatre conductor, or emcee, are even more demanding.[7] In this totally unplanned situation, anything can happen at any time, especially when the stories become serious, and the conductor must know how to hold the ritual space. At the School of Playback Theatre in New York our maximum class size is fifteen and after the basic training, consisting of about forty days of intensive classroom work over a minimum of two years, students often express a humble sense of incompletion. This is appropriate, since pursuit of Playback Theatre is in many ways like an Eastern spiritual practice, and we are always learning. Furthermore, Playback Theatre demands a very high level of maturity and integrity from its practitioners. You have to know, in brief, where your own self ends and the other begins. This is

---

7.   See Hosking, Bev & Hutt, Jenny (2005), "Playback Theatre: A Creative Resource for Reconciliation." Working paper of the Recasting Reconciliation through Culture and the Arts fellowship program, Center for Ethics, Justice & Public Life, Brandeis University, 35.

often a deeply challenging task and takes years to master. It can be especially difficult when one's moral education has been truncated by adverse social conditions.

In the context of development, however, there is pressure to transmit knowledge as efficiently and inexpensively as possible. The trainings in Burundi consisted of two short workshops more than a year apart. The participants included not only Tubiyage actors but also others the NGO wanted to bring together, and numbered over twenty-five. With such a group size, it is hard to achieve the intimacy and cohesiveness necessary for deep learning. During the second training the Tubiyage actors responded to a traumatic story with an inadequate portrayal because, despite their good will, they had not had enough training to be able to handle very serious stories. So they hid behind the short, abstract form we call a "fluid sculpture." How do we persuade Search or any other NGO, which must raise funds for each program and is under pressure to achieve positive results, to support the necessary small group work, an ongoing laboratory program of training lasting many years, and performances for small audiences? Admittedly, Playback Theatre has not yet fully proven itself as a tool for peacebuilding, but it does hold significant promise.

In developing Playback Theatre training programs for the future in regions like Burundi, I would enter into realistic talks with funding partners about expectations and results, trying to find a compromise between need for extensive exposure and support and practical concerns of time and money.[8] I would also make an effort to ally with local institutions that can offer the Playback group(s) logistical and personal support. I would promote the idea that by studying Playback Theatre, the cohort groups of performers will receive an extensive education in personal development, listening nonjudgmentally to others, and teamwork, which will be a significant human resource for their communities in addition to the Playback Theatre skills. I would argue for the training to be in-depth enough for students to acquire the skills of the Playback Theatre method as it has developed over thirty years before adapting it to the needs of their societies.

8. See Chapter 16, "Unexpected Resilience of the Participant Performance Model," for further thoughts about viable program design.

CONGRUENCE. The period of political colonization may be over, but globalization perpetuates the dominance of the Western countries. No matter how deep my respect for the Africans I met, the fact remains that I, a white American, was the teacher, with commensurate stature and authority. My colleague on the second trip was a white Swiss. Looking back, we might have deliberated more before sending two white trainers to Burundi rather than a person of color, preferably of African descent. It is only in recent years that we have gained the awareness that before spreading the knowledge to Africans, it is important to reach out to interested African Americans and other people of color in our own communities. If our own unconscious racism, lack of social awareness, and failure of commitment to redress social injustice keeps us from including people of color in our Playback Theatre work at home, then our desire to spread the work in Africa can be questioned.

On its part, no matter how admirable its objectives of assistance and peace building, Search for Common Ground in Burundi has tremendous power. Its funding comes from US and European sources. Under the direction of an American, it sent me, another American, to teach the locals a new technique, one of a series paraded before them. Knowing they are poor, it pays them transportation money and feeds them. The actors are professional only insofar as Search and other NGOs employ them. Are they coming to learn theatre, to learn tools for change in their country, eat a good meal, to make a connection that will someday take them to the developed world—or what combination of these? And who is benefiting most? Personally, I get a trip to Africa, a tremendously stimulating new experience, and a new item for my resume. I even get paid. To the extent that I may be successful, the work will become "fodder for the imperialist international gaze." (Edmondson 2005: 473) Even my writing this chapter becomes suspect, since it will appear in a book not readily available to my Burundian colleagues, or written in a language they can understand.

Since our training trips to Burundi, we have made big strides as US Playback Theatre practitioners in the direction of congruence following several years of determined effort. In 2006 we were able to respond to the devastation in New Orleans from Hurricane Katrina by sending Playback teams there to act out the stories of evacuees, and the teams consisted primarily of persons of color to match the demographic of our audiences. We are now in a much better position to employ experienced Playback Theatre trainers of color for future trainings in Africa.

SUSTAINABILITY. The issues raised above become starker when we fail to secure the means for the work to continue after we have come and gone. NGOs are continually addressing themselves to problems of sustainability. Yet aid project after aid project has failed the test. Is it ethical for me to agree to a training program that is not adequate to the task and cannot be sustainable? Actors new to Playback Theatre performed in a village during my second trip in an attempt to gain an accelerated performing experience. An audience member told a serious story from her seat in the audience (in our customary theatre ritual, we invite the teller to a chair on stage, where she and her story can be held in safety and respect). The audience, an entire village, was so big and unruly that I suspect the teller's isolation was increased, not decreased, by her revelation. The purpose of the Playback was subverted, but more important, the actors failed because they had not learned enough. In such a context, tellers will soon hesitate to tell, and the performers will sense keenly their lack of positive impact. Eventually, they will give up.

Sustainability cannot ever be guaranteed, but at least it can from the outset be a paramount objective. In the future, we would include the issue of sustainability throughout the planning process. Important considerations are the depth of initial training and ongoing support over time.

CULTURE. The philosophical values embedded in Playback Theatre encountered local Burundian cultural values in problematic ways, some of which seemed amenable to solution, some not. Let me cite a few examples.

As a culture still embedded in the oral tradition, Burundians often communicate thorough stories. But the stories have a different flavor than Playback Theatre stories, which champion open revelation and a kind of spontaneous freshness before the experience. Burundian stories are circuitous and often allegorical; the meaning has to be interpreted; communication through stories can be a battle of wits with often much at stake. At first the Tubiyage actors balked at asking direct questions to the audience. Instead of asking the simple start-of-show question asked by Playback Theatre practitioners all over the world, "How was your day today?" they tended to ask a long, complicated conditional query, such as "Suppose you were walking down the street and you bumped into your boss, how would you feel?" After considerable reflection, I decided to urge them to try out the direct method. One reason was my allegiance to the integrity of Playback Theatre; the direct way of telling was essential to what Playback Theatre is. A second reason, however, had to do with the history of the civil conflict in Burundi, the breakdown of the system of justice, and the politicization of truth. Each side had it own version of every atrocity. Until both sides could accept the revelation of those who suffered without judgment, I felt there was little hope for coexistence in Burundi.

WHEN I RETURNED to Burundi the Tubiyage actors excitedly told me about a man who recounted a story in a performance about his struggles with the local town officials regarding a deserved subsidy, and how the town official, also in the audience, had stood up, acknowledge his new understanding of the situation, and promised him his grant. The direct approach works, they had decided.

A second, related cultural issue is not so easily solved, however. To date in Burundi, it is not socially acceptable to be open about ethnicity. Because of years of intermarriage, especially before the period of conflict, one cannot accurately tell a Hutu or a Tutsi by sight. Often people know, but it is not publicly acknowledged. In Playback Theatre stories in Burundi, the ethnic background of the teller will often be an essential element of any story, but if it cannot be brought to the stage, the actors suffer under a restriction that limits greatly their ability to portray truth with artistry. The potential of Playback Theatre to further peace in Burundi depends on the willingness of its citizens to acknowledge each other's ethnic identity.

A third issue concerns the Tubiyage model of including a large number of actors, so that as many as possible can benefit from the group's opportunities. To learn Playback Theatre, however, actors must rehearse extensively in a small ensemble. This aesthetic demand seemed impossible to meet with Tubiyage's membership of over thirty.

A fourth cultural issue concerns the concept of participatory democracy. Playback Theatre, spawned in resistance to cultural hierarchies in North America, is a people's theatre valuing the unheard voice.[9] Its aim is to give space for anyone, even one of lowest rank, to speak and have their story heard. We proclaim that everyone has a story, and deserves to tell it. How to position such an approach in a cultural context that has no democratic tradition? Are we promoting a human right, or are we perpetuating on the level of theatre exchange what so often takes place on the political level, where the rich democracies use their economic and military power to try and impose their own system?

In future trainings I would raise cultural differences between trainers and trainees as an ongoing part of the training, working with local institution and the students themselves to develop experimental applications for solving problems in the applicability of the method taught. Thus the training itself would be accompanied by dialogue about difference and a search for solutions.

In conclusion, one is left suspended between Fanon, with his vision of a world irrevocably split (Fanon 1963: 32), and Desmond Tutu's Ubuntu-inspired vision of all humanity embraced in the same "bundle of life." (Tutu 1999: 31) Despite discouragements, I see Playback Theatre as potentially effective vehicle for promoting individual agency and communal dialogue. I also share Tutu's spiritual conviction of the presence of a feeling that is "not to be achieved but to be received as a gift freely given," a condition that transcends cultural, economic, and political differences. (Tutu 1999: 85)

9. See Chapter 1, "A Changing Landscape."

The gap caused by history, economic disparity, race, politics, and culture seems wider than the ocean. Yet while preparing this chapter, I received an email from one of the Tubiyage actors, Melchiade Ngendabanyikwa. This is what he wrote:

> Playback Theatre does not cease operating its cures even in prison, to give a fresh memory to those which lost it because of these ceaseless wars. I have just lived a beautiful experiment in central prison of Bujumbura, where I spent a small moment with prisoners who cannot even appear before the judges because they actually forgot what happened. After a funny story of one of the prisoners that they played themselves—without artistic perfection of course—a second arose to also tell his funny story as a history of the insane. But he started to add elements which referred to his cause of arrest. Suddenly he made a volte face and found the true memory of the events. The second day he asked me to seek a lawyer to report all that occurred. With the end of this meeting I distributed some soaps according to my small means (Personal communication, 27 July 2006).

Such a story gives me new hope. From it I learn of a new possibility for Playback Theatre, discovered by Melchiade, in helping repair a "broken narrative" (Lederach 2005: 147). But I also find that to my surprise, even without any ongoing support, Playback Theatre in Burundi remains alive.

References

Bruner, Jerome. (1990). *Acts of Meaning: Four Lectures on Mind and Culture.* Cambridge, MA: Harvard University Press. Reprint edition 2007.

Edmondson, Laura. (2005). "Marketing Trauma and the Theatre of War in Northern Uganda," *Theatre Journal* 57: 451-474.

Fox, Jonathan. (1994). *Acts of Service: Spontaneity, Commitment, Tradition in the Nonscripted Theatre.* New Paltz, NY: Tusitala.

Fox, Jonathan. (1992). "Defining Theater for the Nonscripted Domain," *The Arts in Psychotherapy* 19: 201-207.

Fanon, Franz. (1963). *Wretched of the Earth.* New York: Grove Press,

Herman, Judith. (1992). *Trauma and Recovery.* New York: Basic Books. Reprint edition 1997.

Lederach, John Paul. (2005). *The Moral Imagination: The Art and Soul of Building Peace.* New York: Oxford University Press.

Salas, Jo. (1993). *Improvising Real Life: Personal Story in Playback Theatre.* Dubuque, IA: Kendall/Hunt. 3rd edition 1999, New Paltz, NY: Tusitala.

Tutu, Desmond. (1999). *No Future without Forgiveness.* New York: Doubleday.

STORIES IN THE MOMENT: PLAYBACK THEATRE FOR BUILDING COMMUNITY AND JUSTICE[1]

Jo Salas (2011)

PLAYBACK THEATRE GREW, starting in 1975, from Jonathan Fox's idea of a grassroots theatre in which ordinary people would make theatre on the spot from the true stories of other ordinary people.[2] This theatre would release drama's magic from the rarefied world of proscenium stages and the finely crafted stories of fictional characters, and return it to its place as an accessible part of ordinary life.

Jonathan, myself, and others who were attracted to this vision of a new theatre began to explore how to make it work, forming an ensemble which was simply called Playback Theatre, now often referred to as the "original company." We developed forms and protocols so that audience members would feel both the trust and the excitement necessary to come forward with their stories. That essential but paradoxical task of creating safety along with the artistic embrace of the unknown has been a major focal point of training for Playback Theatre practitioners.

At this point, thirty-six years later, Playback Theatre is established in about sixty countries and used in an extraordinarily wide variety of settings. With reference also to projects in Kiribati and Angola, this chapter focuses mainly on projects in the US

---

1. First published in *Acting Together: Performance and the Creative Transformation of Conflict*, Vol 2, eds Cohen, Varea and Walker. Oakland, CA: New Village Press, 2011. This two-volume anthology is associated with the ongoing multimedia initiative Acting Together on the World Stage, https://www.atwsresources.com/.

2. This chapter is edited and shortened from the original.

(addressing school bullying) and Afghanistan (working with victims of war)—two very different applications with the common element of training members of the intended audiences to become performers for their peers.

Playback Theatre embodies these principles:

Emergence: the events of the show emerge out of the moment and are not preset. Stories or tellers are never chosen prior to the show.

Any story is welcome.

We honor the teller and the story: we want her or him to feel heard, comprehended, and respected.

The story of the group is ultimately significant. It takes shape through attending fully to one person at a time.

Playback Theatre's versatility is both a strength and a weakness. Those of us engaged in this work wrestle endlessly with questions posed by others, and sometimes by ourselves—"What *is* it? And what is it *for*?" Ultimately, in my view, it is for dialogue and the building of connection and empathy—the moral imagination—through the potent medium of theatre, which means invoking aesthetics, imagination, and the physical self.

Robert Wright, the author of *The Evolution of God* (2009a), defines the moral imagination as "the ability to put ourselves in the shoes of other people, especially people in circumstances very different from our own" (2009b, p. 1). Both in peaceful settings and in situations of conflict, the exchange of stories in the ritualized space of Playback Theatre has the capacity to engender empathy and create or strengthen community bonds as multiple voices are heard with respect and responded to with creativity.

Context in Playback Theatre

Playback's impact depends on a subtle weaving of artistic and social-interactive elements. And, to add enormously to the challenge, the requisite balance between these elements varies according to context.

In the early, idealistic days when people outside the original company began to adopt the work, our message to them was open and encouraging—sure, anyone can do it! We did not know enough ourselves to articulate the reality that this work is complex and highly context-sensitive. "Anyone can do it" is much too simple. Anyone can tell a story, yes. As Jenny Hutt and Bev Hosking[3] write below about Kiribati, it is a basic value of Playback Theatre to accept and enact any true story, whether joyful, tragic, disturbing, funny, anecdotal, or epic (which does not mean that all stories are handled the same: those that embody trauma, for example, or prejudice, demand special considerations, which I'll write more about later in this chapter). But who can enact a story, who can do Playback, depends on the context.

Playback Theatre takes place in both workshop and performance formats. In a workshop setting, the work is at its most intimate and informal, with a trained leader, or two, but not a performing team nor a defined audience. The members of the group, whether one-time or ongoing, a class, co-workers, children, etc., take turns telling stories and acting them out for each other. In this contained context, almost anyone can enact a story in a way that has meaning for the teller and the other group members. (The rare exceptions are people who lack the personal stability to step into the role of another, or a person who is unable to access even a small degree of spontaneity.) It requires minimal skill or training on the part of the "actors" for the process to work. The teller readily enters a mild trance state—the creative space of lending your imagination and your belief to what you are seeing. (Any theatre performance must evoke this trance if audience members are to believe in the characters and events on stage.) In that trance the teller is likely to accept the enactment, however simply or even poorly done, and feel that the actors have captured his story effectively.

However, in performance settings, with a defined audience and team of performers (actors, conductor, and musician), the actors

---

3. Bev Hosking is a Playback Theatre practitioner and trainer from New Zealand. Jenny Hutt is a New Zealand/Australian writer and former PT practitioner.

have to convince not only the teller but also a roomful of others who are not so easily caught up in the trance—unaided, in this kind of theatre, by sets, costumes, or lighting.[4] The requirement for skill becomes much higher. The larger or more heterogeneous the audience, the more necessary it is for the performers to be competent, not only in their stage skills but also in their ability to work as an ensemble. Without those skills the performance will fail both as art and as dialogue because in Playback Theatre they are indivisible. The artfulness enables the dialogue; the dialogue is the basis for the art.

It is important to say that the kind of dialogue that can happen in Playback is not cognitive: it is not a process of discussion, of thought and logic. Instead, it is a dialogue in the language of story, image, emotion, and physical action; an embodied, imaginative dialogue.[5] We call it a dialogue because, in the unfolding of a show, the stories are summoned and prompted by each other, often unconsciously—it may not be until long after the event, if at all, that one can discern the actual pattern of the dialogue, the "red thread" (Hoesch, 1999). (This metaphor, common in the German language, is borrowed from weaving, where a red thread allows the weaver to follow the pattern in process.) The teller is welcome to say something after seeing his or her story enacted, but there is no invitation to the audience to comment or analyze. Instead, they're invited to offer the next story.

In a performance in which conflict arises, participants' opinions may not necessarily change. But each person's comprehension of their own and others' experience is altered and expanded, however subtly. I've noted, as a teller myself, that when my experience is reflected accurately in the spontaneous, artistic, and physical expression of others, I have the kinesthetic conviction that I have been understood. Others speak of a similar experience. That sense of certainty creates a kind of softening and relaxation, and an increased openness to another point of view. Listeners, hearing the human voice of the teller and seeing her story brought to life, find a

4. See Chapter 4, "What is 'Good' Playback Theatre?"
5. See Chapter 8, "What We Mean by 'Dialogue' in Playback Theatre."

little more space within themselves to accommodate the humanity of that person and her perspective. The moral imagination grows.

Story is itself to some degree an indirect communication. Stories are multifaceted, allowing a listener many entry points to understanding or learning. Jonathan Fox notes that "in stories, the value, the meaning, often reveals itself only indirectly."[6]

IN 1998-99 Bev Hosking and Christian Penny[7] from New Zealand taught Playback in two villages of the South Pacific nation of Kiribati (pronounced Kiribahss), as part of an overseas development project funded by the New Zealand government. The project complemented other training aimed at increasing the participation of women in decision-making, and tested whether Playback Theatre could influence and empower women within their families and local communities.

Bev and Christian used Playback Theatre to work with the whole community and all its stories, rather than focusing explicitly on the topic of enhancing women's role in the community. As stories from women and men were told and performed, enough trust developed between them for some of the core stories and conflicts around gender to emerge. This happened privately in the workshop sessions and then more publicly in the performances.

A woman told of her relationship with her father, which involved criticism, an overuse of power, and physical beating. Her father had told her that she was bound to marry a good-for-nothing man. In fact she married a fine man who involved her in decisions, shared his successes and difficulties with her and was respectful of her. The teller and the audience were deeply affected by the enactment of this story.

The workshops provided an environment for modeling and enacting equality in the relationships between men and women. The trainers demonstrated an equal and respectful working partnership. Women aged from fourteen to fifty-six years participated actively and equally as participants in the training workshops, in

6. See Chapter 5, "A Ritual for Our Time."
7. Christian Penny is a theatre artist and trainer in New Zealand.

group decision-making during the workshops, and in leadership groups established in each community. They willingly told stories about their experiences, which made visible and acknowledged their contribution to community life. Impacts of the project were immediately observable: the women's shyness and self-consciousness dropped away and their confidence in presenting themselves in front of the group increased noticeably.

The process of learning the basic skills of Playback Theatre in the training workshops created many opportunities for a growing understanding and strengthening of the relationships between women and men. They worked closely together and built on each other's work in creating dramatic enactments. They regularly chose actors to play roles in their stories without reference to gender and there was little difficulty in playing roles of the opposite gender. Stories of ordinary daily activities from the lives of both women and men were listened to without judgment and the dramatic enactments were received with appreciation and delight. New pictures and possibilities of relationships between women and men were beginning to be voiced and witnessed in the community.

One participant in the group was marginalized in his community because of his sexual orientation. He was isolated in the group, and often on the receiving end of harsh jokes. The trainers worked hard to include him at different points in the workshop and to value what he had to contribute. They also worked to build a strong enough relationship with him and with the group to create the conditions conducive for him to tell a story.

> When we finally invited him to tell a story he accepted and came to the teller's chair with a vulnerability that was very poignant to witness. He told a story about building, then losing, a close friendship. His love for this friend was evident and there was a sense that perhaps for the first time he was able to say his friend's name in public. As they listened, the group was able to go beyond their stereotyped view of this man and to see his humanity. They enacted his story with a great deal of tenderness, compassion and respect. This proved to be a turning point in

the relationship between this man and the group. That evening we observed a warmer, more expressive connection between a number of the participants and this man. For the rest of our time together we noticed a marked decrease in people singling him out for ridicule. (Hutt and Hosking, 2004)

As I said above, the necessary level of skill for the actors depends very much on whether the event is an intimate workshop or a performance, and what kind of performance. However, in contrast, the conductor requires sophisticated skills in any context. This role is by far the most demanding in Playback Theatre, calling on those of us who adopt it to synthesize a distinct set of abilities and learning. We must be able to listen deeply to any individual story with courage and openness; we must be able to build, read, and guide the dynamics of an audience or group of (usually) strangers, taking care to include those who are isolated, as in the Kiribati community described by Jenny Hutt and Bev Hosking; we must have the artistic sensibility of a storyteller or theatre director as we hear the story and elicit key information; we must be able to pace and shape an event so that it remains engaging for all present; we must be educated about the world that our audience members and tellers live in; we must have the humility to remember that we're part of a team, not a soloist; we must have the knowledge to respond wisely to stories that contain danger or pain for teller or audience. This knowledge encompasses both a deep understanding of the form—of how to use Playback Theatre—and of the human psyche.

It takes long training and solid experience to be a competent conductor—and likewise to be an effective performing ensemble. (Most Playback companies aspire to last indefinitely, and several have been going for twenty years or longer, giving them time to develop enduring relationships within the group as well as considerable skills.) This inescapably long learning curve has been an obstacle in the use of Playback in troubled parts of the world where extended time for development is unrealistic and resources for in-depth training are not available.[8]

8. See Chapter 19, "Playback Theatre in Burundi: Can Theatre Transcend the Gap?"

The participant performance model

What I am now calling the participant performance model is emerging as a use of Playback that may allow for the impact and scope of performance without requiring the years of development that ordinary performing companies need.[9] Playback practitioners over the years have carried out projects which, as I look back, were akin to this model, but I am now suggesting that we name and develop the concept as an alternative to other designs. Participant performance has the potential to make Playback Theatre more portable and adaptable in situations of crisis. While a typical Playback company strives both for longevity and the ability to perform for any audience, the participant performance model is based instead on training a small number of members (10 to 20) of a particular interest or population group to carry out performances *for other members of that same group*, often for a time-limited project. Because of this very specific focus, it is possible to perform effectively after a relatively short, targeted training, which builds knowledge and skills relevant to the purpose at hand. The performing team is congruent with the audience and tellers—they come from the same community, they share background and concerns, and may be known to each other. The actors' portrayals of stories, even if not highly skilled, are convincing and satisfying to the audience because actors draw on the life experience they share with the audience: the audience's trance is successfully evoked at a lower level of artistic sophistication than in more traditional uses of Playback.

Training for participant performance varies according to various factors: the existing skill and relevant experience of the performers; their maturity and emotional readiness in relation to the stories they will be called upon to act; the number and variety of the performances that are planned. The trainers themselves (ideally two, so that one person can support from the actors' team while the other guides the overall process) need to be seasoned practitioners with the wisdom and perspective to distill the aspects of practice most essential to the task at hand. Training might take place in a two-month series of weekly workshops (as with the

9. See Chapter 16, "Unexpected Resilience of the Participant Performance Model."

children in the anti-bullying work) or in intensive trainings lasting from six to twelve days at a time (as in Afghanistan and Angola, described below).

Some important questions about participant performance are not yet answered: most pressingly, what about the conductor or conductors? There seems no way to shortcut the training process of a conductor, and without a high level of competence a conductor can get into deep water, especially in situations of social fragility and individual or collective trauma. In some situations it may also be necessary to include one or more experienced actors along with the participant-group actors. What does this mean about offering Playback Theatre in a place where there are no trained conductors or experienced actors? If the work is too risky without them, these key figures may need to be imported, raising logistical and practical questions (funding, language, duration) and also questions about the congruence of the leadership; how to make this resource available without being yet another Western-derived form dependent on Westerners for implementation. I'll discuss these issues more after describing the two participant performance projects I mentioned earlier: one in the conflict zone of schools in the United States; and one with victims of war in Afghanistan.

Participant performance and school bullying

Emma—not her real name—is a seventh grader. She's small for her age, slender, very smart, very artistic. She's not part of the "popular" crowd in her class. Emma's interests are different, she doesn't make friends easily, she can be a bit sarcastic and prickly. For a long time, she's been the target of daily, relentless, cruel bullying. She comes to school every day knowing that other kids are going to make fun of her, isolate her, and humiliate her. She feels powerless to stop it. She's talked to her teachers and her parents. Her parents have talked to the assistant principal. The assistant principal has scolded the bullies. Nothing seems to help. She says: "It feels like they're tearing my heart out." All she wants is for the other kids to leave her alone. She would also like it if a couple of the other girls would ask her about her artwork.

Emma has five more years of school. She doesn't know how she's going to survive.

Old problems, new initiatives

The problem of school bullying is far from new. Kids have been brutal to each other for generations. In his autobiography *Goodbye to All That* the British poet Robert Graves described being viciously teased and humiliated at school because he enjoyed studying more than sports, he didn't wear the same expensive clothes as the other students, and he had a German middle name (Graves, 1929). His description of how he was treated could have been written yesterday—but he's talking about 1910, not 2010. Many adults have vivid memories of experiencing or witnessing bullying as children, and the memories may remain raw and painful throughout their lives. In mid-life Graves wrote: "I suffered an oppression of spirit that I hesitate to recall in its full intensity" (1929, p. 38).

In those times, and until relatively recently, school bullying was accepted—even condoned—by adults who justified it as normal behavior, an inevitable part of growing up. Now, at last, teachers, parents, community members, and researchers are attempting to do something about it. We're no longer shrugging our shoulders and pretending that the damage is insignificant. In the past 20 or 30 years there has been a deliberate and growing trend to figure out what's going on when kids treat each other cruelly, and how to stop it. School bullying is a profound problem without easy solutions: in spite of these decades of attention and concern, it seems to get worse, with the development of online weapons for bullies and the enormous tragedy of young people who have been literally bullied to death (Katz, 2010).

Defining bullying

There is still a considerable amount of confusion, among both children and adults, about what school bullying is and how to deal with it. The differences between bullying and fighting are not always understood, for example. A teacher who sends a bully and his victim to peer mediation, with the implication that both share responsibility for the conflict and the power to end it, may be subjecting the victim to further trauma. Another common misperception is that children can and should deal with bullying by ignoring it, or by standing up for themselves. Such tactics may work for some kids, but many who are targeted are not equipped to defend themselves, nor will the abuse end if it is ignored. It is essential to understand the salient elements of bullying if we are going to address it effectively. A number of key features define bullying, such as the invariable presence of a power differential, but the most essential is this: bullying is deliberately hurting or humiliating another person. The personalities of the children involved are a factor, but bullying is not primarily a matter of individual personality, nor is it generally a dyadic interaction. Bullying happens within an ecology of peer group, school, family, and community: "Internal factors in the individual interact with the social environment, which then serves to reinforce bullying and/or victimization behaviors" (Swearer and Doll, 2001, p. 19).

Bullying is a group phenomenon: one child may initiate bullying but other children are almost always involved as active supporters and enablers of the bully as well as passive bystanders. A bully generally wants and needs an admiring audience. The group nature of bullying creates a crucial opportunity, since peer involvement can be mobilized for positive, not negative ends.

Why does bullying happen?

Why do children bully? There is little truth to the stereotype of a bully as someone who hurts others because he or she feels bad about himself, although there is some correlation between bullying behavior and harsh punishment in the child's home (Ohene et al., 2006). But there are plenty of bullies among the "popular" kids—the pretty girls, the athletic boys. The attractive girls from prosperous families who tormented 15 year-old Phoebe Prince to death in Massachusetts were not lacking in self-esteem (Cullen, 2010). The explanation for why some children bully others is elusive and complex, not a simple matter of victims turning on others to make themselves feel better. Nor is it accurate, in fact, to speak of "bullies" as though this is a fixed identity. Many (though not all) children move between the roles of bully, bystander, and victim: in a given incident there may be a clearly defined bully, but on another occasion that same child may be a witness, or a victim.

Bullying is impossible to comprehend or address without looking at a much larger picture. It is a phenomenon that has to do with the legacy and challenges of being human. We are all capable of cruelty as well as compassion and we make decisions—not always conscious or rational—throughout our lives about which aspect of ourselves we are going to develop and express. Young people whose innate empathy and altruism are supported by the adults around them, who are treated with respect and empathy themselves, are more likely—though not guaranteed—to strengthen that part of their character (Strayer and Roberts, 1989). And conversely, kids who see cruelty and disrespect modeled and tolerated, or even rewarded, in their family and close community, are more likely to show that kind of behavior (Olweus, 1980).

The human capacity for cruelty is enacted throughout society. Our species is magnificently capable of kindness, empathy, and altruism. But children also see heartlessness and disrespect replicated on every level, from family and community interactions to television shows and video games, to local, national, and even international politics: the United States, where I live, is viewed as a bully by much of the rest of the world. Children constantly absorb images and stories of adults being hateful and unjust to other adults, treating them unkindly, disrespecting and excluding people on the basis of differences.

The role of negative adult modeling is evident in cyberbullying. The anonymity of the Internet allows people to publicly express their worst selves without consequences to themselves. It used to be that anonymous letters—the old-fashioned kind that arrived in the mail—were generally viewed as morally unacceptable, a very low form of aggression. That distaste seems to have vanished: anonymous comments that are rude, intolerant, offensive, and intentionally hurtful have become ubiquitous online. These comments would not be made face-to-face, nor if the commenter's identity were known. If all online discourse had to be identified, can anyone doubt that it would quickly become more civil? I believe that we cannot begin to address cyberbullying among youth without facing this adult version of it.

Expecting young people to end school bullying within this wider framework of human harshness may seem a gargantuan, even hopeless task. And yet the cycle of cruelty and indifference to suffering must be interrupted wherever possible. Idealistic as it may sound, a generation of children who learn to treat each other well, to stand up for what they know is right, may grow up to be a generation of adults who bring consciousness, compassion, and justice to all their interactions and decisions. In their New York Times op ed "There's Only One Way to Stop a Bully" Susan Sandstrom and Marlene Engel wrote: "Our research on child development makes it clear that there is only one way to truly combat bullying. As an essential part of the school curriculum, we have to teach children how to be good to one another, how to cooperate, how to defend someone who is being picked on and how to stand up for what is right" (2010).

Conversely, as another team of researchers discovered, if bullying is not prevented, "middle schools may unfortunately serve as laboratories for the development of individuals who feel indifferent to the victimization of others" (Jeffrey et al., 2001). Unfortunately, in the absence of intervention, children's natural capacity for altruism decreases as they get older and their capacity for cruelty or indifference becomes stronger.

Playback Theatre and bullying

The first systematic approach to addressing school bullying was based on research conducted in Norway in the 1970s by Dan Olweus (1993). By now there are numerous other anti-bullying approaches as well, all of which can help if certain basic principles are met:

> *There must be a school-wide and preferably district-wide commitment to address bullying in a long-term way. Controlling bullying is a multi-faceted, never-ending task.*

All the adults involved—teachers, aides, administrators, bus drivers, as well as parents, ideally—need to be educated about bullying and prepared to respond consistently and promptly to any instance or report of bullying.

Interventions need to be based on knowledge and research about bullying.

Along with consistent consequences for children who bully, the approach must actively foster respect and empathy.

The Playback Theatre approach that my ensemble has developed, called "No More Bullying!" (NMB),[10] works along-side programs such as OBPP (Olweus Bullying Prevention Program)[11] deepening and extending their impact (Salas, 2005). We use Playback Theatre to engage personal stories, emotions, and the physical self with the intention of fostering empathy and the capacity to take responsibility for fairness. As a theatre-based form, NMB draws on the unique potency of the arts, which invoke creativity, synthesis, vision, and imagination. Artistic expression is available to all children, regardless of gender or other identity factors, and allows them to access their fullest selves in dealing with the complexities and challenges of their world. Art engenders new vision and new possibilities—for example, a school where everyone is safe, welcomed, and respected. Change begins with vision: the educator Maxine Greene says: "It is imagination that draws us on, that enables us to make new connections among parts of our experience, that suggests the contingency of the reality we are experiencing" (1995, p. 30).

In Playback Theatre performances, children are invited to speak about an experience as a victim, a bystander, or a bully, then watch as their feeling or story is enacted on the spot either by a team of professional adult actors—or, using a participant performance model, by student actors and adults together. The

10. Hudson River Playback Theatre began developing NMB in 1999 and has worked with over 35,000 children. We have trained other PT companies in the US, Canada, Israel, Japan, and Russia in this approach. Japanese teams use a culturally adapted version in a nationwide, government-funded program.

11. https://olweus.sites.clemson.edu/

performances take place in an atmosphere of respect and safety in which children, often including the most hurt or isolated, feel empowered to speak up. This atmosphere arises from several elements: the consistent modeling of respect on the part of the adults; the immediate addressing of any instance of disrespect during the show; the structuring of space and time to create a sense of containment; and the welcoming, nonjudgmental embrace of every comment or story that the students offer.

(An important caution: there is far more to the NMB method than described here. Playback practitioner readers interested in using this approach should acquire specific training before attempting it with children. It is difficult work and there is a real possibility of doing harm if undertaken without thorough knowledge.[12])

These live performances have a different kind of impact from other presentations. If you're a child, you can sit in an assembly and tune out a visiting speaker or a video. You can ignore the slogans in mass-produced posters along the hallway. But if someone in your class is right there in front of you, telling her story and feeling her feelings, if her story is then enacted by real people who use her words and embody her emotions, you're likely to be riveted and your own feelings stirred. You are likely to remember that story.

NMB ACKNOWLEDGES the innate capacity that young people have for empathy and decency, and seeks to strengthen this capacity so that it is more resilient than the impulse for cruelty. The program is also based on the fact that, as I mentioned earlier, bullying is essentially a group phenomenon. It is not a problem between two students. It is a problem both of the immediate group of kids who are involved in an incident as bullies, bystanders, and victims; and of the larger group of the school and the community. But if the group is an essential component of bullying, it also has the potential to be an essential part of the solution. The greatest potential power to shift the climate of a school towards safety and respect lies with the majority of students who are neither bullies nor targets. Most

12. Information about training is available at www.hudsonriverplayback.org.

are troubled when they witness bullying but do not know what they can do about it—nor do they realize how many others share their feelings. NMB focuses on the role of the witnesses or bystanders, empowering them by letting them realize how numerically strong they are, and by offering a creative setting in which they can identify and rehearse actions that are practical, accessible, and effective.

Although we sometimes use the more traditional performance model in this work, particularly with young children, we prefer whenever possible to use the participant performance model—training a group of children to become actors in performances for their peers. (Whether we include student performers or not depends on the school's choice and resources as well as grade level: elementary school students are too young to take on the considerable responsibility of enacting sensitive stories.) We call it the No More Bullying! Leadership Program, because many of the young people who are involved become leaders in the school, with the knowledge, courage, and solidarity to stand up to bullying in an ongoing way.

For the NMB Leadership Program, school personnel choose about fifteen students, representing the school's diversity in terms of age, gender, ethnicity, ability, and social standing, to take part in a series of training workshops led by two Playback Theatre leaders. Over a period of seven or eight weeks, meeting once a week, students learn the basics of Playback, and they also learn about bullying—an expanded version of the learning that takes place for audience members during the performances. They all have a chance to tell their own stories, which they enact for each other, developing considerable empathy as well as concrete knowledge about what bullying is and how students can address it. (The necessity to elicit and emphasize this knowledge contrasts with the fundamentally emergent nature of Playback Theatre: fulfilling both makes the work exceptionally demanding.)

By the time the performances take place, the students have bonded well and are confident in their skills. They join adult performers in rotating teams so that all have a chance to take part: each team consists, typically, of four students and two or three adults, including the conductor. Student observers from the group make notes and report on what they notice.

For the audience members, seeing their peers onstage increases the impact of the content: as one of our teenage actors said afterwards when we were evaluating the project: "Grown ups are always telling us about drugs, and bullying, and things we shouldn't do, but if a child hears it from a child, they listen." The young people's performance skills of course do not approach those of the professional actors, but they make up for it in unselfconscious authenticity and familiarity with the audience members' frame of reference.

Over the course of this two-month experience of training workshops and performances, the student group members also become empowered to be anti-bullying leaders in the school in an ongoing way. This capacity emerges organically: as they learn in depth about bullying, they feel their own power to take action, knowing that they are not acting alone. Their comments at the close of this project consistently express notable insight and the resolve to do what they know is fair and right. A ninth grader said: "It made me think a lot, to bend a bit. I feel like I learned a lot because it made me more open to how people are different from me and to look at who they are and not where they come from or what they can and can't do."

The performances

Performances generally take place with an audience of between 25 and 50 students. They can be at any grade level from kindergarten to 12th grade, though it's most effective with 4th to 9th graders (9 to 15 years old). Prior to the show, teachers receive a lesson plan with guidelines for helping students focus their thoughts about bullying (as well as a lesson plan with follow-up activities). The show begins with performers speaking briefly about and enacting their own experiences relating to bullying. Then we invite audience members to generate a definition of bullying, and to describe what kids actually do to make other children feel bad. Students typically bring up physical and non-physical bullying, and cyberbullying. We make sure there's a clear understanding about the difference between bullying and fighting.

Once we've all generated a definition of bullying—a vocabu-
lary—we begin a kind of dialogue through theatre: we ask the
children about their thoughts and observations and feelings about
bullying, and we perform their responses on the spot.

"What's it like for you when you see someone being picked on?"

"I feel sad."

"Let's watch," and then the actors enact that feeling with
sound and movement, along with improvised music. Watching,
everyone in the room understands what that child meant. They
understand it viscerally—it's not just about the words, it's about the
physical expression. The kinesthetic response mentioned earlier
plays an important part. If you're the "teller," seeing your feeling
expressed in the bodies, faces, and voices of the actors allows you to
know beyond doubt that you've been heard and understood. This
certainty is very significant, especially for children who've been
victimized and are very painfully aware that their feelings are not
usually understood at all.

We hear from a number of students in response to a series
of questions, and then we invite them to co-create a short scenario about an imaginary character who's being bullied, played
by one of our adult actors. (Role play is not a traditional part of
Playback Theatre, but it's helpful in this context to intensify focus
on the topic and the actions we want to explore.) Other actors, as
well as volunteers from the audience, play bullies and bystanders.
Audience members are asked to make suggestions about what
bystanders could do to help, and we act out each suggestion.
Invariably, children suggest getting an adult to help; befriending
or supporting the victim; and telling the bullies to stop. We also
emphasize the importance of not making the situation worse by
joining in (a temptation, since the bullying may look like fun).
Sometimes a child suggests violent retribution for the bullies. We
don't enact that suggestion, instead pausing for discussion about
the way that violence tends to backfire.

Once the set of constructive actions has been identified and
practiced, we explore in further vignettes how they can also be used
with cyberbullying. These commonsense actions, springing from

the sense of fairness, altruism, and responsibility that is the basis of decency and good citizenship, readily translate to the world of online bullying.

And then we invite children to tell their own stories, which we act out on the spot—stories about when they might have felt like the character in our scenario, or like one of the bystanders. Or a bully. In each enacted story, we spotlight the actions that bystanders took, or failed to take, or that the teller wishes they had taken. Each story becomes an opportunity to revisit and further rehearse the empowerment of the bystanders.

Children who are isolated and vulnerable often respond to this opportunity to be heard. We are aware of the delicacy of such stories, and the risk that telling them might make things even worse for the teller. However, such consequences do not seem to ensue. We have not been told of instances where a teller was further victimized as a result of telling his or her story. (So far, resources have not permitted extensive follow-up: however, occasional follow-up surveys and informal reporting from school personnel and children themselves over twelve years of performances have indicated only positive outcomes. We are currently developing a research project with Fordham University to further explore and measure outcomes of the project.)

Several factors account for the fact that vulnerable children are apparently able to tell their stories safely. One is the norm of respect that is established strongly at the outset of every show and maintained throughout. We may explicitly recruit the audience's respectful attention when a story unfolds to reveal a particularly tender situation. Following the show, we make a point of ensuring that a responsible adult will take action to address any ongoing unresolved situations that emerged in the stories, and that any child who is especially in need of support will receive it.

Emma, the seventh grader I mentioned at the beginning of this section, told her story in one of our shows. It was hard for her to come forward. She waited until the show was almost over. She decided to speak up because, as she said, "This is the end of the trail"—meaning she felt it was her last chance to make things change. She's tried everything else. The only thing that can make life better for her is for the kids who witness the bullying to speak up, do something, be friendly and supportive to her.

When she told her story the fifty children in the room were silent and attentive. The student actors, her peers, listened intently. At the end of the show, two-thirds of the children present raised their hands solemnly when we asked if they felt they could take one of the actions we'd explored the next time they witnessed bullying.

After the performance ended and the audience left, the student actors spoke urgently about Emma's story, which had shocked them. They resolved to find out more about her artwork, and to stand up for her if they ever saw her being bullied.

Adults can and must help too, but they cannot solve the problem without the students' involvement. Emma herself certainly cannot solve it. It would be nothing but cruel to tell her to ignore the bullying, not to let it bother her.[13]

Participant performance in Afghanistan

A very different example of participant performance appears in the Afghanistan project created by Hjalmar Jorge Joffre-Eichhorn, a theatre practitioner of Bolivian and German background who had worked in Theatre of the Oppressed (TO) for some years and had participated in several Playback Theatre workshops. This discussion is based on Hjalmar's written accounts (2010, 2011) as well as emails and conversations. His work shows the use of Playback Theatre in an extremely fraught context where trauma, both historical and current, is constantly present. As he describes, Playback Theatre's impact has been both constructive and at times problematic. For myself and other longtime practitioners, Hjalmar's work presented a new frontier for Playback Theatre— could it really work in this shattered and volatile setting? As the project unfolded, email bulletins such as this seemed to indicate that yes, it could:

13. I met with Emma a year after she told her story. She had grown taller, and seemed relaxed and confident. She told me she was no longer bullied. Although still not in the "popular" crowd, she had no wish to be. She had one very close friend, a girl who shared her passionate interest in art.

"Now I understand the power of Playback Theatre" is what one of the participants of our participatory theatre training said after performing for a group of thirty widows, earlier this afternoon. The performance was almost cancelled, as the women initially did not accept any (young) male actors and insisted that only our four women plus me as the foreigner could perform. In the end, they accepted all of us and we had a very strong 1h 40 min performance, with many tears, laughter and small moments of beauty, such as when an old woman put her leg on the (female) conductor's leg to calm her down. Tomorrow and the day after tomorrow we will have another two performances for victims' groups, and then finish off the week with performances at Kabul University, a children's residence and an organization that works with hearing impaired children and adults... ten performances in six days... Playback has arrived in Afghanistan..." (Joffre-Eichhorn, 2009 email)

Hjalmar first came to Afghanistan in 2007 to work as a civil peace worker. In 2008 he joined UN-Habitat, United Nations Assistance Mission in Afghanistan, and the Afghanistan Independent Human Rights Commission as a theatre consultant, planning to combine theatre and transitional justice (TJ) activities.[14] After decades of violent conflict and human rights abuses without hope of official redress—and with a recent ruling on amnesty for war criminals (Mojumdar, undated)—the idea of transitional justice was embraced by many Afghan citizens and organizations, although viewed with mistrust by officials.

In 2008 Hjalmar created a project that would offer Theatre of the Oppressed and Playback Theatre as well as more conventional theatre approaches as a vehicle for victims of violence to address transitional justice. He recruited 24 men and six women, training them first in TO and then in Playback Theatre. Between them they represented 15 different organizations.

14. The International Center for Transitional Justice website defines transitional justice as "a response to systematic or widespread violations of human rights. It seeks recognition for victims and to promote possibilities for peace, reconciliation and democracy. Transitional justice is not a special form of justice but justice adapted to societies transforming themselves after a period of pervasive human rights abuse."

Hjalmar has written elsewhere about the project in its entirety (Joffre-Eichhorn, 2011) but here the focus will remain on the Playback Theatre segment. The Playback training consisted of an introductory six-day Playback Theatre training which he led, followed by 16 "on-the-job training" performances for various audiences of 20 to 30 people, including victims' and widows' groups, children, and the hearing impaired. (Hjalmar speaks Dari but also used Pashto and, at times, Afghan Sign Language translators for the workshops and performances.) Six months later, fifteen participants—the group reduced in part because of a change in location—took part in a further six-day workshop with Karin Bettina Gisler, the founder and director of Playback Theater Zürich and a graduate of the Centre for Playback Theatre in New York. The training with Karin was again followed by multiple performances.

In early 2009 ten of these participants, with Hjalmar's support, created an Afghan-led community-based theatre platform, the Afghanistan Human Rights and Democracy Organization (AHRDO). Hjalmar writes: "AHRDO was founded with the desire to bridge ethnic and gender conflicts as well as run a largely non-hierarchical local organization (something basically non-existent in Afghanistan). Originally, there was a total gender balance in terms of the theatre staff. Lately, this has changed as some of our female staff got married and have consequently left AHRDO" (Joffre-Eichhorn, 2011, email).

The ensemble, which also includes people of different ages and two hearing-impaired men, uses both TO and Playback as well as more conventional theatre approaches. Their goal as they set out was to provide opportunities for Afghan men and women to explore human rights, democracy, and transitional justice. They also hoped that through the theatre projects, victims' groups would build contact and cooperation among themselves, allowing them to speak with a coordinated and stronger voice in their discourse with policy makers.

During 2009 and 2010 AHRDO carried out more than fifty performances, most of them in Kabul, though they also ventured to other parts of Afghanistan. In the ethnically divided capital, members of the ensemble had to face their own prejudices and fears as they performed for different communities. In the end they found it expansive and rewarding to encounter these diverse audiences and to hear the stories of fellow-citizens who had previously seemed alien to them.

The performances took place in sheltered circumstances with small (30 or fewer) audiences. Hjalmar had conducted shows within the training, but in these and subsequent performances, the conductors as well as actors and musicians were Afghans, dealing as best they could with the very daunting challenges of guiding the Playback process with people whose painful stories were so raw. As is always the case in Playback Theatre, the actors also carry a major responsibility for realizing and embodying the stories: the enactments are a co-creation of teller, conductor, actors, and musician.

Audience members embraced this structured, ritualized opportunity to speak about what had happened in their lives. They spoke of appalling hardships, losses, abuses, injustices. Most were people of low social standing, many of them women, who had not had other opportunities to tell their stories. They lived silently and alone with their tragedies, unreflected in the official accounts of Afghanistan's history. An audience member, coming forward as a teller with the full attention of the performers and the audience as she told her story, gained affirmation and the knowledge that others heard, comprehended, and respected her experience. After the shows, tellers often spoke of a sense of empowerment as well as emotional relief. Pride and dignity were restored as they told their stories in this respectful context.

> I was forced to marry when I was 12 years old. During the civil war my husband disappeared and I was left alone with four children, two girls and two boys. I worked very hard for all of us to survive but one day, because of the cold weather, one of my sons died. Shortly after, both my daughters married when they were around 11 years old. Now I am basically alone and do not have enough money to put food on the table. (Audience member in Kabul)

Tellers also learned, through the responses of the audience, that their stories were shared by others who were present—a mitigation of the terrible isolation so often suffered by victims of violence. The informal ritual of tea together following performances deepened the experience. "In this post-performance space one could see that a bond had been created among the group, suddenly allowing people with different and sometimes opposing life histories to sit down together and meet each other in their full humanity" (Joffre-Eichhorn, 2010, p. 32).

Playback Theatre invites the telling of stories by those who have lived those stories. For audience members all too familiar with the tendency of national and international NGOs to speak on their behalf, this was an important step in rebuilding a sense of agency. And in a society where personal testimony has been deliberately suppressed, the exchange of stories within a Playback Theatre performance became a means of keeping them in the public memory, as Hjalmar comments:

> In a Playback Theatre event, when memories are (re-)told, they transgress the original boundaries of the individual storyteller's space, time and body, and are relocated in the bodies and minds of the performers and audience. The experience of others becomes our own as we participate in a performance, whether as a teller, a performer, or an audience member. Theatre as a memory-creating process can invite people to transform traumatic personal memory into collective historical memory and consequently help society to move on.
>
> In summary, I strongly believe that Playback Theatre contributes to "build[ing] up a network of stories to reconstruct the trauma of what happened … a counterflow of little stories, anonymous tales, tiny incidents and statements … which condense … a plural and open feeling. The truth is there, we have to look for it and it has the form of a story—not a single story. We have to build this truth; we have to go and look for it. No single subject holds it entirely. We have to create channels for information to flow" (Piglia/Garavelli, 2001). Telling their

stories can provide the victims of torture and atrocity a way back from atomization and disconnection. It can also be an extremely painful renewal of their own experience. We saw both effects during the various performances with victims' groups in Afghanistan. And yet, the overall feedback from the tellers was overwhelmingly positive. They expressed a deep sense of gratitude that someone finally bothered to come and visit them in their own community, truly interested in getting to know them and their stories, without forcing them to share what they might not want to speak of. This happened in an environment where the vast majority of people have never seen or even heard of theatre, and certainly have not participated in any performance. It suggests that Playback Theatre might have a role to play in creating spaces of trust and respect in which those who have been silenced by the historical narrative can legitimize and document their own experiences.

Two of the widows who told their stories during one of our performances expressed afterwards that they had not been able to tell their stories when approached as part of a more formal truth telling initiative a few weeks before. When asked why, both said that they had not felt enough trust to do so and bemoaned the formality of the questioning procedure. "We had never seen any theatre before but this theatre is really useful for our country. It is respectful and we felt like there was no difference between you (the performers) and us. Please do more of this theatre" (Joffre-Eichhorn, 2010, pp. 35–36).

Challenges

In a context such as Afghanistan it is clearly crucial to have performers who emerge from the same population as their intended audiences—"citizen actors," in Fox's term—and who are trained especially to enact their stories. It is hard to imagine performers who did not share the audience members' background being able to effectively enact their stories, with all their specific details and unspoken resonances, and even harder to imagine audience members' entrusting their stories to outsiders.

On the other hand, that commonality also means vulnerability on the part of the performers. At times performers—both conductor and actors—were overwhelmed by the tragic content of the stories, so reverberant with their own.

Asking people to tell their stories shaped by a war setting makes for stories penetrated by life and death, fear and pain, horror and sadness. For example, a woman told this story:

"During the civil war in Kabul, my husband was killed and I left with some of my children for Bakh province. When the fighting started in Bakh, I left the city with one of my sons to escape into the mountains. On the way we saw a lot of people killed and injured. There I lost my son. I finally reached Kabul, where another of my sons was living but once I had arrived there I was informed that my third son had been killed as well."

Faced with the almost impossible task of representing stories such as this, there is a danger of the actors losing themselves in a role rather than remaining critically detached from it. Some of the actors could not hold back their tears while listening to such stories. Listening to and enacting these difficult, almost unbearable stories places an enormous burden on performers, the majority of them having their own histories of painful loss and the incommunicability of permanent war.

Others in the audience also reacted strongly to what they heard and saw. In some cases, the whole audience would engage in collective crying. In other moments audience members nodded in silence whenever they recognized similarities with their own lives. These spectators become witnesses and co-owners of each other's stories through the very act of listening. (Joffre-Eichhorn, 2010, p. 3)

Potential conflict among audience members presented another challenge. In a country with so many intertwined and contradictory histories, it is inevitable that renditions of the past are sometimes at odds. Playback Theatre honors the subjective account of the teller, trusting that the sequence of stories within an event will yield a collective story that has meaning for those present—the "red thread" or dialogue of themes, perceptions, and images that I spoke of earlier. It does not and cannot seek to establish an objective account of the past. Hjalmar describes a performance in Bamyan province in Central Afghanistan where two audience members of different ethnicities accused each other of distorting history. The conductor was eventually able to help them reframe their dispute by seeing themselves both as victims of violence rather than perpetrators. But sometimes the disparity between perspectives is too great to be encompassed. As Hjalmar comments, "the result of a transitional justice-focused Playback event is often a highly fragmented, partial and seemingly incomplete account of what could be called the truth of the past" (Joffre-Eichhorn, 2010, p. 30). Because of the potential contentiousness of this aspect of Playback, the AHRDO ensemble decided to work with more homogeneous groups before attempting again to bring together people whose historical understanding is widely divergent.

Other weaknesses apparently arose from choices or mistakes made by the newly trained performers. Hjalmar described moments during performances when the process went awry: in one performance, the conductor broke down and wept, only to admit later that he did so in order to stimulate more "meaningful" stories from the audience. Some actors were at times carried away with their prowess on stage and become more interested in impressing the audience than honoring the story.

Most difficult of all was the constant pivoting between a constructive, healing exchange of stories and the danger of re-traumatization, about which I'll comment more below. Virtually everyone in the room at these events, including the performers, had suffered violence and loss: a performance presented a minefield of trauma. Sometimes the process broke down in the face of unbearable pain. And yet, reading Hjalmar's bulletins as the project unfolded, I was struck by the degree to which audience members evidently embraced the shows and welcomed the chance to tell, hear, and witness stories.

Reflections

Any written account of a theatre project must necessarily be fragmented, partial and seemingly incomplete, as Hjalmar characterizes
Playback stories themselves. Although I did not witness the trainings or performances in Afghanistan, I understand from Hjalmar's
account that this project gave an extraordinary opportunity to many
women and men, victims of the brutal wars in Afghanistan, to find
insight, meaning, and dignity in their stories, to affirm commonality
with other victims, to release feelings of pain and anger that had
not previously found expression, to comprehend the humanity of
those whose experience or backgrounds were different, and to record
stories in the public memory that otherwise might be forgotten or
suppressed. The members of the performance ensemble, addition-
ally, experienced the satisfactions of using theatre in service to their
fellow-citizens' stories and "to help society to move on."

The ensemble also faced the considerable challenges and dilemmas that predictably accompanied the use of Playback in such a
fraught setting. How to ensure that the process is constructive and
not re-traumatizing? Stories of uncontrollable weeping among performers and audience (and in one case, fainting on stage) suggest
that there may have been times when the performers, particularly
the conductors, were not equipped with the depth of knowledge that
they needed. It remains a question, in my mind at least, whether
the intensive training they received was enough in this exceptionally
difficult situation, and whether it may have been preferable for more
experienced conductors to remain in this role. The degree to which
the project was successful warrants its continuation, but the questions also demand some re-thinking of the content and design of the
training and the ongoing support of the performers. (They routinely
debriefed after shows, which must have been essential to cope with
the intensity of the performances.)

PLAYBACK THEATRE IN A WAR ZONE is guaranteed to elicit stories
of trauma, as is Playback following natural disasters such as the
Indian Ocean tsunami and Hurricane Katrina in New Orleans.[15]

15. See Chapter 17, "Enacting Testimony: Trauma Stories in Playback Theatre."

Victims of these and other catastrophes have welcomed the chance to tell their stories and see them enacted (in Tamil Nadu by an experienced local company; in New Orleans by a visiting team of playbackers who stayed long enough to start and support a local ensemble). Preparation for such work must include performers' telling and enacting their own stories within the safe space of rehearsals. And the training for a participant performance project, though necessarily streamlined, must ensure that certain basic "rules" are thoroughly absorbed and upheld in order to create a resilient and capacious container. For example, a teller of a full-length story sits beside the conductor. This is a safety measure, so that the conductor is physically close enough to monitor how the teller is responding as she tells and watches her story. Sometimes would-be tellers are reluctant to leave their less visible seat in the audience. But the conductor must insist, gently but firmly.

Stories of trauma can emerge in any performance. We can never know who is in the audience and what stories they may tell. So it is essential to know the capacities and flexibility of the form, and for performers to be sufficiently strong within themselves to take on the enactment of someone else's anguish, especially if it might resonate with their own. As Jonathan Fox wrote, "You have to know ... where your own self ends and the other begins."[16]

With adequately prepared actors and a highly skilled conductor, trauma stories told in Playback Theatre can indeed contribute to the transformation of experience from traumatic to narrative memory for both individuals and the community. When a teller is ready, telling a traumatic story to a group "represents a transition toward the judicial, public aspect of testimony" (Herman, 1992, p. 221). There are by now some established principles and techniques for using Playback Theatre with trauma. For example, stories that are evidently or potentially traumatic for the teller should not be enacted literally. The teller needs to "see" his or her story, but in a way that maintains a safe distance from it. Horrific events like a bombing or a rape can be depicted with minimal gestures, narration, or suggested offstage. The conductor might instruct the actors

16. See Chapter 19, "Playback Theatre in Burundi: Can Theatre Transcend the Gap?"

to use a short form rather than enact a story more fully, even if the teller is already in the teller's chair. In a recent performance for incarcerated women on World AIDS Day, a teller could not bear to watch even the stylized enactment of her story of violence and tragedy. We paused and talked, and with her agreement, enacted only the key feelings, not the events, of the remainder of the story, using short sound-and-movement responses with few or no words. This was satisfying to her and to the audience.[17]

Playback Theatre has the tensile strength to work with here-and-now conflict or shock. Bev Hosking recounts an experience:

> In Angola an incident occurred where we were able to apply Playback Theatre in an immediate situation very effectively. Part way through the performance someone in the audience had an epileptic fit. At first it was very unclear what was happening and everyone experienced some degree of fear, panic and shock. Nearly everyone, performers and audience members alike, fled screaming from the jango (compound). The young man recovered well and was taken outside to rest.
>
> The question then was if and how to proceed. Everyone was still in shock and it seemed important at least to bring people together, even briefly, before we finished, and the actors and the conductor agreed to this. The conductor invited the audience to talk about their experience of what had just happened. The first person told of feeling confused and not knowing what was happening, the second told of having felt really shocked and frightened and the third person told of feeling worried and concerned for the man. The actors were quite courageous and did some wonderful work playing these back as fluid sculptures. The second fluid sculpture very accurately mirrored the experience of the shock and there was awkward laughter and murmurs of recognition in response. My own experience with this sculpture was feeling the "shock" leave my body.
>
> Following this, everyone seemed to be able to relax and wanted the performance to continue. There was one last sto-

17. This incident is described in more detail in Chapter 17.

ry and we finished with some singing and dancing. Although
rather shocking in itself, this incident provided a very immediate experience of using Playback Theatre to work with a tense
and difficult moment in the life of this community. (Hutt and
Hosking, 2004, pp. 13–14)

Although not described at the time as participant performance
Playback Theatre, this series of performances was carried out by
an Angolan conductor, actors, and musician who had received a
short, focused training from an outside trainer, and then performed
for audiences of Angolans. Audience and performers alike shared
the background of their country's civil strife.

The need to respond creatively and constructively to traumatic
stories comes up occasionally in the anti-bullying shows. (Many stories depict problematic situations without being traumatic.) Those
stories tend to announce themselves with the young teller's body language: the lowered head, the barely audible and shaky voice warning
that tears are not far off. The conductor and adult actors must be
instantly alert at such times, guiding the telling and the enactment to
give this moment the greatest possible chance of being empowering
and healing for the child. It can feel too risky to have a student as
teller's actor (the actor playing the teller), even though customarily
that choice is left to the teller. When Emma told her story, the conductor, recognizing the delicacy of the story and of Emma's state
of mind, asked me to take Emma's role in the enactment. (I was in
the musician's spot for that particular show.) She felt, and I agreed,
though we had no chance to discuss it, that it was too big a challenge
for one of the students. The student actors did a wonderful job in
their supporting roles as the mean kids and the adults who tried but
couldn't help.

Hudson River Playback Theatre also carries out frequent performances with groups of mostly Latin American immigrants, many of
them undocumented.[18] Unprompted by us, audience members have
wanted repeatedly to tell the trauma stories of how they came to the
United States—the despair of living without resources or hope; the

18. See Chapter 20, "Immigrant Stories in the Hudson Valley."

terrifying, dangerous journey across river and desert. Tears flow, and yet over and over again our audience members insist on telling these stories. They find relief in bringing these stories to a semi-public forum and seeing them transmuted into artistic form. An audience member wrote: "It helps us to know that someone listens to us even though sometimes we tell our stories with pain."

Trauma is not the only challenge that Playback teams may face. Stories occasionally express prejudice, unconscious or otherwise. On the one hand, we are committed to honoring the teller and his or her story. On the other, we are committed to justice. Again, it takes awareness, intentionality, and skill to negotiate these values.[19] The conductor and the actors must find a way to distance themselves from the teller's prejudice. If they do not, they perpetuate it and they risk alienating those in the audience who are hurt by it. The story from Kiribati illustrates how the Playback process addressed prejudice gently but effectively—made possible by the fact that the group was together over time. The trainers themselves (male and female, Maori and Pakeha/European) modeled respect, equality, and acceptance. They did not confront those who taunted the gay man, but nurtured the relationships within the group to the point where it became possible for him to tell his story. In a briefer event, such as a single performance, other actions might be necessary— an actor playing the object of the teller's prejudice, for example, could make a point of bringing out that person's humanity in such a way that the audience, at least, would know that the performers do not share the teller's views. Or, with tact and compassion, the conductor might find a way to question the teller's problematic assumptions.[20]

In a world where personal story is increasingly commodified it is important that Playback Theatre is clearly based on values such as respect, authenticity, and inclusiveness.[21] Manipulation of the teller or the audience—as in the example of the conductor who wept in

19. Training in all aspects of Playback Theatre practice is available through the Centre for Playback Theatre and its international affiliates: www.playbackcentre.org.

20. See Chapter 6, "The Wider World."

21. See Chapter 13, "Telling Stories in Public."

order to stimulate "meaningful" stories—is unethical by any standard, and particularly out of place in Playback where stories are invariably told because they are important to the teller. A joyful story, or an apparently slight story, can hold great meaning for all present, if listened to with open ears and heart and enacted with creativity.

Playback Theatre offers the possibility of a socially contained but artistically unlimited space in which ordinary people can listen to each other and accept each other's stories. It holds promise as a resource in situations of conflict, where moral imagination has been truncated. In the organic dialogue of the stories, in the spontaneous exchange of images, memories, and allusions, a group of people may create a new collective story that embodies new understanding, new connection, possibly new hope. The women in Kiribati enacted their rightful place in their society and found space within themselves and their community to accept an outcast. Children dealing with bullying in schools acquired the empathy and practical tools they needed to stand up for what they knew to be fair. Audience members in Afghanistan spoke the unspeakable to each other and shed some of the voluminous tears built up in thirty years of violence. An outdoor audience of displaced people in Angola, in the midst of telling stories of terrible loss, used the Playback process to cope with a moment of immediate shock.

The use of Playback in troubled areas has so far been limited by the assumption that it is necessary to have a fully trained, ongoing ensemble, on the model of the permanent companies established in the Western world. The participant performance concept that I have described here—a reiteration of the original idea of the citizen actor—may prove a more portable model for Playback in the future, and perhaps a more accessible structure in cultural settings where group participation and membership are traditionally fluid. Training local performers is both congruent and efficient. A project may be conceived as time-limited: lasting indefinitely, on the model of the Western Playback ensembles, does not have to be a goal.

The success of future participant performance projects will depend on conceptualizing and carrying out training that distills knowledge and principles fundamental both to Playback Theatre and to the issue at hand; and, in an area of conflict, this must include training in addressing trauma. Moving in this direction also demands on an honest assessment on the part of Playback community: what does it take to be ready to lead such projects and how can we best prepare these courageous trainers?

I look forward to seeing, and taking part in, this new development of Playback Theatre. Many stories await the chance to be told.

References

Cullen, Kevin. (2010). "The Untouchable Mean Girls." *The Boston Globe*, January 24, 2010.

Graves, Robert. (1929; 1957). *Goodbye to All That*. New York: Anchor Books.

Greene, Maxine. (1995). *Releasing the Imagination: Essays on Education, the Arts, and Social Change*. San Francisco: Jossey-Bass.

Herman, Judith. (1992). *Trauma and Recovery: The Aftermath of Violence—from Domestic Abuse to Political Terror*. New York: Basic Books.

Hoesch, Folma. (1999). "The Red Thread: Storytelling as a healing process." In *Gathering Voices: Essays on Playback Theatre*, eds. Dauber, H. & Fox, J. 46–66. New Paltz, NY: Tusitala, 1999.

Hutt, Jenny, & Hosking, Bev. (2004). "Playback Theatre: A Creative Resource for Reconciliation." www.brandeis.edu/ethics/peacebuildingarts. Waltham, MA: International Center for Peace, Justice, and Public Life. Brandeis University.

Jeffrey, Linda R.; Miller, DeMond; & Linn, Margaret. (2001). "Middle school bullying as a context for the development of passive observers to the victimization of others." In *Bullying Behavior: Current Issues, Research, and Interventions*, eds. Geffner, R. A., Loring, M., & Young, C. 154. Binghamton, NY: Haworth Press.

Joffre-Eichhorn, Hjalmar J. (2009). Email, January 24, 2009.

Joffre-Eichhorn, Hjalmar. J. (2010). *Tears into Energy: Theatre and Transitional Justice in Afghanistan*. Unpublished draft.

Joffre-Eichhorn, Hjalmar J. (2011). *Tears into Energy/Das Theater der Unterdrücken in Afghanistan*. Hannover, Germany: Ibidem Verlag.

Joffre-Eichhorn, Hjalmar J. (2011). Email, March 3, 2011.

Katz, Neil. (2010). "Schools Battle Suicide Surge, Anti-Gay Bullying," CBSNews.com, October 11.

Ohene, Sally-Ann; Ireland, Marjorie; McNeely, Clea; & Borowsky, Iris W. (2006). "Parental expectations, physical punishment, and violence among adolescents who score positive on a psychosocial screening test in primary care." *Pediatrics*, 117, 441–447.

Olweus, Dan. (1980). "Familial and temperamental determinants of aggressive behavior in adolescent boys: A causal analysis." *Developmental Psychology*, 16, 644–660.

Olweus, Dan. (1993). *Bullying at School*. Carlton, Australia: Blackwell Publishing.

Mojumdar, Aunohita. (Undated). "War Crimes Amnesty Adds to Afghan Women's Grief," Women's eNews.

Piglia, Ricardo. (2001). Speech at a seminar at the University of the Mothers of the Plaza de Mayo, quoted in "Tales Rescued from Oblivion: The Construction of Collective Memory" by Maria Elena Garavelli. *Interplay*, 1.

Salas, Jo. (2005). "Using Theater to Address Bullying." *Educational Leadership*, September 2005, Vol 63, 1, 78–82.

Sandstrom, Susan, & Engel, M. (2010). "There's Only One Way to Stop a Bully." NYTimes.com, July 23, 2010. www.nytimes.com/2010/07/23/opinion/23engel.html

Strayer, Janet, & Roberts, William. (1989). "Children's Empathy and Role Taking: Child and Parental Factors, and Relations to Prosocial Behavior." *Journal of Applied Developmental Psychology*, 10, 227–239.

Swearer, Susan, & Doll, Beth. (2001). "Bullying in Schools: An Ecological Framework." In *Bullying Behavior: Current Issues, Research, and Interventions*, eds. Geffner, R. A., Loring, M., & Young, C., 7–24. Binghamton, NY: Haworth Press.

Wright, Robert. (2009a) *The Evolution of God*. New York: Little, Brown.

Wright, Robert. (2009b). "Why We Think They Hate Us: Moral Imagination and the Possibility of Peace." https://www.cato-unbound.org/2009/06/08/robert-wright, page 1.

Stories by Firelight: Playback Theatre in the Jordan Valley[1]

Jo Salas (2013)

WE ARE IN THE GENTLE HILLS of the Jordan Valley, under a starry sky, in a Bedouin village of several families on land that they have owned and grazed for centuries. The air is pungent with sheep dung. There is no electricity in the village—they are not permitted to have electricity, nor to build permanent structures—but along the ridge of the hills just a couple of hundred yards away marches a line of poles and wires carrying electricity to the nearby Jewish settlements and to the massive army base just down the road.

The Freedom Bus performers and their helpers are setting up a stage area.[2] They're going to do a Playback Theatre show under a spreading doma tree hung with lanterns whose light is augmented by a blazing campfire on the side. The team is traveling with ten or so internationals on a three-day solidarity trip, visiting Bedouin, farmer, and herder communities, planting olive trees and making mud bricks, eating together, and doing Playback shows so that the villagers can tell their stories.

I've joined them just for this evening, driving from Jenin with Abu Naji, a famed Zajaal poet whose traditional form of improvised poetry and song will play a part in the performance. We drove through lush farmland and villages and into an exquisite

1. First published at www.thefreedomtheatre.org.
2. The Freedom Bus is a long-term project of the Freedom Theatre in the Palestinian city of Jenin, initiated by Ben Rivers in 2011. Palestinian Playback performers, sometimes accompanied by international visitors, travel to villages in the occupied West Bank and spend several days in each one, participating in tasks like brick-building and tree-planting as well as offering Playback shows.

valley of scattered olive trees and wildflowers. And then we see Israeli soldiers walking down the road, guns at the ready. A little further there is a checkpoint. Cars are stopped, engines off, people waiting in the warm breeze. The word is that they have closed the checkpoint because two boys in the last village threw stones at the soldiers, who are now hunting for them. In the car we are quiet but anxious. If we can't get through this checkpoint it will take several hours to reach the village. We'll be late for the performance. After twenty minutes the soldiers start letting cars through. They peer at us, suspicious, but let us go.

Abu Naji and Adnan in the front seat are on their cell phones, trying to find the village where we are heading. The instructions lead us onto a small side road, and then into a field. We follow a long stony track, driving very slowly. Up in the crook of the hills we find the village, and our friends.

A gaggle of excited children surround Fidaa, a storyteller from the Freedom Theatre who has been telling stories and playing with them since the team arrived earlier in the day. They chant together— the children know long verses by heart. They leave for school at 5:30 each morning, walking a long distance to the bus: the village is not permitted to build their own school. I sit on a bench that someone has dragged down to the doma tree and after a while the children come and join me. One tiny child snuggles close and holds my hand, gazing up at me with solemn eyes. The others are shrieking, apparently convinced that if they raise their voices I'll understand Arabic. We get as far as exchanging names and the number of siblings we each have. They have many—seven, eight, nine.

I talk with two men who are part of a solidarity organization in a nearby town. One of them, a lawyer, tells me that when he was 17, during the first intifada, he was imprisoned for 28 months for throwing a stone. "They counted us many times a day," he says. "They would wake us up at two o'clock in the morning to count us."

A few days ago I finished teaching a Playback Theatre workshop in Beit Jala in which the Freedom Bus performers took part and we are happy to see each other again. I watch them preparing to perform, in the dark, in the dirt, in this rather chaotic atmosphere, and I marvel at their dedication and good humor. They are fueled by their passion for resistance and justice. As Palestinians they live every day with humiliation and deprivation. They are committed to reaching out to the people of this valley who are victimized perhaps the most of all—the poorest of the poor, invisible even to many other Palestinians, voiceless and powerless, but unshakably determined to stay on their land.

The performance begins. Abu Naji steps out and sings his welcome. I do not understand the words but his expansive gestures and full-throated voice invite us all to listen, to embrace this moment together. The conductor speaks to the audience, this odd assembly of villagers and their children, local Palestinian activists, dreadlocked young Europeans and Americans, the Freedom Bus team, and a few other visitors like myself. A man from the village expresses bemusement when Dabdoub, the conductor, asks everyone how they are doing. "It's very strange that you're here, with us who have nothing." The actors play back his comment, and he laughs—"That was strange!"

Several others speak up, and then Dabdoub invites someone to come to the teller's chair on the stage area to speak at more length about something from their lives. A middle-aged man accepts the invitation. The soldiers came to demolish his house. He pleaded with them to let him take out some of his belongings first. They refused, and destroyed his house, and beat him, and arrested him.

The musician plays his oud and the actors enact the story. Hassan, playing the teller, picks up a handful of dirt and lets it sift through his fingers. The man watches, absorbed, and nods when it is over. A woman comes next. She talks about living in a firing zone. The children are in danger but the soldiers don't care, she says. We hear later that people from other villages are afraid to come to this one, because of the frequent shooting. It has kept them away from the performance.

Abu Naji's powerful voice interweaves with the action, the ornate contours of his music linking these stories of the present to centuries of music and story in this historic land.

The third story is told by a younger man. One day the soldiers accosted him out in the hills. They said that the land was a natural resource and sheep were not permitted there. He argued that the land belonged to him. His family had always grazed their sheep on it. The soldiers arrested him and took him away. They did not give him a chance to find someone to look after the sheep. Later when he was released he took his case to court. After a long struggle his right to graze sheep on his land was affirmed. But now, he said, the soldiers do not respect this decision. They still threaten and harass him.

The performance ends with Abu Naji's voice once more. There is no resolution for these stories, no redemptive vision of change or hope. But there is the echo of centuries and declaration of resolve. There is the telling, and the listening. Someone stokes the fire and the conversations continue.

GARLAND OF FLOWERS[1]

Jonathan Fox (2017)

EXHAUSTED AFTER THE 24-hour journey from New York, having survived the sudden storm as we approached the Kathmandu Valley, then finally disembarking into the gloom of an airport that had lost electricity, I staggered around in the darkness looking (in vain) for my suitcase, eventually wandering out into a shadowy hall to be met by a handful of beaming strangers bearing prayer scarves. Later, finally settled in a hotel room (with backup generator), I shocked myself by catching sight of my bleeding forehead in the bathroom mirror—when and how had I sustained this injury?—finally realizing that the red was not blood, but dye from a ceremonial welcome *tika* that I did not remember.

I awoke the next morning to sunlight and views of a bright colored stupa and rooftops with flowers. At breakfast when asked, "Coffee or tea, sir?" I answered proudly in Nepali. But when I tried to tell the waiter how I knew Nepal forty-eight years ago, my words failed. I sighed and said in English: "Peace Corps Volunteer."

That first day was a day of meetings—drinking tea and discussing the Playback Theatre project run by the Berlin Centre for Integrative Mediation (CSSP) and Pro Public, partnering NGOs from Germany and Nepal. Traveling by taxi from one place to another I glanced at a city transformed—ten times bigger than I had known before, choked with cars and motorcycles, with pedestrians wearing facemasks against the foul air and litter everywhere. Time had not been kind to Kathmandu.

1. First published, with photo illustrations, at www.PlaybackTheatreReflects.net, 2018.

Entitled EnActing Dialogue, the project was an ambitious attempt to use theatre for peace building. In the decade surrounding the new century over 14,000 Nepalis had died in an armed conflict. The insurgents had made use of child soldiers. These ex-combatants, now young adults, were struggling to integrate into civil life. The EnActing Dialogue program involved "dialogue facilitators" acting out the stories of villagers using an interactive approach of which I was a founder.[2] Hence my invitation to be a trainer. The goal was to encourage mutual understanding in the post-conflict period.

I had been a Peace Corps Volunteer in its early days, when the US government had not hesitated to send liberal arts graduates to teach technical subjects they knew nothing about, such as converting to modern agricultural systems.[3] The assumption was that an educated, Western, American youth was so smart, so pragmatic, he or she could figure out anything. Of course I couldn't. In actuality, despite three months of special training, I arrived in my assigned village in the flat, rice-growing region of Nepal called the Terai unable even to recognize the difference between planted wheat and rice.

My ignorance made little difference, however, due to the dysfunctionality of the Nepali infrastructure and government. The improved seeds and fertilizer upon which my work depended never arrived in my region. There was nothing to do. For two years. That Nepal was the most isolated and poorest of all the countries to which the US sent volunteers did not help (we were well off with a salary of $1 per day). Conditions were truly challenging. The weather excessively hot. I was the only English speaker for dozens of square miles, my handful of cohorts equally isolated. With no occupation, no nearby companions, and an absence of support from supervisors, my life in Nepal then was a kind of waking nightmare, which I only survived by dulling my spirit and kidding myself that things would improve tomorrow.

The ordeal of my experience and the absurdity of my mission had been the reason why, despite a career of traveling the world as

2. See Chapter 16, "Unexpected Resilience of the Participant Performance Model."
3. See Chapter 1, "A Changing Landscape."

the founder of a now widely-practiced theatre method, I had never returned to Nepal, even though I had long been aware that in some vague way my work owed its genesis to there. I had been loath to be a tourist and relive some of the gross disparities I had experienced in the '60s. Moreover, I couldn't get over my fundamental embarrassment that the US had plunked me down in a Nepali village and expected that I would transform villagers' lives.

Yet being back on the noisy streets of Kathmandu, buying sandals in a tiny, open-air shop and discussing the price in my slowly return-ing Nepali language, shaking my head from side to side to mean Yes the way Nepalis do, taking in colors and smells that had not changed in a half century, was exhilarating. Once more in Nepal! "Namaste!" I said to everyone in the hotel. I looked at the prayer scarfs my new colleagues had welcomed me with, now carefully placed across the back of a chair, and welled up with joy. I had waited a long time for a good reason to return, and it had finally come.

PLAYBACK THEATRE is a more-than-entertainment approach that sometimes takes place in box office theatres, but mostly occurs in community settings. Its improvisational basis—the performers enact real stories of audience members—demands an attunement to each new place and each new group of people. Not unlike what I observed at festival performances in Nepal, where a vil-lage cultural event was affected by demands of weather and other local considerations.

There was another, even more obvious, way that the discovery of Playback Theatre was influenced by my time in Nepal. Playback Theatre's nonscripted nature connected it to preliterary recitation, and my daily life in Sunwal village, surrounded by mostly illiterate neighbors, was nothing if not an immersion in a culture where every speech was a performance and stories could not stand inde-pendent of the persons narrating them.

I had known something about this when I first arrived in Nepal, since I had learned about the oral tradition in my university days. Of course, there was a distinct difference between studying a subject (reading Gilgamesh in the library) and living it.

The EnActing Dialogue project was organized in two tiers of participants. First were theatre artists from Kathmandu, who had learned the basics of Playback Theatre in order to instruct the locally-based dialogue facilitators, the mixed teams of ex-combatants and community members who would perform in villages in the post-combat era.

The EnActing Dialogue project, and Playback Theatre itself for that matter, is based on a belief that the narrativizing of identity is beneficial. In a case cited in project reports, a woman had told about losing her married sister when she was a child, then being wed herself to the same brother-in-law, a much older man. Soon after the wedding, this man was killed in the war. She was suddenly the sole parent of two stepsons. She spoke about her aloneness and her struggle to care for the boys, despite her original reluctance for the ill-fated match. The neighbors had been suspicious of this young woman. But after the enactment of her story, they had new understanding and decided to support her.

On my second day in the country one of the theatre artists asked me if I knew the words, "*Bhannelaai phulako mala*" frequently proclaimed at the end of a recited story. In translation, it goes:

> *To the teller, a garland of flowers,*
> *To the listener, a garland of gold,*
> *May our story go to heaven,*
> *And come back to be told again.*

I was astounded. This little poem summed up my life's work! I did not know "*Bhannelaai*." But perhaps I had known it before, then forgotten?

"Let us tell you about the name we have chosen for Playback Theatre in Nepal," said the theatre artists. After trying out one name and another, they ended up hitting upon the correspondence between the *chautari* tradition and Playback Theatre. *Chautari* refers to spots reserved for travelers to rest and refresh themselves. In a mountainous country, often without roads between settlements, much commerce of all kinds was undertaken by foot. Villagers would plant a bal or pipal tree (sometimes both, then "marry" them in a special ceremony), and build a wall of stones around it for passers-by to sit on. These *chautari*, located throughout the country, in the flat Terai region, where my own village had been located, as well as in the hills, are known not only as places to rest, but also to chat, to relax, and share stories. Hence Playback Theatre in Nepal is called *Chautari Natak*, or *Chautari* theatre.

When I looked back, there had been that big pipal tree across from my verandah. It must have been a Chautari! (I had brought a camera with me on my original sojourn, and I came across a note I had written early in my stay: "so far I haven't taken any pictures here, but as soon as I feel comfortable, I will.") I never did. So there is no photographic record of the pipal tree, or the mud hut I slept in, the public pump I bathed in, the house whose family I ate my meals with, or the people who stared at me as I went about the necessities of life.

The words came pouring out, hard to catch at times, but the events were clear. In my first training a man told this story about his baby niece:

> She was only a year old. Her mother gave her a wedge of orange to suck. Then the baby started to choke on one of the little seeds. We couldn't dislodge it. There was no way to call an ambulance due to the political demonstrations. We managed to get a car to rush her to the local hospital, but the roads were blocked by demonstrators, and when we got through we learned the hospital's equipment was not good enough. We had to transfer her to Kathmandu, more than seven hours away. All this time she could barely breathe. We finally arrived. But it was too late. We lost her.

His face flushed, the teller watched intently as the actors portrayed his story. He was, in fact, a manager of the dialogue project, taking advantage of the chance to tell his story—the uncle who despite his considerable professional skills at organizing and getting things done, was helpless to save a member of his own family. His close colleague told me afterward that she was glad to hear him tell this story, since it had been bottled up inside him.

The project hosts had asked me to carry out two trainings, one with the theatre artists, located high on a ridge in the Kathmandu valley with a spectacular view of hills and high mountains (where the project manager told his story), and the other, for a group of dialogue facilitators, in the Terai city of Butwal, in the heart of one of the former conflict areas.

I knew Butwal, because it was close to my village of Sunwal. It had been one of the towns I trekked 15 miles to for a haircut or a decent meal. What a coincidence! "We should go to Sunwal, even do a performance there!" said my new friends. I demurred. What would be the point? Who would remember me after so many years? Who would care? "Thik hola," I said, politely, shaking my head, Nepali style. "Maybe."

The training space for the first week was a light-filled room looking out over steeply falling terraced hills. On one side was draped a brightly colored cloth that waved in the breeze. It took the place of the wall that had been destroyed in Nepal's terrible 2015 earthquake. Signs of earthquake damage were everywhere, in crumbling buildings and roads—almost a year later the funds for restoration had reportedly still to be released.

Despite the breeze blowing in from the open wall, it was a beautiful place to practice Playback Theatre. But as soon as we got down to work, I realized how new these actors were to the form, and how much learning lay in front of them. In sudden doubt, I reviewed in my mind the history of the EnActing Dialogue project. While Pro Public was the local partner, the impetus had come from Anne Dirnstorfer, a long-time Nepal peace worker and theatre practitioner with a history of working with the Theatre of the Oppressed. She had first encountered the Playback idea from a foreigner in Nepal, but had learned more back home in Germany, where there is an active Playback Theatre movement. She had then enlisted a German Playback practitioner and fellow peace worker to be her co-trainer in teaching the Nepali theatre artists a year before.

The funding for the project, in fact, was coming from a German government's foreign aid program channeled through CSSP, an organization devoted to international peace building, which had in turn invited the involvement of Pro Public.

Was I being hoodwinked once again, just as when I joined the Peace Corps? My job now was to run two trainings. But trainings were often the Big Macs of international programs, easy to deliver, easy to consume, and often of little sustenance. (When I taught Playback Theatre in Burundi, another poor country dependent on handouts, I had learned from my students that they had had a storytelling workshop the week before my visit and a conflict resolution training the week before that.[4])

"How much are people getting paid to be part of this program?" I asked Anne, knowing that in many cases the real reason locals participate is the stipend and the meals.

"Only transportation," she said, explaining her thinking that refusing to offer stipends was the only way to ensure genuine motivation.

To know that the dialogue facilitators were volunteers, albeit carefully selected, reassured me. And as I continued to find out more from Anne as the days continued, I grew in respect for her sensitivity and ethics. Anne had been researching and working in Nepal over much of her adult life. She had long-term relationships with Nepalis, and knew the language and culture well. She cared about questions of sustainability and genuinely wanted to help build peace, goals that I shared. In our modern, superconnected world, how else should it be, I rationalized, than wealth being redistributed by gift as well as commerce? I reminded myself that in fact even in the developed world Playback Theatre rarely lives only from the market economy, but is sustained by grants and volunteering.

Although EnActing Dialogue called in foreign trainers to get it off the ground, from the start the goal of the program was to involve only Nepalis, and despite the performers' only recent exposure to the Playback forms, villagers had unquestionably responded to the invitation to be tellers during the performances, even of their most serious stories. Even more important, their neighbors had paid attention. "*Bhannelaai phulako mala.*" Garlands of flowers for the

4. See Chapter 19, "Burundi Journal."

tellers, and for the listeners, garlands of gold. I decided to hang in there, do my best, and keep my eyes and ears open.

ON THE WAY FROM Bhairawa airport to Butwal, our second training site, the jeep broke down. "Oh no," I thought, imagining a long delay by the dusty road (we were now in the Terai, and it was hot). But ten minutes later we were on our way again. (With my status as elderly founder, I rode in front-seat comfort—a far cry from the old days, when I was once one of 19 riding in a similar jeep on this road.)

Even though the second training took place in a high-end hotel for Butwal, the meeting room was far from my usual standard. It was too long and narrow; the floor was too hard; and the temperature too hot (there was air conditioning, but only when the electricity worked, of course). But within a day, I adapted.

One of the Nepali trainers told a story. Now an established actress in the capital, she belonged to the Tharu people, a Terai tribe often disparaged by high caste Nepalis. Her story was about her resolve to go to school:

> We were very poor. I asked my elders if I could start school with the other children. They all said my job was to herd the goats, not go to school. I was only five. But I was determined. I kept hounding them. Finally my mother said if she could find the money—we needed 5 rupees to pay the teacher [about 5 cents US]—maybe I could go. She was eventually able to get it by selling rice at a festival. Then I had to get the right clothes to wear, which I did by stealing my older brother's shirt and making it into a school dress. It was a big effort, but in the end I made it.

The teller paused. "That's not the end of the story, of course," she said. "Each year I was first in my class."

FORTY-EIGHT YEARS BEFORE, I had had a brief taste of the resilience needed to get by from day to day in Nepal, where in my village life there had been no electricity at all, no running water, no sealed roads, and no way to keep rats out of my living quarters. I learned one did not need shoes to survive; or peace and quiet; or three meals a day; or indoor heating and cooling; or even clean water. Eventually I came to feel that there was comfort in living so close to the earth and its natural rhythms, a counterbalance to the claustrophobia of isolated village life.

After Nepal, I deliberately opted out of comfort as a career objective. Put another way, there seemed something positive about a life that demanded simplicity, daily problem solving, and resilience. As I looked out my hotel window at leaves glistening from a late afternoon shower, I wondered, could my experience in a remote Asian village have sparked the creation of a contemporary theatre in New York? A theatre in which the actors, time and again, starting at zero for each successive story, faced the challenge of giving intelligibility and aesthetic shape to ordinary persons' lives? Playback Theatre was the epitome of "poor" theatre, requiring no elaborate sets or costumes. But it asks a lot of its performers, for when they miss the essence of a story, the audience always knows it, as does the teller. On the other hand, when one succeeds, it feels wonderful to have risen to the challenge of the unforeseen moment. (This sense of reward, perhaps a fundamental human feeling, is one reason why members of Playback Theatre companies tend to remain in their ensembles for years.)

While the shadow of a colonialist pattern may have flickered over my new assignment in Nepal, my visit also represented a kind of homage. I felt thankful to the culture that had given me my lesson in hardship and inspired an idea based on creativity and courage.

WHEN I TRIED TO RECALL details of my experience all those years ago, they were elusive. I knew I had taken my meals with a family, but had forgotten their name (and never written it down). I remembered they made me eat on their porch because I was not, like them, a high-caste Hindu. I don't know how much I paid, but I do remember how meager the meals were. The young wife, who made the food, was kept out of bounds to me. And despite my extreme loneliness and a general love of kids, I knew to keep my distance from the five young girls in the family.

I remembered that my arrival in the village had caused conflict, but not why. Something about the house (one-room mud hut) they had promised to build, then delayed, then overcharged me for. Had I been a pawn between political factions?

The faces of my Peace Corps supervisors were still clear in my mind, but not my constant struggle to counter their neglect of me, as the months stretched out to my two years without meaningful work or any helpful intervention. It was so long ago.

Anne Dirnstorfer did not let go of the coincidence of the closeness of our training site to my old village. The Pro Public staff visited Sunwal. The local leaders readily accepted the idea of a performance. So on our last full day of the training we all climbed in a bus and took a half-hour field trip (there was a sealed road now). The bus broke down only two times on the way, on both occasions quickly fixed. The students, full of enthusiasm, sang and danced in the aisle.

Sunwal, now a town on the East-West highway, had completely transformed, from a place with no shops to dozens. It even had a hall to perform in. And while the students prepared the space for the performance, I went outside. Speaking in Nepali to the oldest person I saw, I told him my story: I lived here 48 years ago. I advised in agriculture. I ate with a family. I don't remember their name. But the father was the village pandit.

"Was it Paudel?" he asked. "Yes!" I said at once. "I think it might have been Paudel." The man walked up to a younger woman, who took out her cell phone and made a call.

The performance started. The troupe entered with a song. The musician played. The actors stood facing the audience while the conductor made an introduction. The Playback Theatre ritual was underway. Before long audience members were sharing about their everyday, and the performers were playing it back. So far, so good. But would the team, I wondered, be able to motivate and hold the audience as the show progressed? I was curious, since this was my first public performance in Nepal. In Playback Theatre a common safety valve is that audience members, faced with actors who are not up to understanding or staging the stories, simply stop wanting to tell. The energy shuts down. I would not have been totally surprised to see it happen here. But the tellers kept coming, and as the show went on, the stories grew more revealing rather than less—a definite sign of success.

It became apparent that the authenticity of the dialogue facilitators, volunteers from towns just like Sunwal, coupled with their natural human creativity and knowledge of the local culture, helped them fulfill the Playback idea and enabled them to carry the event.

Behind me there was a commotion. I turned, and there she was, the young mother and maker of my food. She had the same chiseled face, but it held a different kind of beauty now. She was white-haired, as was I. We recognized each other at once. One of the daughters was at her side. She had been less than 10, now almost 60. I recognized her, too. They handed me an exuberance of bougainvillea blossoms plucked from their garden. There was no time to talk. The performance unfolded, as we watched.

It was a rare experience watching that show, my hands full of flowers, my faced flushed with emotion because of two people sitting near me that I had never expected to see again. What would have happened if mother Paudel and I had each told a story in that Playback Theatre performance in Sunwal? Might each of us have been surprised? Might I have ended with more understanding of her situation then? (In fact, since my appearance in Sunwal was the pretext for the performance, the conductor might well have invited us to be tellers, but she did not). I might have learned that this young mother of five resented having to prepare extra meals twice a day at her husband's orders; or resisted her husband ordering her to restrict the food she gave me, so that they could save more of the money I was paying them; or that she delighted, albeit from her shadow inside the house, in the presence of this exotic stranger.

To my surprise, at the end of the performance I was asked to stand up and address the audience. Speaking in a Nepali that seemed to flow from me without hesitation, I said how happy I was to be back in this place that I had lived in almost 50 years ago, and how beautiful the natural surroundings were. And I thanked the Paudel family for taking care of me at that time.

Later after a walk to their house (a new structure built on the same land as the old one), we talked.

"You were so good with the children," the (now) grandmother said. (I remembered only my distance from the children).

"You were always so polite, and said that the food was good," she said. (I remembered only my frustration eating on the porch and the monotony of the same food day after day.)

"You brought us cauliflower seeds. We were the first to have them." (No memory.)

"She used to tell us about you," a granddaughter said. (What could she possibly have to tell? We never talked!)

"I told them you would come back one day!" her grand-mother said.

We were but two small players in a minor international exchange, who had barely interacted. Yet here we were, after so many years, each with such warm feelings for the other. Anne, the instigator, the teacher, the intermediary, looked on happily. Evidently our worlds were not irrevocably divided.

BEFORE FLYING AWAY from the Butwal/Bhairawa region and back to my home I took the opportunity to visit Lumbini, the reputed birthplace of Buddha. Wearing gracefully its centuries of venera-tion, the renowned Bodhi tree stood serenely in the center of a large grassy park. Birds sang. The sun shone. Monks in bright orange sat together and prayed. I thought of the stories I had heard—of the power and powerlessness of parents, of obstacles sometimes over-come, but often unsurpassable, of lives cut short and lives allowed to flourish. Of the danger of an orange pip and the promise of a school dress. Of villagers finally accepting a widowed neighbor. Of years passed. And the opportunity we all have. To tell. To listen. And to bring the stories back to tell again wherever we may be on our one earth.

★ ★ ★

APPENDIX

CODE OF ETHICS FOR
PLAYBACK THEATRE TRAINERS
AND PRACTITIONERS

AS PRACTITIONERS AND TRAINERS of Playback Theatre, we agree to uphold the following Code of Ethics:

RESPECT: *We interact with our audiences, students, tellers, company members, and colleagues with respect at all times. We acknowledge and affirm the integrity of the other party and behave in a way that does not seek to undermine or shame the other. We understand and respect the rituals, traditions, principles, and practices of Playback Theatre, and undertake to acquire that knowledge.*

INCLUSIVENESS: *We are open to any story and also ready engage with ethical complexities within a story. We seek to include voices that are often unheard in our communities.*

EMERGENCE: *We allow the events of a performance to emerge out of the moment, without being preset or manipulated. Stories or tellers are not chosen prior to the show (unless in exceptional situations, which should be transparent.)*

COMPETENCE: *We commit to ensuring that we have sufficient training and supervision for any Playback Theatre project that we undertake, acquiring further training as needed. We commit to practicing and/ or teaching Playback Theatre at the level of our competence and not beyond.*

HUMAN RIGHTS: *We promote the human rights of all those present and not present. When necessary we take appropriate action to address prejudice that may be expressed consciously or unconsciously by a teller or workshop participant.*

COLLEGIAL RELATIONSHIPS: *We strive to maintain respectful, co-operative, and supportive relationships within the Playback Theatre community. We respect boundaries between companies and undertake to be transparent with our colleagues, particularly in areas which may have financial or professional impact, including in relation to financial supporters. We respect each other's proprietary material including company names, publicity materials, and project descriptions. When companies, training entities, or trainers are in geographical proximity they need to negotiate and respect regional agreements.*

PRIVACY AND CONFIDENTIALITY: *We acknowledge that stories told in a performance are not subject to confidentiality. However, we undertake to repeat or write about stories only in a respectful and discreet way.*

For trainers of Playback Theatre

ETHICS TOPICS IN TRAINING: *As trainers, we commit to developing self-awareness and awareness in our students of ethical issues in Playback Theatre.*

SUPERVISION: *As trainers, we commit to an adequate level of supervision.*

ACKNOWLEDGMENTS

WE ARE GRATEFUL to Laurie Frederick, Norbert Ross, and Rickie Solinger for reviewing and commenting on our plan for this book, and to Rickie and Norbert for their detailed comments on our first chapter. Hannah Fox, Maddy Fox, and Sarah Urech also read the opening chapter and gave us valuable reflections. Further thanks to Rickie Solinger and to Tilman Reitzle for their painstaking work on the index.

Our thanks also to our worldwide Playback Theatre community, our fellow Playback pioneers from the early days, and Hudson River Playback Theatre, all of whom have accompanied us on this lifelong journey and enriched every step. So many people—more than we can name—have been influential in our Playback lives, teaching us about theatre, about justice, about the subtleties of group life and inner life, challenging us, inspiring us, surprising us, supporting us. If you think you are one of these people, then you are. We do want to acknowledge Judy Swallow, an integral member of the original company and part of our lifelong conversation.

And gratitude beyond words to our daughters Hannah and Maddy and their families who fill our days with liveliness and love.

ABOUT THE AUTHORS

JONATHAN FOX was artistic director of the original Playback Theatre company from its inception in 1975. From 1993 until 2010 he was director of the Centre for Playback Theatre in New York. He earned a BA from Harvard University in English, where he studied the oral tradition under Albert Lord; an MA in political science from Victoria University in New Zealand, studying under a Fulbright scholarship; and in 2008 a D. Phil. h.c. from the University of Kassel in Germany for his artistic and scholarly contribution to theatre. He is also a Trainer, Educator, and Practitioner of the American Society of Group Psychotherapy and Psychodrama. Jonathan is the author of *Acts of Service: Spontaneity, Commitment, Tradition in the Nonscripted Theatre*; *Beyond Theatre: A Playback Theatre Memoir*; and *The Playback NR Workbook*. He also edited *The Essential Moreno: Writings on Spontaneity, Psychodrama and Group Method*; and co-edited *Gathering Voices: Essays on Playback Theatre*. Since 1980 he has been teaching Playback Theatre in a variety of settings around the world.

JO SALAS is the cofounder of Playback Theatre and the founder of Hudson River Playback Theatre. She graduated from Victoria University in Wellington, New Zealand with a BA in English literature, and from New York University with an MA in music therapy. Jo has taught Playback Theatre workshops in 27 countries and was a keynote speaker at the academic symposiums on Playback Theatre held at the University of Kassel, Germany, and Arizona State University.

Jo's publications on Playback Theatre include numerous articles, contributions to anthologies, a TEDx talk "Everyone has a story," and the books *Improvising Real Life: Personal Story in Playback Theatre*, now published in ten languages and a 20th anniversary edition, and *Do My Story, Sing My Song: Music Therapy and Playback Theatre with Troubled Children*. She co-edited the bilingual publication *Half of My Heart/La Mitad de Mi Corazón: True Stories Told by Immigrants*. She has also published short stories and a novel, *Dancing with Diana*.

Jo and Jonathan have two daughters and three grandchildren. They live in upstate New York, surrounded by woods, fields, and mountains.

INDEX

CPSIA information can be obtained
at www.ICGtesting.com
Printed in the USA
JSHW041348010421
13120JS00004B/4